THE CONSTITUTION OF

Professor Dyzenhaus deals with the urgent question of how governments should respond to emergencies and terrorism by exploring the idea that there is an unwritten constitution of law, exemplified in the common law constitution of Commonwealth countries. He looks mainly to cases decided in the United Kingdom, Australia and Canada to demonstrate that even in the absence of an entrenched bill of rights, the law provides a moral resource that can inform a rule-of-law project capable of responding to situations which place legal and political order under great stress. Those cases are discussed against a backdrop of recent writing and judicial decisions in the United States of America in order to show that the issues are not confined to the Commonwealth. The author argues that the rule-of-law project is one in which judges play an important role, but which also requires the participation of the legislature and the executive.

DAVID DYZENHAUS is Professor of Law and Philosophy at the University of Toronto. He is a Fellow of the Royal Society of Canada, and has worked in South Africa, the United Kingdom, Germany and New Zealand.

Thank you!

David

THE CONSTITUTION OF LAW

Legality in a Time of Emergency

DAVID DYZENHAUS

CAMBRIDGE
UNIVERSITY PRESS

CAMBRIDGE UNIVERSITY PRESS

Cambridge, New York, Melbourne, Madrid, Cape Town, Singapore, São Paulo

Cambridge University Press
The Edinburgh Building, Cambridge CB2 2RU, UK

Published in the United States of America by Cambridge University Press, New York

www.cambridge.org
Information on this title: www.cambridge.org/9780521677950

First published 2006

Printed in the United Kingdom at the University Press, Cambridge

A catalogue record for this publication is available from the British Library

ISBN-13   978-0-521-86075-8 hardback
ISBN-10   0-521-86075-X hardback

ISBN-13   978-0-521-67795-0 paperback
ISBN-10   0-521-67795-5 paperback

For Alexander and Sophie

CONTENTS

ACKNOWLEDGEMENTS

The book is a revised version of a manuscript I prepared as a basis for the J. C. Smuts Memorial Lectures, four lectures delivered to the Faculty of Law of the University of Cambridge in November 2004. I am grateful to the Faculty of Law and especially Joanne Scott for the invitation to deliver these lectures and to those who attended.

I have incurred many other debts both in writing and revising these lectures. Robert Leckey performed the unusual research task of preparing on the basis of several of my published articles and many works in progress not only a detailed memorandum about how to organize the lectures but also a rough cut-and-paste version of how the lectures might go. While much has changed during the course of initial revisions and since, his work made it possible for me to get started during a busy term. Emily Hammond gave me challenging comments on my first set of revisions and also has sought in the past to educate me in the intricacies of Australian constitutional law. Mike Taggart provided me with comments on two successive drafts and much encouragement. Murray Hunt gave detailed answers to questions throughout the period of preparation. It would be remiss not to mention that my debt to Mike and Murray goes far beyond these lectures. They are great friends and great teachers.

As I mentioned at the start of my first lecture, much of what I write about the rule of law is inspired by Trevor Allan, whose book on the rule of law is, in my view, the most important work on this topic since A. V. Dicey. Trevor's questions at the lectures have prompted me in new directions, and Mark Walters and Amanda Perreau-Saussine also pressed me to think harder about my central claims. My colleague, Kent Roach, gave me comments on a draft. More important is that the ideas I present have been forged in discussion with him over several years, as they have been with Mayo Moran, whose work on influential authority has enriched my understanding of legality.

Geneviève Cartier gave me comments and the influence of her doctoral thesis 'Reconceiving Discretion: From Discretion as Power to Discretion as Dialogue' is manifest in many parts of this book. Rueban Balasubramaniam compiled an insightful memorandum on my discussion of the two wartime decisions of the House of Lords discussed here and I owe much to discussions with him about the continuum of legality. Lars Vinx has provided me with many insights about the relationship between political and legal philosophy and his interpretation of Hans Kelsen's view of legality in his thesis 'Legality and Legitimacy in Hans Kelsen's Pure Theory of Law' has greatly assisted my arguments. I owe the same kind of debt to Evan Fox-Decent, and to the ideas he developed in his doctoral thesis, 'Sovereignty's Promise: The State as Fiduciary'.

Matt Lewans, Jonathan Lewis, Sean Rehaag and Rayner Thwaites considerably helped me with either research assistance or comments or both and three reviewers for Cambridge University Press gave me very useful feedback on the manuscript of the lectures. I particularly want to thank reviewer number 3, who managed to combine encouraging comments about my work with highly critical questions about the arguments in the manuscript. Jonathan Masur, with whom I got in touch after reading his excellent article on themes similar to mine, kindly read most of the manuscript and gave me very helpful comments.

Finally, Luc Tremblay of the Faculty of Law of the University of Montreal arranged a seminar on the penultimate version of the manuscript and I thank him for this wonderful opportunity to reflect for the last time on the manuscript and in particular three people who have already figured in these acknowledgements, and who at the seminar provided at short notice insightful commentaries on my arguments: Geneviève Cartier, Evan Fox-Decent, and Robert Leckey.

I have received generous support over the years from my two academic homes, the Law Faculty and the Philosophy Department of the University of Toronto. In particular, the Law Library under the direction of Beatrice Tice and with the able help of Esmé Saulig made available a document and book delivery service that is a boon to research. I have been supported throughout this project by research funds from the Social Sciences and Humanities Research Council of Canada.

I mentioned that the first drafts of the lectures were put together during a busy term. While I did not set out to write or to revise the lectures this way, in retrospect I know that only anxiety-produced insomnia of a rather extreme sort provided me with the hours I needed. It is impossible not to disturb one's partner when one regularly begins work between 2.30 and 4.30 in the morning and it takes true love not to display impatience with such nocturnal weirdness until the very end of the process. For that, and much more, I thank Cheryl Misak.

TABLE OF CASES

TABLE OF STATUTES

Introduction

Is the rule of law optional for liberal democratic societies? In the wake of the attacks on the United States on 11 September 2001, the Bush administration seemed to say that it is. And in the wake of the attacks on London in July of 2005, Tony Blair has indicated that the rule of law is a luxury, dispensable when the going gets rough. In particular, he has indicated that judges have to be reined in from their disposition to enforce the rule of law against the executive, even if this requires both legislating how they are to balance liberty against security and amending the Human Rights Act 1998. In contrast, the Spanish government elected in the immediate aftermath of the attacks on Madrid on 11 March 2004 did not see fit to renege on a commitment to the rule of law.

Blair's comments fit within a trend whereby many liberal democracies since 9/11 have used either legislation or executive order to create a variety of legal black holes, situations in which individuals suspected of being threats to national security are detained indefinitely. In the United Kingdom, they were detained because, while they were aliens who would ordinarily be deported after a determination that they threatened security, the government is committed to not deporting anyone to a country where that person faces a serious risk of torture. In this situation, the government's respect for one human right – the right not to be tortured – leads to an individual being stripped of another human right, that is the right not to be detained except for certain legitimate purposes, for example, that one is awaiting trial on a criminal charge or that one's deportation is imminent. Thus, when the United Kingdom amended its anti-terrorism law to provide for this kind of situation, it also expressly derogated in advance from its domestic and international human rights commitments in regard to detention.

In some respects, those detained were not altogether in a legal black hole, a lawless void, as they were able to contest the validity of the determination that they were risks to national security before the Special Immigration Appeals Commission (SIAC), a tribunal with expertise

1

in law, immigration, and security. Moreover the anti-terrorism statute required periodic reviews by SIAC of the particular decisions to detain and the statutory provisions allowing for indefinite detention expired unless renewed on a set date. But, given the assumption of the government that the terrorist threat it faces is permanent and that threats do not have to be imminent to justify emergency measures, the detainees were in a legal black hole in that they faced detention without criminal charge for the foreseeable future.

Even more dramatic are the legal black holes created by the government of the United States. Notorious here is the situation of aliens detained off-shore at Guantanamo Bay, which the government claimed to be beyond the jurisdiction of the federal courts. These individuals are not detained because the US government refuses to deport them to face torture. Indeed, the government of the United States has deported people in order that they will be tortured in countries in which torture is condoned. More-over, its own treatment of detainees has raised questions about whether it practises torture, spurred by signals from the highest reaches of the Bush administration that torture is acceptable, given the severity of the emergency. Rather, they are detained because it is alleged that they fall into the category of 'enemy combatants', a category which is beyond the reach of both domestic and international law. In addition, there is the situation of those citizens who are detained within the United States, but who are by executive order placed in the same enemy combatant category.

It is hardly a new claim that in a time of emergency even liberal democracies have to suspend the rights which those subject to the law enjoy in ordinary times in order to preserve themselves. All that is new is the prevalence of the claim that this emergency has no foreseeable end and so is permanent. For those who are troubled by the trend towards permanent emergency powers, that is the normalization of the exceptional, the central question has become how such a trend might be resisted.

I will argue that a response to emergencies, real or alleged, should be governed by the rule of law. My conception of the rule of law is substantive: the rule of law is a rule of fundamental constitutional principles which protect individuals from arbitrary action by the state. Substantive conceptions of the rule of law are often contrasted with procedural ones, where the contrast is between what kinds of decisions are made and how they are made. For example, the procedural right to a hearing before a decision is made is not a substantive right to a particular decision. But I will argue there is more to the rule of law than principles that are procedural in the sense that all they protect is rights to how decisions are made. The principles do constrain the decisions of those who wield public power in a way that protects the interests of the individuals subject to those decisions.

While a substantive conception gives a significant role to judges, it also requires the cooperation of the legislative and executive branches of government[1] in what I call the rule-of-law project. There are limits to judicial competence and it will sometimes take imaginative exercises in institutional design to craft solutions to problems about how to impose the rule of law on certain kinds of executive decisions. Decisions about national security considerations, for example, decisions to detain individuals as risks to security, starkly pose such problems and SIAC, the tribunal just mentioned, is an attempt at a solution. A substantive conception of the rule of law has to find a way of coordinating the roles of the judiciary and the other branches of government, when the latter are productively engaged in the rule-of-law project.

But what is the judicial role when such cooperation ceases altogether or is half-hearted? An example of total cessation is when the statute that responds to the emergency either explicitly exempts the executive from the requirements of the rule of law or explicitly excludes judicial review of executive action. Half-hearted cooperation comes about when a tribunal is put in place to police decisions about security, but its procedures make it look more like a rubber stamp for executive decisions than a forum in which executive claims are properly tested. In the first example, the legislature seeks to create a legal black hole, a situation in which there is no law. In the second, the legislature seeks to create a hole that is grey rather than black, one in which there is the façade or form of the rule of law rather than any substantive protections. As we will see, the appropriate judicial reaction to a black hole will vary according to the way in which it is created. But judges should avoid any part in the creation of grey holes; indeed, they should try their hardest to turn the form of the rule of law into something substantive, to turn grey holes into situations which are properly governed by the rule of law. For grey holes are disguised black holes, and if the disguise is left in place governments will claim that they govern in accordance with the rule of law and thus garner the legitimacy that attaches to that claim.

These concerns might, as I have already suggested, seem misplaced if the thought is right that a substantive conception of the rule of law has no or little role in an emergency situation. It would follow that responses to emergencies have in the nature of things to be partly or even wholly

---

[1] I will at times use 'government' and 'executive' interchangeably.

exempted from the requirements that we associate with the rule of law in ordinary or normal times. The government or the legislature or both in tandem cease to cooperate in the rule-of-law project, not out of ill will, but because of a good faith judgment about necessity. Necessity has no law, as the saying goes; and we will see that the fascist legal theorist Carl Schmitt challenged liberal theories of the rule of law on the basis that even liberals have to recognize that the rule of law has no application in a state of emergency.

I will respond to that challenge in arguing that judges have a constitutional duty to uphold the rule of law even, perhaps especially, in the face of indications from the legislature or the executive that they are trying to withdraw from the rule-of-law project. Indeed, the legislature and the executive have that same duty to uphold the rule of law in emergency times no less than in ordinary times, which is why judges are entitled to assert the rule of law in the face of what seem to be legislative or executive indications to the contrary.

My claim that judges have this duty because of a shared commitment of all three branches of government to the rule of law is questionable, not only because of the issue about necessity. It might also seem viable only when judges are explicitly given the constitutional resources by their legal order to stand up to a legislature or executive which chooses to depart from the rule of law. If, that is, one equates the rule of law with the rule of fundamental constitutional principles, it might seem that a duty exists to protect those principles against the legislature and the executive only when judges have the resource of an entrenched bill of rights which makes them guardians of those principles. While judges might have a moral duty always to uphold the rule of law, only the existence of a bill of rights can turn that moral duty into a legal one, let alone a constitutional one.

However, if the argument about necessity is right, the existence of a bill of rights is irrelevant during a state of emergency. The thought that the law applicable in normal times has no or little application during a time of emergency extends to all law, including a bill of rights. Moreover this book is titled 'The Constitution of Law' because my argument is that, in circumstances when a society chooses to rule through law, it also chooses to subject itself to the constitutional principles of the rule of law, whether or not it articulates those principles in a bill of rights.

Law presupposes the rule of law, in the substantive sense. Therefore, if there is no written constitution, these principles will be unwritten or implicit; in common law legal orders, they will be part of the common law constitution. For this reason, my argument will rely for the most part on cases drawn from jurisdictions where there is or was no bill of rights which protects the principles of the rule of law, from, that is, countries which belong to the common law family of the Commonwealth. My overall argument is that what we might think of as the Commonwealth constitution exhibits the values of a substantive conception of the rule of law and that these values make the exercise of legal authority legitimate.

At one level, then, my ambition is to sketch the basis for a productive account of the relationship between the three powers – the legislature, the government, and the judiciary. I will try to show that it is better to understand their relationship in terms of what they share and not in terms of what separates them, since their separation is in the service of a common set of principles. The powers are all involved in the rule-of-law project. They are committed to realizing principles that are constitutional or fundamental, but which do not depend for their authority on the fact that they have been formally enacted. In order to count as law or as authoritative, an exercise of public power must either show or be capable of showing that it is justifiable in terms of these principles.

The countries from which most of my examples are drawn are the United Kingdom, Canada, and Australia. Together they present a fertile ground for testing my claims because, until quite recently, Canada and Australia had what I will refer to as a 'division of powers constitution', a constitution which set out the parameters of the country's federal structure. Even today, Australia has not decided to adopt a bill of rights and the move into the era of domestic human rights documents by the United Kingdom through the enactment of the Human Rights Act 1998 does not give judges the authority to invalidate legislation. Instead, that Act requires them to interpret statutes in such a way that they are rendered consistent with the United Kingdom's human rights commitments. If a statute cannot be so rendered, then the judges are entitled only to declare it incompatible with the human rights commitments, a declaration which leaves it up to the government and the legislature to decide whether to amend the statute. Moreover, the Canadian Charter of Rights and Freedoms explicitly gives Canadian legislatures the power to override most judicial determinations that legislation is unconstitutional. So my argument is that there are continuities across the United Kingdom, Australia, and Canada that transcend in importance orthodox distinctions based on (a) an unwritten constitution, (b) a federal constitution but no enacted bill of rights, (c) an enacted but not entrenched bill of rights, and (d) a federal constitution and an entrenched bill of rights. That is why I speak of the Commonwealth constitution.

The idea that the legal rights of the subject, even when protected by an authoritative written source of law, may be overridden by the legislature is the direct result of the fact that the common law tradition of these countries is one in which the common law coexisted in the same space as a doctrine of parliamentary supremacy.[2] One view of that tradition is that judges are entitled to interpret legislation in the light of the values of the common law until the point where Parliament decides to use its supreme legislative authority to override them and, as I have indicated, it is when Parliament is considered more or less supreme, in the sense that it can override judges, that one has the best testing ground for a claim about the unwritten constitution of law. Only when judges must resort to an unwritten constitution to unearth the principles of the rule of law because their legal order does not entrench rights, can one investigate the hypothesis that the choice to rule through or by law necessarily involves ruling in accordance with constraints that make that rule legitimate. So it is in exploring the idea that constitutional constraints can be both genuinely binding and yet overridable that we begin to understand what is involved in the political choice to rule by or through law.

The claim that rule by law presupposes the rule of law is controversial. For example, the central theme of a recent collection of essays on democracy and the rule of law is the distinction between rule by law and the rule of law, where the former means the use of law as a brute instrument to achieve the ends of those with political power while the latter means the constraints which normative conceptions of the rule of law place on the instrumental use of law.[3] The contributors argue that the normative conception of jurists is a 'figment of their imagination'.[4]

Law, they say, is not an autonomous constraint on actions but a constraint which those with political power will accept or not depending on their relative strength. If accepting the constraint is the only way to maintain their power they will accept, otherwise not. Not only is the choice to abide by the rule of law a matter of political incentives, the same is true of the choice to use rule by law to achieve one's ends. It follows that the weaker one's relative position, the closer one will find oneself to the normative, rule-of-law end of the continuum that stretches between rule by law and rule of law. One who is in a very powerful position will submit to

---

[2] See Stephen Gardbaum, 'The New Commonwealth Model of Constitutionalism' (2001) 49 *American Journal of Comparative Law* 707–60, for a detailed analysis of these features.

[3] José María Maravall and Adam Przeworski (eds.), *Democracy and the Rule of Law* (Cambridge: Cambridge University Press, 2003).

[4] *Ibid.*, 'Introduction', p. 1.

ruling at various points away from the rule-by-law end of that continuum only when it is expedient to do so; for example, when it is convenient to have public attention and thus also possible hostility deflected onto officials such as judges.

I will argue that as one approaches the rule-by-law end of the continuum not only does the rule of law disappear entirely but even the claim that there is rule by law starts to seem implausible. The choice to order a society through the institutions of legality entails a commitment to abiding by the rule of law so that where one does not have the rule of law, one finds that there is also no rule by law. Moreover, we will see that the idea of overridable constraints affords a new perspective on the rule of law, one which shows that the operation of the rule of law is not confined to limiting public power. The rule of law is also constitutive of a certain kind of power – of legal authority; and with the aid of that insight, we can also see why the different institutions should not be understood in terms of 'competing supremacies',[5] but rather as involved in the rule-of-law project. The rule of law turns out, then, to be constitutive in that legislatures and executives which understand their role in its maintenance will undertake experiments in institutional design in order to make law's rule into reality; and judges have a crucial role in keeping these institutions of government on that path.

I will also argue that the principles are inherent in the constitution of law itself. So, at another level, my claim is about law or legal order, including international legal order, not just about the values inherent in the law of a particular legal order or family of legal orders. Moreover, I want to claim that only by understanding the rule of law and its limits can we understand the nature of law. With Sir Hersch Lauterpacht, but perhaps unlike most contemporary legal theorists, I believe that the question of the limits of the rule of law is the central question of jurisprudence.[6]

It is important at this juncture to mark the distinction between 'the legal order' and 'legal order' because the model of the Commonwealth constitution that I am proposing recognizes that one positive legal order will differ from another in terms of the positivized or determinate content

---

[5] See Murray Hunt, 'Sovereignty's Blight: Why Contemporary Public Law Needs the Concept of "Due Deference"' in Nicholas Bamforth and Peter Leyland (eds.), *Public Law in a Multi-Layered Constitution* (Oxford: Hart Publishing, 2003), pp. 337–70.

[6] 'As in any other system of law, so also in that which governs the relations of states *inter se*, the question of the limits of the rule of law is the central problem of jurisprudence'. Hersch Lauterpacht, *The Function of Law in the International Community* (Oxford: Clarendon Press, 1933), p. vii.

of its laws, including its constitutional law. Legal orders will also differ from each other, sometimes quite dramatically, in the way they arrange the institutions that are principally involved in bringing the principles of the rule of law to realization. In fact, the Commonwealth constitution is just one example of institutional arrangement. But what the model shows is that the idea of legal order, of government in accordance with the rule of law, is an aspirational ideal,[7] an attempt to make the law serve justice, which has the result that judges legitimately understand the positive law in terms of that inspiration. Their interpretative duty then is not, as legal positivism might have it, first to determine the content of the positive law without relying on their own moral sensibilities and, second, to apply that content. Rather, their duty is to determine the content of the law in accordance with the aspirations of (ideal) legal order; and the legislature and the executive have exactly the same duty.

It is not, I must hasten to add, that the content of the enacted texts of a legal order, statutes and constitutions, become secondary considerations for judges who share this understanding of duty. But in the cases I will discuss such texts were never sufficient in themselves for the judges, often they were of little or no assistance, and sometimes obviously unhelpful. The texts were never sufficient in themselves because any claim about how precisely a particular text spoke to the question the judge had to answer could not be extracted from the text alone. Rather, it relied on an interactive process of interpretation that moved between the text and the judge's understanding of the ideal, or political point of legal order. And because that process is interactive or two-way, the judge will work up the ideal from the text as well as work down in constructing the meaning of the text in light of the ideal.

The best account of this interpretative process is that of Ronald Dworkin. He argues that judges who approach the interpretation of positive law with the right set of questions will find that the law provides principled answers to those questions, answers which show the law in its best light, by which Dworkin means the best moral light. For Dworkin, the leading candidate to shed this light is the political principle of liberalism that the state should treat all individuals with equal concern and respect.[8]

But while I accept Dworkin's interpretive approach to understanding legal texts, it does not suffice for the situation in which there is little or no text that is relevant. This situation can come about because it is

---

[7] See Lon L. Fuller, *The Morality of Law* (rev. edn, New Haven: Yale University Press, 1969).
[8] Ronald Dworkin, *Law's Empire* (Cambridge, Mass.: Belknap Press, 1986).

the case that all would agree that no legal text speaks directly or at all to the question the judges have to answer. Of course, judges can draw on principled solutions that rely on the positive law in domains other than the one in which the question arises. And Hercules, Dworkin's ideal judge, is supposed to survey the legal order as a whole in order to arrive at his solutions. But it is important to keep in mind that in an emergency situation, the question can arise as to whether texts that would dictate a solution in ordinary times are relevant. Text is no help when the question is whether text is relevant.

In addition, there is the situation where the texts are obviously unhelp-ful, for example, where there is no bill of rights and the legislature explicitly gives to the executive the power to operate unconstrained by principles of the rule of law, which express the ideal of legal order. When texts are recal-citrant to interpretation in the light of the ideal, Dworkin has suggested that judges might simply have to step outside of the interactive process because they can no longer find any purchase within law's texts for the principle of equal concern and respect.[9]

My argument is that the details of what is involved in such a step, indeed, the question whether judges are ever forced to take it, cannot be elaborated by attention only or even mainly to the principle of equal concern and respect, or to any other candidate for the ultimate principle of liberalism. Getting the details of that step right is one of the central tasks of this book. But to get them right is not just a question of close attention to the facts. As we will see, characterization of those facts depends here as elsewhere on theory, on my argument for a rule-of-law project common to the judiciary, the legislature, and the executive.

In setting out this argument, I will have to contend with what I will call the rigid doctrine of the separation of powers. This is the doctrine that asserts that the legislature has a monopoly on law-making, the judiciary a monopoly on interpretation of the law, while the executive is left with the task of implementing the law. I will argue that we should not even regard a unitary common law legal order as one in which sovereignty is divided between Parliament and the judges, as one in which there is a 'bi-polar' constitution, to use Stephen Sedley's term.[10] If anything, as I have indicated, the constitution is tri-polar, divided between Parliament, the judges and the executive. But even that description smacks too much of

---

[9] Ronald Dworkin, 'A Reply to Critics' in Marshall Cohen (ed.), *Ronald Dworkin and Contemporary Jurisprudence* (London: Duckworth, 1984), pp. 247–300 at pp. 254–60.

[10] For a recent essay on this theme, see Stephen Sedley, 'Everything and Nothing: The Chang-ing UK Constitution' (2004) 26 *London Review of Books* 10.

the language of competing supremacies and so I will support a conception of the powers of government which is divided more by function than by areas of exclusive power or jurisdiction.

A further foil for my argument is legal positivism, which manifests itself in a family of loosely connected positions: the conceptual version which argues on theoretical grounds that there is no necessary connection between law and morality, or as I prefer to put it, between legality and legitimacy; political positivism, the Benthamite and neo-Benthamite positions which argue on political grounds for an understanding of law which will maintain the legislature's supremacy over judges; constitutional positivism, the version developed by judges who work within a common law legal order which they make sense of in accordance with the rigid doctrine of the separation of powers; and, finally, functionalism, a theory of the administrative state that seeks to tame the judiciary in order to facilitate the work of public officials.

Finally, I will set out a conception of the judicial role that is rather different from Dworkin's Herculean one, where judge Hercules is regarded as the guardian of the abstract principle of equal concern and respect. Rather than looking to such abstract principles of political philosophy, I will argue that we should look to the principles of the rule of law or legality which are by way of being structural principles of the integrity of legal order. Here I will rely on Lon L. Fuller's idea that legal order must aspire to realize principles of an 'inner morality of law'.[11] It is such principles which provide us ultimately with the basis for understanding how judges should approach the cases discussed in this book. They can rightly be seen as mediating between liberalism as an abstract political doctrine and an account of how judges are to decide cases in which the rule of law is at issue. Certainly, when there is compliance with the principles, the results will be consistent with liberalism's concern for the rights of the individual and their inclusion into an account of judicial duty is not hostile to the spirit of Dworkin's approach.[12]

However, as already indicated, the realization of the principles of the rule of law is as dependent, if not more, on legislative and executive

---

[11] Fuller, *Morality of Law*.

[12] Indeed, in more recent work Dworkin has come to rely more on the idea of legality as an organizing principle of legal order: see Ronald Dworkin, 'Hart's Postscript and the Character of Political Philosophy' (2004) 24 *Oxford Journal of Legal Studies* 1–37. He has also suggested that judges need not be the only site for the moral elaboration of the requirements of law: Ronald Dworkin, *Freedom's Law: The Moral Reading of the American Constitution* (Cambridge, Mass.: Harvard University Press, 1996), pp. 33–4.

commitment as it is on judicial guardianship. I will show that the commonality of the rule-of-law project requires that judges adopt an appropriate stance of deference not only to their legislatures, but also, and more controversially, to the executive, even when the executive is engaged in interpretation of the most fundamental legal values. Further, that same project raises questions about the most effective institutional arrangements for implementing the rule of law – and answers to such questions might well require imaginative experiments in institutional design which only the legislature and the executive can undertake, and in which it might be appropriate that judges have only a marginal role.

Thus, even though judges play an essential role in my argument, they will also be somewhat demoted from the supreme position they are sometimes accorded in legal theory. Nevertheless, even if judges cannot undertake the institutional experiments in which I think the legislature and the executive must engage in order to support the rule-of-law project, and even though once these experiments are under way, judges might play only a marginal role in them, judges still retain a central role in prompting the legislature and the executive to undertake the experiments. For the moment, at least, judicial reasoning remains the main site for articulating the principles of the rule-of-law project.

My conception of the judicial role is thus neither of the two versions offered by legal positivism: the judge as the mouth through which the law (understood as the determinate content of rules) speaks; nor the judge as a mini-legislature, who has to make law because rules do not dictate an answer. Nor, as I have already suggested, is it only the judge as Hercules. Rather, it includes the judge as weatherman, an idea partly inspired by Bob Dylan, though, contrary to his claim, I think that one needs a weatherman to know which way the wind blows.[13] But mostly the image comes from Thomas Hobbes and from the most famous chapter in his work, chapter 13 of *Leviathan*,[14] where Hobbes sets out the state of nature.

Everyone remembers that Hobbes defines the state of nature as a 'warre, as of every man, against every man'.[15] But not everyone recalls that Hobbes also says that the war he has in mind need not be actual fighting, but the 'known disposition thereto', just as the 'nature of Foule weather, lyeth not in a showre or two of rain; but in an inclination thereto of many days

---

[13] See 'Subterranean Homesick Blues'. First release, 'Bringing it All Back Home'.

[14] Thomas Hobbes, *Leviathan*; edited by Richard Tuck (Cambridge: Cambridge University Press, 1996).

[15] *Ibid.*, ch. 13, p. 88.

together . . .'.[16] I will be referring to Hobbes at various points and will at the end rely heavily on his political and legal theory to make sense of what I have called the constitution of law. Such reliance might seem counterintuitive since Hobbes is widely considered to be both the founder of legal positivism and to have supposed that the sovereign is, as H. L. A. Hart described it, an 'uncommanded commander':[17] his authority is absolute. Indeed, Carl Schmitt regarded Hobbes as the most important precursor to his own work on the relationship between law and politics and liked to quote Hobbes' dictum that authority, not truth, makes law.[18]

But I will argue that for Hobbes judges have the role of alerting the commonwealth to the storm clouds on the horizon when the rule of law which secures the fabric of civil society is put under strain. This is quite a modest role for judges. It does not say with John Rawls that the first virtue of political and legal institutions is liberal justice, in the sense of an independent resource of liberal principles whose natural guardian is the judiciary.[19] Instead, it looks to a kind of justice located within the law, justice in the administration of the law. Authority and not truth makes law. But one who wants to be an authority has to accept the constraints of the rule of law. And these constraints are both moral and the constitutive or constitutional conditions of being an authority.

I will also argue that even the diminished prominence of judges in this regard is a somewhat contingent matter. When legislatures and executives self-consciously identify their own roles in the project, they too provide important sites for articulating the principles of the rule of law. Nevertheless, as I will seek to demonstrate, judges can instruct us in what it is we are committed to when we are committed to upholding the rule of law and thus in what we are entitled to demand of a government that claims to govern through law.

I should mention right at the outset that I will not at any point go into much detail about what I claim to be the content of the rule of law. In summary, my position is that legislation must be capable of being interpreted in such a way that it can be enforced in accordance with the

---

[16] *Ibid.*

[17] H. L. A. Hart, 'Positivism and the Separation of Law and Morals' in H. L. A. Hart, *Essays in Jurisprudence and Philosophy* (Oxford: Clarendon Press, 1983), pp. 49–87 at p. 59.

[18] Carl Schmitt, *The Leviathan in the State Theory of Thomas Hobbes: Meaning and Failure of a Political Symbol*, translated by George Schwab and Erna Hilfstein (Westport, Conn.: Greenwood Press, 1996), p. 55.

[19] John Rawls, *A Theory of Justice* (Oxford: Oxford University Press, 1980) p. 3 read in conjunction with John Rawls, *Political Liberalism* (New York: Columbia University Press, 1993).

requirements of due process: the officials who implement it can comply with a duty to act fairly, reasonably and in a fashion that respects the equality of all those who are subject to the law and independent judges are entitled to review the decisions of these officials to check that they do so comply. I will also argue that our understanding of concepts such as fairness, reasonableness, and equality is inevitably influenced by our evolving view of the individual who is subject to the law, the legal subject for short, and thus in recent times by the claim that the legal subject has to be regarded primarily as a bearer of human rights.

In other words, my conception of the rule of law is a rather bare common law one, enriched by the way in which such a conception has to be updated, most recently because of the central place taken by an international and domestic discourse of human rights in our thinking about law. Indeed, the relationship between international law and domestic law is a central theme of this book. It arises because of the willingness of some judges to draw inspiration from international human rights law for their understanding of the rule of law, a willingness which is matched by the hostility of others to this interpretative strategy. The former declare themselves willing often in cases where the individuals who seek their protection are in the most vulnerable category of all, the alien who is suspected by public officials of being a security risk.

It is often at the point where judges decide how to deal with this category that one can most sharply pose the question whether the people who get the protection of the rule of law are the citizens – those who are already in the political community, or whether it is enough to be a legal subject – an individual who is subject to the law of that community. And if it is the latter, is that subject to be treated by the law as bearer of human rights, an individual who has the same rights as a citizen? This last question raises the important issue of the relationship between the rule of law and human rights and that issue is of course not confined to immigration cases.

For one should never neglect law's capacity to move people in and out of categories – 'law's role in producing the alien within'.[20] Law is capable of shifting the category of alien enemy out of the legal arena in which it often goes unnoticed because we don't care much about those who have fragile legal status in our societies, or even want them out as soon as possible – those with names like Rehman, Al-Kateb, Teoh, Suresh, that is,

---

[20] Audrey Macklin, 'Borderline Security' in Ronald J. Daniels, Patrick Macklem and Kent Roach (eds.), *The Security of Freedom: Essays on Canada's Anti-Terrorism Bill* (Toronto: University of Toronto Press, 2001), pp. 383–404 at p. 398.

refugee claimants and people subject to deportation because they are not yet citizens. In addition, it shifts the category of the alien into the ordinary law of the land, where the ineliminably vague and political understandings of 'terrorist' and 'national security' give to the executive a wide scope for dealing conveniently with those it considers to be its enemy.

Nevertheless, I hope to show that even my bare conception of the rule of law has significant consequences for legal theory, for our understanding of constitutionalism, and for our sense of what we are entitled to demand of our legislatures, our judges and our governments. At the least, it tells us that any plausible conception of the rule of law is one that both links procedural constraints to substantive values and requires that all three branches of government regard themselves as participating in a common project of realizing those values.

As I have suggested, participation requires choice and any of the branches may choose at times against the rule of law. I hope to show that the pathologies that result from such choices help to understand what a commitment to the rule of law involves. But it is important to keep in mind that talk of a choice to govern through the rule of law can be somewhat misleading, except in transitional societies. These are societies which are trying to develop the rule of law as part of a more general task of escaping from an authoritarian past and in their regard it makes complete sense to talk about a choice to have the rule of law.

In contrast, in societies that are already governed by the rule of law, any attempt to articulate what that rule involves will express already exist-ing fundamental commitments to certain principles and to institutional arrangements which seek to implement the principles. And these prin-ciples and institutions will often have been developed over centuries. In this kind of society, the issue of choice often arises as a choice against the rule of law, one which will come into conflict with deeply embed-ded values and institutional arrangements which will slow a drift towards authoritarianism and thus help to maintain that society's place among the civilized nations. For such a society, the choice against the rule of law is thus quite difficult and will in fact be made up of many particular choices that incrementally amount to a drift in the direction of authoritarianism. But there are moments in these societies when the issue of commitment to the rule of law is starkly illuminated and my selection of cases is always with an eye to such illumination. Moreover, as I have also suggested, while at times the issue is how to ensure that a society maintains its institutions in such a way as to continue the rule-of-law project, at other times, the issue is how best to design new institutions in order to perform that same task.

When I originally planned the lectures on which this book is based, it seemed that the natural way to divide them was by allocating to the judiciary a role equal to the treatments of the legislature and the executive. But I came to realize that the judiciary did not deserve separate treatment. The constitution of law is revealed through the detailed discussion of a few judicial decisions so that the judiciary plays a role throughout. Such a methodology will seem suspect both because of the element of selectivity and because it might appear designed to rig the game in favour of judges with the inevitable result that they turn out to win the competition for supremacy. I hope to deal with the suspicion of selectivity by demonstrating that my account has the theoretical resources to deal convincingly with alleged counter-examples. I will also deal with the suspicion about what might be termed judge worship by, as indicated, elaborating a relatively modest role for judges in the rule-of-law project.

The judgments I will discuss fall roughly into three categories. First, there are judges who think that they have a duty to uphold the rule of law in the sense of fundamental principles only when there is a bill of rights that imposes such a duty. They also tend to think that in an emergency situation legal rights, including entrenched constitutional rights, have no or little application. Second, there are judges who articulate and follow through on such a duty, despite the fact that they have no bill of rights to rely on, and despite the fact that the legislature and/or the executive claims that there is an emergency situation. Third, there are judges who reach the same conclusions as judges in the second category, but who avoid making explicit their constitutional commitments.

A large part of my argument will consist of elaborating the claim that it is important for judges to make their commitments explicit. Only then can we see why it makes sense to say that judges are under a constitutional duty to uphold the rule of law, despite the fact that they might not always be able to fulfill that duty in the face of an executive and legislature determined to operate without the rule of law. Moreover, there is more than a theoretical point riding on the claim that judges should reach their rule-of-law preserving conclusions by articulating fully the theory that sustains those conclusions. As I will show, judges who avoid making their commitments explicit risk lending support to judges in the first category as well as to future legislative and executive departures from the rule of law.

Not all of the cases I discuss deal with emergencies. But my argument is in part based in the fact that the kinds of claims that are made about states of emergency occur also in quite ordinary situations, for example, claims that the rule of law does not apply to some ordinary exercises of official discretion. In addition, in seeing why ordinary exercises of official discretion are subject to the rule of law, we can also see how what often seems to be the exercise of discretion writ as large as possible – the executive's discretion in deciding how to respond to emergencies – is similarly subject.

The main objective of chapter 1 is to set out Carl Schmitt's challenge: the claim that a response to an emergency situation has in the nature of things to be partly or even wholly exempted from the requirements that we associate with the rule of law in normal times. I will show how Schmitt's challenge is supported by much of the history of the way in which judges in the Commonwealth have failed to impose the rule of law during times of emergency. And I will also show how in the United States, academic debate about how best to respond to emergencies tends to support that challenge. Yet, I will argue, there is still a basis for claiming that the law contains moral resources sufficient to respond to the challenge.

The rest of the book explores these resources. Chapter 2, 'Constituting the legislature', discusses the fundamental values that constitute legislative authority whether or not there is a written constitution. It also introduces the doctrine I call constitutional positivism, the kind of legal positivism deployed by judges who are faced with deciding constitutional questions. Chapter 3, 'Taking the administrative state seriously', focuses on the role of the executive in maintaining the rule of law. Chapter 4, 'The unity of public law', weaves the threads of the entire argument of the book together via a discussion of the relationship between international human rights law and domestic law, as exemplified in the recent *Belmarsh* decision of the House of Lords,[21] which found that the indefinite detention of aliens was incompatible with the United Kingdom's commitments to human rights.

---

[21] *A v. Secretary of State for the Home Department* [2005] 2 WLR 87.

Legality in a time of emergency

Introduction

This book explores the idea that there is a constitution of law, exemplified in the common law constitution of Commonwealth countries. It looks mainly to cases decided in the United Kingdom, Australia, and Canada in order to show that law provides a moral resource that can inform a rule-of-law project capable of responding to situations which place legal and political order under great stress, for example, states of emergency or executive decisions about national security. My argument is that the rule-of-law project is one in which judges play an important role but which also requires the participation of the legislature and the executive.

Two obstacles to such an argument will strike anyone familiar with the history of legal responses to such situations. First, in such situations the government usually claims that the exceptional nature of the situations requires a departure from the rule-of-law regime appropriate for ordinary times and so whatever role one accords to judges in ordinary times has to be significantly rethought. And often the government will follow through on this claim by procuring through a statute powers for itself which seem to permit it to act outside of the ordinary constraints of the rule of law. The government could be wrong in the claim that it needs such powers, but, and this is the second obstacle, as a matter of fact the judicial record in enforcing the rule of law in such situations is at worst dismal, at best ambiguous, and this fact might serve to buttress the government's claim.

There are different explanations of this record, and these hinge to a large extent on whether one thinks that the executive is right when it claims that exceptional situations require departures from the rule of law. If one thinks that such a claim is wrong, one might be tempted to infer that the dismal judicial record comes about because judges are in dereliction of their duty to uphold the rule of law: judges simply fold in the face of executive claims, whether or not these are supported by statute. Alternatively, one might think that the judges are not so much spineless as prudent: judges want to avoid provoking the executive on this occasion so that, on a later more important occasion, they will be able to act effectively. They are, in other words, keeping their powder dry in the long-term interests of the rule of law.[1] But if the executive's claims are right that the rule of law does not apply in exceptional situations, then neither judicial spinelessness nor prudence is the issue. Rather, the judicial record is not so much in itself dismal as reflective of the dismal fact that the rule of law has little or no role to play in policing exceptional situations. Finally, it can be argued that the judicial record is not dismal. Rather, judges are still upholding the rule of law in the cases that make up the record because, as long as the executive has its authority to respond to exceptional situations from the law, the situations are governed by law, which is to say, by the rule of law.

This last explanation equates the rule of law with rule by law, whereas the explanations that rely on judicial spinelessness or prudence, as well as the one which relies on the peculiar nature of exceptional situations, do not make this equation. That is, unless one equates the rule of law with rule by law, one will regard the rule of law as substantive in nature so that it does not suffice to have the rule of law that the executive can claim a statutory warrant for its actions. They require not only such a warrant but also that the executive's actions comply with the principles of the rule of law. Thus only the explanations that rely on judicial spinelessness or prudence presuppose that a substantive conception might apply in the exception.

While there is something to each of these competing explanations, in practice they tend to boil down to two: either judges are in dereliction of their duty to uphold the rule of law or, on the contrary, they are doing precisely what their duty to uphold the rule of law requires given the exceptional nature of the situation. As we will see, when questions about the legality of executive action or the validity of legislation arise out of emergency situations, judges are reluctant to adopt a political questions doctrine and say that the questions are so quintessentially political that they are not regulated by law. Because interests like the interest in liberty will usually be at stake, judges prefer to find that the situation is regulated by law and therefore subject to the judicial imprimatur which certifies whether or not the executive is acting in accordance with (the rule of)

---

[1] This view is often associated with Alexander M. Bickel, *The Least Dangerous Branch: The Supreme Court at the Bar of Politics* (2nd edn, New Haven: Yale University Press, 1986).

law. Thus, rather than find that what the executive does is beyond the reach of law, judges will find that, given the situation, they should, as a matter of law, defer to the executive's judgment about what is required. In other words, the political questions doctrine, a doctrine that says that certain questions are not justiciable or amenable to judicial review, is replaced by a doctrine of judicial deference. Similarly, judges who adopt the stance of prudence and who fail to uphold the rule of law now for the sake of the rule of law in the long term will not say that on this occasion the executive is acting outside of the rule of law. Precisely because the point is to keep the executive friendly to the rule of law, judges must find that on this occasion the executive is acting in accordance with its rule, understood in a more formal or procedural way, so that later they can enforce a more substantive conception of the rule of law.

In short, at the level of legal theory, the explanatory contest is between a substantive conception of the rule of law and a more formal one, which equates rule by law with the rule of law. And since that contest is about which conception is appropriate, it is not just about explanation but also about justification – about what judges ought to do.

In order to clarify this contest, I will start with an account of the judicial record, one which seems to support the claim that it is either dismal or at best ambiguous. Indeed, I will show that there is a plausible argument that when judges assert that they are maintaining the rule of law in exceptional situations, they make things worse not better from the perspective of a substantive conception of the rule of law. For they maintain that they are upholding the rule of law when at most there is rule by law, a statutory warrant for the executive.

I will then set out the view that in fact a substantive conception of the rule of law has no application in an exceptional situation. As we will see, this view was mostly starkly presented by the fascist legal theorist, Carl Schmitt who, during the Weimar period, argued that law cannot govern a state of emergency or exception. I will show that recent attempts by academics in the United States to respond to an allegedly different post-9/11 world turn out to support Schmitt's view. Indeed, they might make things worse, in much the same way as do judges who claim to be upholding the rule of law when there is merely rule by law. However, I will conclude that we still have a basis for not giving up on the idea that law provides moral resources sufficient to maintain the rule-of-law project even when legal and political order is under great stress. The rest of my book will take up the challenge of providing the argument that will sustain that idea.

Judges and the politics of the rule of law

My doctorate dealt with the South African judiciary during apartheid. I tried to show that the different approaches judges took to interpreting the laws of apartheid illuminated debates in philosophy of law about the relationship between law and morality. My main focus was on the statutory regime put in place to maintain national security and on the way in which the majority of South African judges had reneged on their commitment to the rule of law. The crucial moment, one which set the course for nearly all judges for most of apartheid, happened in 1961 in *Rossouw* v. *Sachs*.[2]

In issue were the conditions of detention of Albie Sachs – later a judge of South Africa's Constitutional Court – who had been detained under s. 17 of the 90-Day Law. This statute said nothing about the conditions under which detainees were to be held, only that they were to be detained for 'interrogation' for a period of up to ninety days until 'in the opinion of the Commissioner of Police' they had 'replied satisfactorily to all questions'.[3]

The case came to the Appellate Division, then South Africa's highest court, by way of the government's appeal against the decision of two judges of the Cape Provincial Division, which had said that to deprive Sachs of reading matter would amount to 'punishment' and that it would

---

[2] (1964) 2 SA 551 (A).
[3] The '90-day detention law' was the name given to s. 17 of Act 37 1963, enacted to assist the government in countering the underground activities of the African National Congress and other liberation organizations. Section 17(1) provided that:

> Notwithstanding anything to the contrary in any law contained, any commissioned officer . . . may . . . without warrant arrest . . . any person whom he suspects upon reasonable grounds of having committed or intending . . . to commit any offence under the Suppression of Communism Act . . . or the Unlawful Organizations Act . . . or the offence of sabotage, or who in his opinion is in possession of information relating to the commission of such offence . . . , and detain such person . . . for interrogation . . . , until such person has in the opinion of the Commissioner of Police replied satisfactorily to all questions at the said interrogation, but no such person shall be so detained for more than ninety days on any particular occasion when he is so arrested.

Section 17(2) provided that no person was to 'have access' to the detainee except with the consent of the Minister of Justice or a commissioned officer, though the person had to be visited not less than once a week by a magistrate. Section 17(3) provided that, 'No court shall have jurisdiction to order the release from custody of any person so detained . . .'

The section was effective for twelve months and thereafter was subject to annual renewal by proclamation of the State President. Security statutes enacted as the political crisis of South Africa worsened provided for indefinite detention and shielded the conditions of detention from the scrutiny of lawyers and courts.

be 'surprising to find that the Legislature intended punishment to be meted out to an unconvicted prisoner'. The discretion of the officer in charge of detention in regard to such issues was, the judges said, 'at all times subject to correction in a court of law'.[4] But the Appellate Division found that it could not order that Sachs be given reading and writing materials, since the intention of the detention provision was clearly to use psychological pressure to 'induce the detainee to speak'.[5] Moreover, the Court said that it was influenced by the fact that

> subversive activities of various kinds directed against the public order and the safety of the State are by no means unknown, and s. 17 is plainly designed to combat such activities. Such being the circumstances whereunder s. 17 was placed upon the Statute Book, this Court should, while bearing in mind the enduring importance of the liberty of the individual, in my judgment approach the construction of s. 17 with due regard to the objects which that section is designed to attain.[6]

This decision laid the basis for a sense among the security forces that they could torture and otherwise mistreat detainees with impunity. As I argued before South Africa's Truth and Reconciliation Commission, the judges were accountable for having facilitated the shadows and secrecy of the world in which the security forces operated and for permitting the unrestrained implementation of apartheid policy.[7] They thus bore some responsibility for the bitter legacy of hurt which was the main focus of the Commission. Moreover, the judges were clearly warned at the time of the consequences of their decisions. In an article aptly titled 'The Permanence of the Temporary', the authors subjected the Appellate Division to a devastating critique and argued that the judiciary had made itself complicit in a government strategy to introduce a permanent state of lawlessness into the ordinary law of the land.[8]

It was inevitable in one sense that the judges of the Appellate Division would reach this result. The National Party government had in the 1950s secured through the appointment process a compliant bench, presided over by L. C. Steyn, Chief Justice of South Africa, from 1959 to 1971. He

---

[4] The decision is unreported. For detailed analysis of the Appellate Division's decision, see David Dyzenhaus, *Hard Cases in Wicked Legal Systems: South African Law in the Perspective of Legal Philosophy* (Oxford: Clarendon Press, 1991), ch. 4.

[5] *Rossouw*, at 560–1.   [6] *Ibid.*, at 563.

[7] For my account of this hearing, see David Dyzenhaus, *Judging the Judges, Judging Ourselves: Truth, Reconciliation and the Apartheid Legal Order* (Oxford: Hart Publishing, 1999).

[8] A. S. Mathews and R. C. Albino, 'The Permanence of the Temporary: An Examination of the 90- and 180-Day Detention Laws' (1966) 83 *South African Law Journal* 16–43.

had been appointed from government service to the Transvaal Provincial Division in 1951, a move which broke with the tradition of appointing only senior members of the Bar to the Bench, and which thus brought a 'wave of protest' from the Bar.[9] Just four years later he was appointed to the Appellate Division at a time of great political and legal controversy caused by the Court's resistance to the government's attempts to use legislation as a means of sidestepping the constitutional protection given to coloured or mixed race voters. In addition, he was appointed Chief Justice in 1959 over the heads of two more senior judges, one of whom, Oliver Schreiner had been the principal defender of rule-of-law principles on the Court. L. C. Steyn ensured that his Court was utterly complicit in the apartheid regime's attempt to claim that it was a rule-of-law respecting government while at the same time the regime gave through statute its officials the power to abuse the human rights of black South Africans and those few white people who rallied to their cause.

However, in order to assist in sustaining the claim that the government respected the rule of law, the judges of the Appellate Division had to show that their conclusions were supported by law. My point about the inevitability of the result in *Rossouw* is not a crude legal realist one that the judges were supporters of apartheid and thus could be counted on to exercise their discretion in favour of the government. While some or many of them might have been with L. C. Steyn enthusiastic supporters of the apartheid regime, it is a mistake to underestimate the influence in their judgments of their understanding of law, one which inclined them to deliver results that favoured the government. I call this understanding of law constitutional positivism, and I will explore its complexities in some detail later. For the moment it suffices to say that constitutional positivism regards the legislature as the sole legitimate source of legal norms and thus in moments of interpretative doubt looks primarily to proxies for actual legislative intent in order to work out what the law requires.

Constitutional positivism was not however the creation of South African judges. Rather, it was the product of the hub of the Commonwealth – the United Kingdom – and of the way in which legal education, under the influence of John Austin, one of the principal legal positivists, and A. V. Dicey, the constitutional lawyer whose book on the English constitution takes much from Austin. Also, despite the fact that South Africa had exited the Commonwealth in 1961, in anticipation of being

---

[9] See C. F. Forsyth, *In Danger for Their Talents: A Study of the Appellate Division of the Supreme Court of South Africa from 1950–80* (Cape Town: Juta, 1985), pp. 14–33.

evicted because of the abhorrence of other members towards apartheid and the political repression required to maintain it, South African judges by and large continued to think of themselves as part of the family of the common law, proudly sustaining its traditions, including that of an independent judiciary whose first commitment is to the rule of law. It was only because South African judges had that self-image and were determined as a result to produce comprehensive legal reasons for their judgments that the apartheid government could make its claim that it respected the rule of law while using the law as an instrument of oppression.

It was thus of great importance to the Appellate Division in *Rossouw* that no less an authority than the House of Lords, the highest court in what Commonwealth judges regarded as the bastion of liberty, had in 1942 in *Liversidge* v. *Anderson*[10] set out a line of reasoning in security matters which they could follow. *Liversidge* concerned a rather different legal situation, the question whether a detention regulation which allowed the responsible minister to detain if he had 'reasonable cause to believe any person to be of hostile origins or associations . . .' should be construed objectively or subjectively. A subjective construal would mean that the minister's say-so was sufficient to ground a claim that a detainee was a security risk. Hence, only if the regulation were construed objectively could judges test the grounds for the minister's claim. The majority of the House of Lords held that, in a wartime emergency, the only possible construal is subjective.

The South African judges rightly took the basic principle at stake in *Liversidge* to be the same as that in *Rossouw*: should authoritative legal texts be read subject to common law values in the face of some legislative indications to the contrary and despite the fact that the executive was dealing with judgments about national security, judgments in which the executive claims and judges often accept it has a special expertise? So *Rossouw* is evidence of the rather depressing fact that within the family of Commonwealth legal orders, the fruit born of the migration of legal ideas from one to another can be bitter.

In my doctorate, I argued that one should not let such depressing facts shape one's understanding of law. Rather one should look to the few South African judges in the lower courts who took their cue not from the judgments of the majority of the House of Lords in *Liversidge*, but from the kind of stance Lord Atkin adopted in his lone dissent in that case. Such judges, in my view, did more than maintain their commitment to the rule

---

[10] *Liversidge* v. *Anderson* [1942] AC 206.

of law. They also showed how law itself contains the moral resources that make it possible for them to resist the attempts by an allegedly omnipotent legislature to undermine the rule of law. My optimism was helped by the fact that I fully accepted at the time the official ideology of English public law that Lord Atkin's dissent represented the true spirit of the common law, so that the majority's reasoning in *Liversidge* should be regarded as an unfortunate aberration in an otherwise unbroken tradition of legality.

But at my oral exam, one of my examiners – Jeffrey Jowell – gently pointed out to me that the official ideology masked the fact that when English judges had after the Second World War confronted the issue of review of national security, they tended to forget about Lord Atkin's dissent in *Liversidge* and to revert in substance, if not in name, to the majority's approach. Jowell was, of course, right at the time. And not only have judges for the most part continued to prove him right in the wake of 9/11 but *Liversidge* was not the first decision of its kind by the House of Lords, which brings me to the First World War decision, *R v. Halliday, ex Parte Zadig*[11] and the recent article by David Foxton, '*R v. Halliday Ex Parte Zadig* In Retrospect'.[12]

Foxton's article does the important service of bringing out from the shadow of *Liversidge* the judgments of the majority of the House of Lords from the First World War in *Halliday* on which the majority in *Liversidge* relied. He also brings out from the shadow of Lord Atkin's dissent in *Liversidge*, Lord Shaw's dissent in *Halliday*, on which Lord Atkin did not rely. The situations were again somewhat different. In *Liversidge* there was no issue about the validity of Regulation 18B, since the Emergency Powers (Defence) Act 1939 clearly gave the Cabinet authority to make regulations detaining people without trial. In the First World War, the Defence of the Realm (Consolidation) Act 1914 did not grant any such power and so the question in *Halliday* was whether the very wide grant of power in the Act included by necessary implication the authority to make detention regulations.[13] But again, the fundamental issue was the same in both: whether an authoritative legal text should be read as if it were intended to respect common law values.

Foxton reports that Shaw was impressed from the outset by Zadig's lawyers' argument that a constitutional convention required that

---

[11] [1917] AC 260.   [12] (2003) 119 *Law Quarterly Review* 445–94.

[13] As I will explain in ch. 3, it was this difference which Lord Atkin relied on to distinguish the cases, though it is, in my view, clear that he was embarrassed by the fact that he had as a lower court judge in *Halliday* concurred in a decision which upheld the validity of the regulation.

Parliament could only suspend habeas corpus by express enactment. But it seems that the 'final catalyst', as Foxton calls it, in Shaw's decision to dissent came through a dinner at the Middle Temple with Jan Smuts, who had come to London to attend an Imperial Conference, and whose name adorns the lectures which are the basis for this book.[14] In Shaw's own words:

> I broke the ice and I discussed this very judgment with him. He saw the crux of the case in a moment, and informed me that the same point had been settled in a case decided in the Privy Council on an appeal from Pondoland. I asked the date, and he gave me the date within six months. I turned up the Reports and found that he was right in every particular, and a page and a half of that judgment is really in that way the work of General Smuts rather than myself.[15]

Foxton continues that Shaw was particularly receptive to Smuts's argument. Shaw had been an opponent of the Boer War. Not only had he protested against demands to dispense with due legal process, but he had organized a petition to the King to prevent the execution of another Boer general. Foxton says that '[p]opular fervour would have demanded the same fate for Smuts. Smuts' presence at the Imperial process, and in the Middle Temple, vividly demonstrated that Shaw had been right to resist popular clamour then . . .'[16]

---

[14] Smuts went from being a Boer general in the war against England to becoming one of South Africa's most distinguished politicians of the twentieth century. As well as a stint as Prime Minister of South Africa, he was a member of the Imperial War Cabinet during the First World War, played a significant role in the foundation of the League of Nations, and was made Chancellor of the University of Cambridge. Whether Smuts would have approved of my arguments is very doubtful. The issue is not only or even mainly that Smuts was a racist, whose own policies in South Africa laid the basis for apartheid: after all, in holding racist views, he was in the mainstream of politics. Rather, he strongly favoured a unitary system of government over a federal one for South Africa because he thought it desirable to have a system of absolute parliamentary supremacy and, correspondingly, wished to avoid giving judges any excuse to arrogate legislative power and thought that a federal constitution offered such excuses. See Bernard Friedman, *Smuts: A Reappraisal* (London: George Allen & Unwin Ltd, 1975), pp. 41–4. Friedman also suggests that Smuts was quite aware that a unitary Parliament in the colonial context might be even more absolute than in Britain since it would be established without the restraining conventions and traditions in place in Britain. Smuts' fondness for the Privy Council decision could perhaps be explained by the fact that he saw it as a blow against colonial authority – not only against the Governor, but also against the Prime Minister, Cecil John Rhodes who, was one of the parties to oppose Sigcau's petition for his release.

[15] Foxton, 'R v. Halliday', 484. The case was *Sprigg* v. *Sigcau* [1897] AC 238.

[16] Foxton, 'R v. Halliday', 485.

In this case, the Privy Council decision upheld a decision of the Supreme Court of the Cape Colony that, in the absence of express delegated authority, the Governor of that Colony could not by proclamation give himself powers to arrest and detain indefinitely and without charge a dissident African chief. So I would like to claim that *Halliday* shows that the migration of legal ideas does not always go from centre to periphery in the Commonwealth and that those that go from periphery to centre can bear good fruit.

But like Lord Atkin in *Liversidge*, Lord Shaw was alone in dissent so the two stories of judges and wartime detention have the same unhappy ending. Together they seem to merge into one to show that Jowell's objection cannot be met by revising somewhat the myth that the majority's judgment in *Liversidge* is an aberration. The line from the majority judgments in *Halliday* through the majority judgments in *Liversidge*, via the Appellate Division's decision in *Rossouw*, to post-9/11 highly deferential decisions such as the 2002 decision of the House of Lords in *Secretary of State for the Home Department* v. *Rehman*[17] is unbroken. In the last decision, the House of Lords articulated an understanding of the separation of powers which requires almost complete deference by judges to executive determinations of the interests of national security – and with it, the House of Lords once again initiated the process of exporting bad legal ideas to the former colonies.

Moreover, even Lord Atkin's dissent can be understood as not achieving much more than lip service to a conception of the rule of law as the rule of fundamental values. Brian Simpson has suggested that Lord Atkin's argument that judges were entitled to read Regulation 18B objectively, so that the Home Secretary was obliged to provide reasons for Liversidge's detention that could be scrutinized in a court of law, was ineffectual. Given the secrecy and duplicity of the secret services and the judicial inability to go beyond their claims about the need to protect their information from scrutiny, the kinds of reasons that will be offered, and with which judges will have to content themselves, will not allow for any genuine testing of the validity of the administrative decisions. Simpson thus concludes that Lord Atkin's dissent in *Liversidge* is itself an example of judicial lip service to the rule of law – an attempt by a judge to shore up his sense of role in the face of the reality of necessarily untrammeled executive discretion.[18]

---

[17] [2002] 1 All ER 123.
[18] A. W. Brian Simpson, *In the Highest Degree Odious: Detention Without Trial in Wartime Britain* (Oxford: Oxford University Press, 1992), p. 363.

If Simpson is right, then Lord Shaw's dissent in *Halliday* is a lonely and futile beacon of the rule of law: lonely because it is the sole exception in the historical record; futile not only because it was a dissent, but also because its potential to inspire future courts could be nipped in the bud by a clearly expressed legislative delegation of authority to make regulations concerning detention. Thus the Emergency Powers (Defence) Act 1939 explicitly gave the Cabinet the authority to make detention regulations because Sir Claude Schuster, a senior civil servant, thought that the lesson of *Halliday* was that a severe power such as the power to detain should be expressly authorized by the statute.[19]

We might thus conclude not only that the judicial record during emergencies is a dismal one, but that it could not be otherwise. Moreover, it might seem, following Simpson, that for judges to try to pretend otherwise, to pay lip service to the rule of law in situations where the rule of law cannot do any work, is likely to make matters worse by giving to government the façade of the rule of law without the judges being able to enforce its substance.

The seriousness of this last concern is graphically illustrated by the political stance of Lord Woolf, a former Lord Chief Justice of England, in the post-9/11 period. Indeed, as I will show, his stance illustrates two further and no less serious concerns. The first is that judicial lip service to the rule of law in exceptional situations has consequences for the way judges deal with ordinary situations. One finds that judges begin to be content with less substance in the rule of law in situations which are not part of any emergency regime, all the while claiming that the rule of law is well maintained. Second, the law that addresses the emergency situation starts to look less exceptional as judges interpret statutes that deal with ordinary situations in the same fashion. As a package, these concerns seem to show that once the exceptional or emergency situation is normalized, that is, addressed by ordinary statutes and treated by judges as part of a 'business as usual',[20] rule-of-law regime, so the exception starts to seep into other parts of the law.

Now the first episode in the story of Lord Woolf's stance will seem to undermine my claims for he condemned publicly, in a lecture at Cambridge University in 2004, the ouster or privative clause which the government intended to introduce by statute to shield immigration

---

[19] *Ibid.*, p. 46.
[20] I take the term from Oren Gross, 'Chaos and Rules: Should Responses to Violent Crises Always be Constitutional?' (2003) 112 *Yale Law Journal* 1011–134.

decisions almost totally from judicial review.[21] He castigated the government for contemplating a measure that would be 'fundamentally in conflict with the rule of law and should not be contemplated by any government if it had respect for the rule of law'.[22] He predicted that the measure would 'bring the legislature, the executive and the judiciary into conflict',[23] thus suggesting that the judiciary might well invalidate it or at the least find some means of reading it down. And he threatened the government with a campaign to enact a written constitution:

> Immigration and asylum involve basic human rights. What areas of government decision-making would be next removed from the scrutiny of the courts? What is the use of courts, if you cannot access them? . . . The response of the government and the House of Lords to the chorus of criticism of clause 11 will produce the answer to the question of whether our freedoms can be left in their hands under an unwritten constitution.[24]

These comments of Lord Woolf caused a public stir and may have been a significant factor in the government's decision to withdraw the measure. Less noticed, however, were his remarks in the same speech about the Nationality, Immigration and Asylum Act 2002. He said that what made the proposed privative clause 'even more objectionable' was that the statute had

> introduced a form of statutory review by the High Court on the papers which is extremely expeditious (taking a few weeks rather than months) and which gives every indication of being successful. The judiciary recommended this new procedure and cooperated in its introduction to prevent abuse of the protection afforded by the courts. Because this process is so speedy, there is no great advantage to be gained from making abusive applications and this is one of the reasons why the number of statutory reviews has, so far, been relatively modest.[25]

---

[21] For an account of the government's strategy, see Andrew Le Sueur, 'Three Strikes and It's Out? The UK Government's Strategy to Oust Judicial Review from Immigration and Asylum Decision-Making' (2004) *Public Law* 225–33 and for a general overview, see Richard Rawlings, 'Review, Revenge and Retreat' (2005) 68 *Modern Law Review* 378–410. Lord Woolf's comments were made in the Squires Lecture, delivered in the Faculty of Law, University of Cambridge, 3 March 2004, now published as Lord Woolf, 'The Rule of Law and a Change in the Constitution' (2004) 63 *Cambridge Law Journal* 317–30. For Lord Woolf's earlier reflections on judicial reactions to statutes that clearly flout the rule of law, which seemed to indicate a limited judicial authority to invalidate statutes, see Lord Woolf, 'Droit Public – English Style' [1995] *Public Law* 57–71 at 69.

[22] Woolf, 'The Rule of Law', 328.   [23] *Ibid.*   [24] *Ibid.*, 329.   [25] *Ibid.*, 328.

In assessing these remarks, it is important to know that this statute put in place the recommendations of Mr Justice Collins, at that time the President of the Immigration Appeal Tribunal, who had designed a process of statutory review to replace judicial review in immigration and asylum cases. This process is regarded by human rights lawyers as vastly inferior to judicial review because it is confined to review by a High Court judge on the basis of written submissions, the applicant has only five days to lodge an application, and the decision of the High Court is final – there is no further appeal to the Court of Appeal or to the House of Lords. Since, as Lord Woolf acknowledged, it is in immigration and refugee matters that important issues about human rights often arise, human rights lawyers were concerned that a particularly vulnerable group of people were being denied the kind of scrutiny by the superior courts that is required when human rights are at stake. Moreover, the government's justification for both the ouster clause and the statutory review procedure is that there is large-scale abuse of the present system. But the government has never produced any hard evidence of such abuse, choosing to rely on what it acknowledges to be 'anecdotal' evidence and on the suggestion that if a large proportion of appeals are failing this shows that there must be abuse.[26]

Collins appeared on 3 February 2004, before the Select Committee on Constitutional Affairs, to answer questions about the process. He was asked if it were possible to have his judgment about whether the process had done 'fundamental injustices', given that he recognized that the process was his idea. He replied: 'No – well, I would say that, wouldn't I but no, I do not think it has and I do not think anyone thinks it has.'[27] At this time, that is, the same time that debate about the privative clause was taking place, a challenge was launched to the statutory review process on both common law and European Convention on Human Rights[28] grounds. The challenge was heard by Mr Justice Collins now sitting in the High Court of Justice on 11 and 12 March 2004. On 12 March, he announced that he was dismissing the appeal with reasons to follow.[29]

---

[26] See Letter from Lord Filkin, Parliamentary Under Secretary of State, Department for Constitutional Affairs, to the Chair of the Joint Committee on Human Rights, Appendix 1a to the Seventeenth Report of Session 2003–04.

[27] Select Committee on Constitutional Affairs, Minutes of Evidence, 3 February 2004.

[28] The Convention for the Protection of Human Rights and Fundamental Freedoms also known as the European Convention on Human Rights, Rome, 4 November 1950, in force 3 September 1953, 213 UNTS 221.

[29] Reasons were given on 25 March 2004. See *R (G and M)* v. *SSHD* [2004] EWHC 588 (Admin).

It is I think intriguing that a judge should preside over a challenge to a statutory scheme, which he himself has designed. It is even more intriguing that on 15 March, just three days after Collins had announced his decision, Lord Woolf welcomed in the House of Lords the government's statement that it was abandoning the privative clause.[30] In his view, this meant that the government was affirming its commitment to the rule of law. He then went on to praise again the success of the statutory review process, thus suggesting by direct implication that it is consistent with the rule of law.

The government has since brought forward a version of statutory review to replace the ouster, which will apply to immigration and asylum generally.[31] Lord Woolf again said that he was pleased that the government had chosen not to come 'into conflict with the rule of law' and seemed to signal that this new provision was not so in conflict because it did give the High Court 'some power of review'. Somewhat strangely, in view of his past interventions, he did this through a letter he deposited in the library of the House of Lords, saying that it would be unwise for him to speak in the debate.[32] This provision was then adopted by Parliament despite the fact that some members took up the human rights and rule-of-law concerns about it that had been raised in a report by the Joint Committee on Human Rights.[33] The appeal against Collins' decision was heard and dismissed by the Court of Appeal.[34]

My claim is not that the Court of Appeal's decision was unequivocally wrong. Rather, it is that the story of Lord Woolf's participation in these debates supports a claim that the privative clause became a 'lightning conductor' to attract concerns about the rule of law so that the government could then slip through a provision that achieved the same substantive ends.[35] In other words, the government manipulated the political process to replace a proposed legal black hole, a space devoid of rule-of-law controls, with a grey hole, a space in which there are some rule-of-law controls. But these controls might not suffice to give to those who find themselves in the hole sufficient protection either from the perspective of the rule of law or from the perspective of the human rights regime to which the United Kingdom is officially committed. Moreover, the issue is

[30] Hansard, HC, vol. 659, cols. 60–61. 15 March 2004.
[31] The Asylum and Immigration Act 2004.
[32] Letter from the Lord Chief Justice to the Lord Chancellor, 29 April 2004.
[33] See Thirteenth Report of Session 2003–04.
[34] *M v. Immigration Appeal Tribunal* [2004] EWCA Civ 1731.
[35] See Sedley, 'Everything and Nothing' 10. Note that Sedley was one of the panel that decided the appeal. It is not that I think that the government was insincere about its desire to exclude judicial review.

not just government manipulation but active participation by the judiciary in legitimizing the rule-of-law credentials of a dubious procedure. Lord Woolf's advance approval bestowed an aura of legitimacy on the provision which is difficult to challenge in court, especially when it is given by the Lord Chief Justice. It seems obvious that had Lord Woolf presided over the appeal against Mr Justice Collins' decision, there would have been unanswerable grounds for the appellants to seek his recusal, as there would have been had Mr Justice Collins been asked to recuse himself. But even without Lord Woolf's presence, concerns remain that he could be interpreted as having publicly decided in advance of his Court hearing the challenge that the statutory review process complies sufficiently with the rule of law and with the United Kingdom's commitments to human rights. Thus it seems that while the judges are prepared to go to the wall to protect some role for themselves – hence the opposition to the proposed privative clause – all that they really care about is that they have a role, not its substance. They turn out to be sheep in rule-of-law clothing.

Now the issue in this story was not one of emergency or national security, but immigration. However, it is important to remember both that immigration law is often the area where executive decisions about those who are considered threats to national security are made and that control over aliens is often claimed to be of a piece with protecting the security of the state. More important is that Lord Woolf's participation in this political debate reflects the positions he had taken earlier in judgments on emergency law.

He was one of the panel of judges which decided *Rehman* and in substance the House of Lords upheld his judgment in that case. And he gave the lead judgment in *A* v. *Secretary of State for the Home Department*,[36] better known as the *Belmarsh* decision because the individuals who were appealing were detained in Belmarsh prison. *Belmarsh* concerned the statutory derogation from the Human Rights Act 1998[37] permitting the government to detain indefinitely non-citizens who are considered security risks but who cannot be deported because they face a risk of torture in their home country. Since the statute does not permit citizens who are security risks, and who cannot in virtue of their citizenship be deported, to be detained, the statute seems an affront to the rule-of-law principle of equality before the law as well as to the principles of any regime which purports to treat all those subject to its power as full bearers of human

---

[36] [2004] QB 335.   [37] See s. 23 of the Anti-Terrorism, Crime and Security Act 2001.

rights.[38] In the Court of Appeal, Lord Woolf, relying on *Rehman*, held that it was 'impossible for the Court to differ with the Secretary of State on the issue whether action was necessary only in relation to non-national suspected terrorists',[39] that aliens are 'objectively' in a 'different class from those who have a right of abode',[40] and that to discriminate only against aliens promotes human rights because one does not then have to discriminate against the class of those with a right of abode.[41]

Lord Woolf thus let the government off the hook of accepting the full political costs of an official disregard for human rights which might be incurred if citizens were indefinitely detained. For if the emergency the United Kingdom claims to face in fact requires indefinite detention of those who are thought to be risks, and thus requires a derogation from the state's commitment to human rights, then all who are thought to pose a threat should be detained. Put differently, if there is no need to detain citizens, then the government's case about the extent of the emergency and the necessity of its response to it is greatly weakened. Indeed, Lord Woolf's reasoning in *Belmarsh* sustains Simpson's charge of judicial lip service to the rule of law as, in an obvious, face-saving ploy, Lord Woolf warned against the dangers of repeating past mistakes when it came to internment of aliens and said that his judgment conserved the rule of law.[42]

Now the House of Lords has with one dissent upheld the appeal against the Court of Appeal's decision largely on the ground that the statutory provision is discriminatory.[43] However, with the exception of Lord Hoffmann, the judges in the majority did not question the government's

---

[38] In particular, it was argued that the derogation was incompatible with Articles 5 and 14 of the European Convention because it permitted discrimination on the grounds of nationality. Article 5 enshrines the right of the individual not to be arbitrarily detained while Article 14 requires that all rights and freedoms secured by the Convention are to be enjoyed without discrimination, including discrimination on the ground of 'national . . . origin'.

[39] *Belmarsh*, at 359–60.   [40] *Ibid.*, at 361–2.   [41] *Ibid.*, at 362.   [42] *Ibid.*, at 348.

[43] [2005] 2 WLR 87. It is well known that the government was successful in its anticipatory challenge to the participation by Lord Steyn, a very different Afrikaner judge from L. C. Steyn, in the panel which has now heard the appeal against Lord Woolf's judgment in *Belmarsh*. Lord Steyn was not considered fit to hear this matter because he had publicly expressed doubt about the government's claim that the United Kingdom faces an emergency of the kind that justifies derogations from its commitment to human rights. In the same speech, Lord Steyn articulated his concern about the American government's willingness to flout the rule of law in its establishment of a 'legal back hole' at Guantanamo Bay and suggested that the House of Lords has perhaps strayed back from the rule of law path in its post-9/11 decisions, including *Rehman*, a decision in which he wrote one of the concurring judgments; Johan Steyn, 'Deference: A Tangled Story' [2005] *Public Law* 346.

decision that there was a state of emergency, only its decision about how to respond to it. Further, none of the judges in the majority confronted the question of how to square their decision with *Rehman*, and thus have set up a tension in English public law between a conception of the judicial role which requires complete deference to the executive and the legislature in a time of emergency and one which gives judges a significant role in evaluating the decisions made by the other branches of government. Finally, the fact that a decision under the Human Rights Act declares an incompatibility between a provision in a statute with human rights commitments without invalidating the provision can be seen as letting the judges off the hook. They can reap kudos from human rights enthusiasts for taking a stand, and so affirm their role in legal order. But the law remains valid with government taking the decision whether or not to amend the statute, either by executive order or through legislation. Indeed, one of the judges in the majority, Lord Scott, seemed to understand the Human Rights Act as forcing him into the non-judicial role of making a political declaration about the content of legislation which could embarrass the government but which had no more legal effect than that.

Later in this book, I will discuss in detail *Halliday*, *Liversidge*, *Rehman*, and *Belmarsh*. Here I want to draw your attention to the complex issues raised by my sketch of judges and their role in maintaining the rule of law in times of emergency. Following Simpson, it would be better for judges to confess that in an emergency situation, they cannot uphold the rule of law. Such a conclusion follows from the last chapter of Simpson's magisterial book on Regulation 18B, where he points to the fact that in ordinary administrative law judges have developed highly nuanced rule-of-law controls on administrative discretion, controls whose worth he seems to recognize.[44] So for him the rule of law has content which judges can develop and enforce, but he does not think them capable of doing that job in an exceptional situation such as that presented by national security.

However, since it is a regulative assumption of the judicial role that judges are under a duty to uphold the rule of law, it might seem that they cannot make that confession and at the same time purport to be doing their job. I will argue later that it does make sense for judges to make such a confession in order to make public the fact that they are not capable of doing their job. They must, that is, be prepared to say that they are no longer able to occupy the role that judges have to take in maintaining the integrity of legal order.

---

[44] Simpson, *In the Highest Degree Odious*, p. 420.

For the moment, I want to explore the idea that it is antithetical to legal theory, as well as to judges, to think that states of emergency lie outside the law, and thus outside the reach of the rule of law. That thought requires one to succumb to the challenge put by Carl Schmitt that the rule of law has no place in an emergency. As I have mentioned, Schmitt issued this challenge during Germany's first experiment with democracy in the Weimar period.

In the opening line of his book *Political Theology*, Schmitt claimed that 'Sovereign is he who decides on the state of exception'.[45] He thus asserted that in abnormal times the sovereign is legally uncontrolled. Schmitt's thought of course goes further. Not only is the sovereign legally uncontrolled in the state of emergency; the quality of being sovereign, he who *is* the sovereign, is revealed in the answer to the question of who gets to decide *that* there is a state of emergency.

Closely bound up with Schmitt's claim about states of emergency is another claim about 'the political'.[46] According to Schmitt, the political is prior to law and its central distinction is between friend and enemy, so that the primary task of the sovereign is to make that distinction. It is in the moment of the emergency that the existential nature of the political is revealed. Since to make that distinction is to make a kind of existential decision, he who makes it has to be capable of acting in a decisive way, which, for Schmitt, ruled out both the judiciary and Parliament, leaving the executive as the only serious candidate.[47]

There is, in Schmitt's view, a continuum of exceptional situations, ranging from a global threat or the situation of war where the state – the political and legal order as a whole – is in danger, to situations which occur within the political and legal order, which are local manifestations of the global external threat. The sovereign must respond to all exceptions. He is the only figure in the political and legal order capable of acting as the guardian of the constitution, since he alone has the power to make the ultimate decision as to who is an enemy. Once one recognizes the possibility of a threat from without that threatens the life of the state, and that it is the sovereign's role both to determine that there is such an emergency and to deal with it, one should also recognize that in more local emergency situations, the sovereign should play the same role.

[45] Carl Schmitt, *Political Theology: Four Chapters on the Theory of Sovereignty*, translated by George Schwab (Cambridge, Mass: MIT Press, 1988), p. 5.

[46] Carl Schmitt, *The Concept of the Political*, translated by George Schwab (New Jersey: Rutgers University Press, 1976).

[47] Carl Schmitt, *Der Hüter der Verfassung* (Berlin: Duncker & Humblot, 1985).

Schmitt's claims, forged in the hothouse of Weimar politics and the disintegration of the attempt to establish democracy in Germany,[48] might seem overblown to the common lawyers of jurisdictions such as the United Kingdom, Canada, and Australia, let alone to lawyers in the United States, given the place of the bill of rights in American political culture. However, as I have indicated, the judicial record largely supports Schmitt's claims, albeit not through the idea that the rule of law has no place in an emergency, but through the idea that only a formal or wholly procedural conception of the rule of law is appropriate for emergencies. But, as I will now argue, the latter idea might make things worse from the perspective of the rule of law, at least from the perspective of a substantive conception of the rule of law, than a total surrender to Schmitt's challenge. Indeed, it might succumb more subtly but also more fully to Schmitt's challenge, since Schmitt also thought that liberals found unbearable the idea that the rule of law cannot constrain the political, so that they prefer to pretend it constrains while recognizing that in substance it does not.

Carl Schmitt's challenge

In what remains one of the leading studies of the state of emergency, *Constitutional Dictatorship*, Clinton L. Rossiter concluded in 1948 that '[n]o sacrifice is too great for our democracy, least of all the temporary sacrifice of democracy itself'.[49] Crucial to his argument was the claim that the dictatorship necessary to respond to an emergency can be constitutional. Here he took his cue from the Roman dictatorship, one that was legally bestowed on a trusted individual whose task it was to 'restore normal times and government' and to 'hand back this power to the regular authorities just as soon as its purposes had been fulfilled'.[50]

Rossiter argued that three 'fundamental facts' provide the rationale for constitutional dictatorship – the complex system of the democratic, constitutional state is designed to function during peace and is often 'unequal to the exigencies of a great constitutional crisis'; thus, in a time of crisis, the system of government must be 'temporarily altered to whatever degree is necessary to overcome the peril and restore normal conditions'; this altered government, which might amount to an 'outright dictatorship',

---

[48] For further discussion see David Dyzenhaus, *Legality and Legitimacy: Carl Schmitt, Hans Kelsen and Hermann Heller in Weimar* (Oxford: Clarendon Press, 1997).

[49] Clinton L. Rossiter, *Constitutional Dictatorship* (Princeton: Princeton University Press, 1948), p. 314.

[50] *Ibid.*, pp. 4–5.

can have only one purpose – the 'preservation of the independence of the state, the maintenance of the existing constitutional order, and the defense of the political and social liberties of the people'.[51]

Rossiter was, however, anxious to stress the importance of the qualifying adjective in the idea of constitutional dictatorship.[52] What distinguishes it from fascist dictatorship is that it is 'temporary and self-destructive' and that the 'only reason for its existence is a serious crisis; . . . when the crisis goes, it goes'.[53] Thus, in his concluding chapter, he listed eleven criteria which have to be met for a dictatorship to remain constitutional. They fell into three main categories: 'criteria by which the initial resort to constitutional dictatorship is to be judged, those by which its continuance is to be judged, and those to be employed at the termination of the crisis for which it was instituted'.[54]

Rossiter's first criterion was that constitutional dictatorship should not be initiated 'unless it is necessary or even indispensable to the preservation of the state and its constitutional order'.[55] The second criterion followed hard on the heels of the first: 'the decision to institute a constitutional dictatorship should never be in the hands of the man or men who will constitute the dictator'.[56] Here Rossiter referred to the institution of Roman dictatorship, in which it was the Senate which initiated the proposal that the consuls appoint a dictator, a citizen who had absolute power but who was limited to a six-month period in office.[57] As Rossiter immediately recognized, this second criterion is not uniformly observed in modern experience with emergency powers, and he remarked that the

---

[51] *Ibid.*, pp. 5–7.   [52] *Ibid.*, p. 4.   [53] *Ibid.*, p. 8.   [54] *Ibid.*, p. 298.   [55] *Ibid.*

[56] *Ibid.*, p. 299. The remaining nine are: '[A]ll uses of emergency powers and all readjustments in the organization of the government should be effected in pursuit of constitutional or legal requirements', that is, 'no official action should ever be taken without a certain minimum of constitutional or legal sanction'; '[N]o dictatorial institution should be adopted, no right invaded, no regular procedure altered any more than is absolutely necessary for the conquest of the particular crisis'; 'The measures adopted in the prosecution of a constitutional dictatorship should never be permanent in character or effect'; 'The dictatorship should be carried on by persons representative of every part of the citizenry interested in the defense of the existing constitutional order'; Ultimate responsibility should be maintained for every action taken under a constitutional dictatorship' – that is, officials should be held responsible for what they have done after termination of the dictatorship; 'The decision to terminate a constitutional dictatorship, like the decision to institute one, should never be in the hands of the man or men who constitute the dictator'; 'No constitutional dictatorship should extend beyond the termination of the crisis for which it was instituted'; '[T]he termination of the crisis must be followed by as complete a return as possible to the political and governmental conditions existing prior to the initiation of the constitutional dictatorship.'

[57] *Ibid.*, pp. 20–3.

'greatest of constitutional dictators was self-appointed, but Mr. Lincoln had no alternative'.[58]

Rossiter had in mind Lincoln's actions during the Civil War, including the proclamation by which Lincoln, without the prior authority of Congress, suspended habeas corpus.[59] Lincoln, he said, subscribed to a theory that in a time of emergency, the President could assume whatever legislative, executive, and judicial powers he thought necessary to preserve the nation, and could in the process break the 'fundamental laws of the nation, if such a step were unavoidable'.[60] This power included one ratified by the Supreme Court: 'an almost unrestrained power to act towards insurrectionary citizens as if they were enemies of the United States, and thus place them outside the protection of the Constitution'.[61]

Rossiter's difficulties here illustrate rather than solve the tensions in the idea of constitutional dictatorship. On the one hand, he wants to assert that emergency rule in a liberal democracy can be constitutional in nature. 'Constitutional' implies restraints and limits in accordance not only with law, but also with fundamental laws. These laws are not the constitution which is in place for ordinary times; rather, they are the laws that govern the management of exceptional times – his eleven criteria. The criteria are either put within the discretion of the dictator – they are judgments about necessity – or are couched as limits that should be enshrined either in the constitution or in legislation.

However, Rossiter does not properly address the alleged fact that judgments about necessity are for the dictator to make, which means that these criteria are not limits or constraints but merely factors about which the dictator will have to decide. Other criteria look more like genuine limits. Moreover, they are limits that could be constitutionally enshrined, for example the second criterion requires that the person who makes the decision that there is an emergency should not be the person who assumes dictatorial powers. Yet, as we have seen, Rossiter's foremost example of the modern constitutional dictator not only gave himself dictatorial powers but, Rossiter supposes, Lincoln had no choice but to do this.

Moreover, if these criteria are constitutionally enshrined, so that part of the constitution is devoted to the rules that govern the time when the rest of the constitution might be suspended, they still form part of the constitution. So, no less than the ordinary constitution, what we can think of

---

[58] *Ibid.*, p. 229.
[59] *Ibid.*, ch. 14: 'The Constitution, the President, and Crisis Government'.   [60] *Ibid.*, p. 229.
[61] *Ibid.*, p. 230, referring to *Prize Cases* 67 US 635 (1863); 2 Black (67 US) 635 (1863) at 670.

as the exceptional or emergency constitution, the constitution that governs the state of emergency, is subject to suspension, should the dictator deem this necessary. This explains why, on the other hand, Rossiter equated emergency rule with potentially unlimited dictatorship, with Locke's idea of prerogative, defined by Locke as '*nothing but the Power of doing publick good without a Rule*'. Locke holds that the prerogative is 'This power to act according to discretion for the publick good, without the prescription of the Law and sometimes even against it'.[62] And Rossiter says, 'whatever the theory, in moments of national emergency the facts have always been with . . . John Locke'.[63]

So Rossiter at one and the same time sees constitutional dictatorship as unconstrained in nature and as constrainable by principles – his eleven criteria. The upshot is that 'constitutional' turns out then not to mean what we usually take it to mean; rather it is a misleading name for the hope that the person who assumes dictatorial powers does so because of a good faith evaluation that this is really necessary and with the honest and steadfast intention to return to the ordinary way of doing things as soon as possible.

In his reflections on politics and law after 9/11, the Italian philosopher Girgio Agamben is thus right to remark that the bid by modern theorists of constitutional dictatorship to rely on the tradition of Roman dictatorship is misleading.[64] They rely on that tradition in an effort to show that dictatorship is constitutional or law-governed. But in fact they show that dictatorship is in principle absolute – the dictator is subject to whatever limits he deems necessary, which means to no limits at all. As H. L. A. Hart described the sovereign within the tradition of legal positivism, the dictator is an 'uncommanded commander'.[65] The dictator thus operates within a black hole, in Agamben's words, 'an emptiness and standstill of law'.[66] Hence, Agamben suggests that the real analogue to the contemporary state of emergency is not the Roman dictatorship but the institution of iustitium, in which the law is used to produce a 'juridical void' – a total suspension of law.[67]

In coming to this conclusion, Agamben sides with Carl Schmitt, his principal interlocutor in his book. While Schmitt had in his first major

[62] John Locke, *Two Treatises on Government* edited by P. Laslett (Cambridge: Cambridge University Press, 1988), p. 375 (author's emphasis).

[63] Rossiter, *Constitutional Dictatorship*, p. 219.

[64] Girgio Agamben, *State of Exception*, translated by Kevin Attell (Chicago: Chicago University Press, 2005, first published in 2003), pp. 47–8.

[65] Hart, 'Positivism', p. 59.   [66] Agamben, *State of Exception*, p. 48.

[67] *Ibid.*, ch. 3, pp. 41–2.

work on the topic of dictatorship made a distinction between commissarial dictatorship,[68] the constitutional dictator who is constrained by his commission, and the unconstrained sovereign dictator, it seems that he did not think that this distinction could work in practice. As I have pointed out, the notorious opening sentence of Schmitt's *Political Theology*, 'Sovereign is who decides on the state of exception', is meant to make the point that the sovereign is he who decides both when there is a state of emergency/exception and how best to respond to that state. And that decision for Schmitt is one based on the considerations that he took to be the mark of the political – existential considerations to do with who is a friend and who is an enemy of the state.[69]

Schmitt's claim is, however, more radical than Agamben's. The space beyond law is not so much produced by law as revealed when the mask of liberal legality is stripped away by the political. Once that mask is gone, the political sovereign is shown not to be constituted by law but rather as the actor who has the legitimacy to make law because it is he who decides the fundamental or existential issues of politics. So Schmitt's understanding of the state of exception is not quite a legal black hole, a juridically produced void. Rather, it is a space beyond law, a space which is revealed when law recedes leaving the legally unconstrained state, represented by the sovereign, to act.

In substance, there might seem to be little difference between a legal black hole and space beyond law since neither is controlled by the rule of law. But there is a difference in that nearly all liberal legal theorists find the idea of a space beyond law antithetical, even if they suppose that law can be used to produce a legal void. This is so especially if such theorists want to claim for the sake of legitimacy that law is playing a role, even if it is the case that the role law plays is to suspend the rule of law.

Schmitt would have regarded such claims as an attempt to cling to the wreckage of liberal conceptions of the rule of law brought about by any attempt to respond to emergencies through the law. They represent a vain effort to banish the exception from legal order. Because liberals cannot countenance the idea of politics uncontrolled by law, they place a thin veneer of legality on the political, which allows the executive to do what it wants while claiming the legitimacy of the rule of law. And we have seen that Rossiter presents a prominent example which supports Schmitt's view.

[68] See Carl Schmitt, *Die Diktatur: Von den Anfängen des modernen Souveränitätsgedankens bis zum proletarischen Klassenkampf* (Berlin: Duncker & Humblot, 1989, first published in 1922).

[69] Schmitt, *Political Theology*, p. 5.

It is a depressing fact that much work on emergencies in the wake of 9/11 is also supportive of Schmitt's view. For example, Bruce Ackerman in his essay, 'The Emergency Constitution',[70] starts by claiming that we need 'new constitutional concepts' in order to avoid the downward spiral in protection of civil liberties when we wait for politicians to respond to each new terror attack by enacting laws that become increasingly repressive with each attack.[71] We need, he says, to rescue the concept of 'emergency powers from fascist thinkers like Carl Schmitt, who used it as a battering ram against liberal democracy'.[72] Because Ackerman does not think that judges are likely to do, or can do, better than they have in the past at containing the executive during an emergency, he proposes mainly the creative design of constitutional checks and balances to ensure, as did the Roman dictatorship, against the normalization of the state of emergency. Judges should not be regarded as 'miraculous saviors of our threatened heritage of freedom'. Hence, it is better to rely on a system of political incentives and disincentives, a 'political economy' that will prevent abuse of emergency powers.[73]

Ackerman calls his first device the 'supramajoritarian escalator',[74] basically the requirement that a declaration of a state of emergency requires legislative endorsement within a very short time, and thereafter has to be renewed at short intervals, with each renewal requiring the approval of a larger majority of legislators. The idea is that it will become increasingly easy with time for even a small minority of legislators to bring the emergency to an end, thus decreasing the opportunities for executive abuse of power.[75] The second device requires the executive to share security intelligence with legislative committees with opposition political parties guaranteed the majority of seats on these committees.[76]

Ackerman does see some role for courts. They will have a macro role should the executive flout the constitutional devices. While he recognizes both that the executive might simply assert the necessity to suspend the

---

[70] (2004) 113 *Yale Law Journal* 1029–91. There are of course many interventions which argue for control by substantive conceptions of the rule of law, for example, Laurence Tribe and Patrick O. Gudridge, 'The Anti-Emergency Constitution' (2004) 113 *Yale Law Journal* 1801–70; Jonathan Masur, 'A Hard Look or a Blind Eye: Administrative Law or Military Deference' (2005) 56 *Hastings Law Journal* 441–521; D. Cole, 'Judging the Next Emergency: Judicial Review and Individual Rights in Times of Crisis' (2002–03) 101 *Michigan Law Review* 2565–95.

[71] Ackerman, 'The Emergency Constitution', 1029–30.   [72] *Ibid.*, 1044.

[73] *Ibid.*, 1031.   [74] *Ibid.*, 1047.   [75] *Ibid.*, 1047–9.

[76] *Ibid.*, 1050–3. Ackerman would also insert a constitutional requirement of an actual, major attack, before the executive may declare a state of emergency (at 1060), and have the constitution provide for adequate compensation for the individuals and their families who are harmed by emergency measures (at 1062–6).

emergency constitution and that this assertion might enjoy popular support, he supposes that if the courts declare the executive to be violating the constitution, this will give the public pause and thus decrease incentives on the executive to evade the constitution.[77] In addition, the courts will have a micro role in supervising what he regards as the inevitable process of detaining suspects without trial for the period of the emergency. Suspects should be brought to court and some explanation given of the grounds of their detention, not so that they can contest it – a matter which Ackerman does not regard as practicable – but in order to give the suspects an identity so that they do not disappear and to provide a basis for compensation once the emergency is over in case the executive turns out to have fabricated its reasons. He also wishes to maintain a constitutional prohibition on torture which he thinks can be enforced by requiring regular visits by lawyers.[78]

Not only is the judicial role limited, but it is clear that Ackerman does not see the courts as having much to do with preventing a period of 'sheer lawlessness'.[79] Even within the section on the judiciary, he says that the real restraint on the executive will be the knowledge that the 'supramajoritarian escalator' might bring the emergency to an end, whereupon the detainees will be released if there is no hard evidence to justify detaining them.[80]

In sum, according to Ackerman, judges have at best a minimal role to play during a state of emergency. We cannot really escape from the fact that a state of emergency is a legally created black hole, or lawless void. It is subject to external constraints, controls on the executive located at the constitutional level and policed by the legislature. But, internally, the rule of law does next to no work – all that we can reasonably hope for is decency. But once one has conceded that internally a state of emergency is more or less a legal black hole because the rule of law, as policed by judges, has no or little purchase, it becomes difficult to understand how external legal constraints, the constitutionally entrenched devices, can play the role Ackerman sets out.

Recall that Ackerman accepts that the reason we should not give judges more than a minimal role is the history of judicial failure to uphold the rule of law during emergencies in the face of executive assertions of necessity to operate outside of law's rule. But why should we accept his claim that we can rely on judges when the executive asserts the necessity of suspending the exceptional constitution, the constitution for the state of emergency, when one of his premises is that we cannot so rely? Far from rescuing the concept of emergency powers from Schmitt, Ackerman's devices for an emergency constitution – an attempt to update Rossiter's model of constitutional dictatorship – fails for the same reasons that Rossiter's model fails. Even as they attempt to respond to Schmitt's challenge, they seem to prove the claim that Schmitt made in late Weimar that law cannot effectively enshrine a distinction between constitutional dictatorship and dictatorship. They appear to be vain attempts to find a role for law while at the same time they concede that law has no role.

Of course, this last claim trades on an ambiguity in the idea of the rule of law between, on the one hand, the rule of law, understood as the rule of substantive principles, and, on the other, rule by law, where as long as there is a legal warrant for what government does, government will be considered to be in compliance with the rule of law. Only if one holds to a fairly substantive or thick conception of the rule of law will one think that there is a point on a continuum where rule by law ceases to be in accordance with the rule of law.

Ackerman's argument about rule by law, by the law of the emergency constitution, might not answer Schmitt's challenge, but at least it attempts to avoid dignifying the legal void with the title of rule of law, even as it tries to use law to govern what it deems ungovernable by law. The same cannot be said of those responses to 9/11 that seem to suggest that legal black holes are not in tension with the rule of law, as long as they are properly created. While it is relatively rare to find a position that articulates so stark a view, it is quite common to find positions that are comfortable with grey holes, as long as these are properly created. As I have indicated, a grey hole is a legal space in which there are some legal constraints on executive action – it is not a lawless void – but the constraints are so insubstantial that they pretty well permit government to do as it pleases. In addition, since such grey holes permit government to have its cake and eat it too, to seem to be governing not only by law but in accordance with the rule of law, they and their endorsement by judges and academics might be even more dangerous from the perspective of the substantive conception of the rule of law than true black holes.

An example of such endorsement can be found in Cass Sunstein's elaboration of the extension to the emergency situation of the 'minimalist' stance which he thinks judges should adopt in deciding all constitutional matters.[81] Sunstein thus differs from Ackerman and others engaged in

---

[81] For the stance see Cass R. Sunstein, *One Case at a Time: Judicial Minimalism on the Supreme Court* (Cambridge, Mass: Harvard University Press, 1999). For the extension, see Cass R. Sunstein, 'Minimalism at War' (2004) *The Supreme Court Review* 47–109.

the American debate because he does not advocate a minimalist role for judges purely on the basis that judges have shown themselves incapable of doing more. Rather, he puts his argument on the basis that judicial minimalism is appropriate during normal times, but even more appropriate during an emergency situation.

According to Sunstein, minimalists favour shallowness over depth. They avoid taking stands on the most deeply contested questions of constitutional law, preferring to leave the most fundamental questions – 'incompletely theorized disagreements' – undecided. Sunstein's hope is that such shallowness can attract support from people with a wide range of theoretical positions or who are undecided about answers to the deep questions. Minimalists also favour narrowness over width. They proceed 'one case at a time', thus avoiding any attempt to resolve more than the case demands, although minimalism, Sunstein says, is consistent with a strategy of which he approves, the strategy of forcing 'democracy-promoting decisions' – decisions which prompt judgments by 'democratically accountable actors, above all Congress'.[82] This aspect of minimalism requires that as little is said as possible about what the legislature should do, thus leaving it up to the democratically elected body to decide how best to respond to the problem identified by the court.

Maximalists, by contrast, favour depth; they adopt foundational theories which they articulate in their judgments, confident in the correctness of their views. And they also favour width, because laying down 'firm, clear rules in advance' cuts down on the judicial discretion which minimalism perforce leaves to judges at the same time as providing a 'highly visible background against which other branches of government can do their work'.[83]

Sunstein argues that minimalism can better reconcile the tension between national security and constitutional rights in a time of emergency than either of two alternatives. These he styles 'National Security Maximalism', which requires a highly deferential role of the judiciary, and 'Liberty Maximalism', which insists that judges must protect liberty to the same extent as they would in peace; indeed, that in emergency times it is all the more important that judges play this role.[84] He rejects Liberty Maximalism both because judges have refused to take this role in the past and because it is 'inherently undesirable': when security is at risk,

---

[82] Sunstein, 'Minimalism at War', 47–8. For a detailed discussion on this point see Sunstein, *One Case at a Time*, pp. 26–39.

[83] Sunstein, 'Minimalism at War', 47–8.   [84] *Ibid.*, 48.

the government has greater justification to intrude on liberty.[85] And he rejects National Security Maximalism for the following reasons. Its reading of the Constitution is tendentious in its claim that the Constitution gives the President exclusive authority in an emergency. The executive is capable of striking the wrong balance between security and liberty especially because deliberation within the executive branch is likely to lead to reinforcement of existing attitudes rather than to checks on those attitudes. And, in the nature of things, the selective denial of liberty for the targets of security measures is likely to have low political costs for the executive.[86]

Courts, he argues, will not have the requisite information to second-guess the executive on the balance between security and liberty; but they can still require clear congressional authorization for any executive action that intrudes on constitutionally protected interests. This requirement both provides a check and 'such authorization is likely to be forthcoming when there is a good argument for it'. Liberty is thus promoted 'without compromising legitimate security interests'. Courts should also 'insist, whenever possible, on the core principle of the due process clause'. Some kind of hearing must be put in place to ensure against erroneous deprivations of liberty. Finally, judges must exercise self-discipline.[87]

In combination, these three features of his minimalist approach will he thinks promote democracy by requiring that executive action has a basis in legislation while still ensuring that judges retain a significant role in upholding the constitutional order. The approach thus amounts to 'due process writ large'. Congressional authorization will ensure attention from a diverse and deliberative body; the hearing requirement before a court 'reflects the most familiar aspect of the due process guarantee'; and the requirement of narrow and shallow rulings from a court means that those not before the court, that is, those whose cases arise later, will be provided with an opportunity to be heard.[88]

Both Ackerman and Sunstein accept that the past teaches us that as a matter of fact one should not expect much of judges in a time of emergency. But Sunstein differs from Ackerman in that he seems unperturbed by the way in which Congress and the executive have reacted to 9/11, in part because he thinks that the judges are doing a good job of upholding the rule of law. In other words, his conception of minimalism is the correct stance for judges to adopt on constitutional questions even in ordinary times. And since that conception is also being displayed in the American

---

[85] *Ibid.,* 51–2.   [86] *Ibid.,* 52–3.   [87] *Ibid.,* 53–4.   [88] *Ibid.,* 54–5.

response to 9/11, there is no special problem from the perspective of the rule of law.

But it follows for Sunstein and for others that decisions which were regarded until recently as badges of shame in American legal history, most notably, the decision of the majority of the Supreme Court in *Korematsu*,[89] have to be seen in a new light. These decisions cannot be unproblematically understood as ones in which the Court failed to uphold the rule of law. Rather, they should be seen 'as a tribute to minimalism – requiring clear congressional support for deprivations of liberty by the executive, and permitting those deprivations only if that support can be found'.[90]

In *Korematsu*, the Court upheld an executive order which two years prior to the decision authorized the evacuation of American citizens of Japanese descent from the West Coast to facilitate their detention so that the military could make determinations of who among them were loyal. Sunstein and other revisionists[91] now wish to point out that in a case decided on the same day, *Endo*,[92] the Court held that the detention of those citizens was illegal. They emphasize that the Court found that there was Congressional authorization for the evacuation order, but not for the detention order.

In *Korematsu*, the order was based on a recent statute which made it an offence 'to remain in . . . any military area or military zone' prescribed by a competent official. In *Endo*, in contrast, Sunstein says, there was no statute on which the executive could base its detention order. Sunstein claims that the conclusion is that the executive survived legal attack only when 'Congress had specifically permitted its action'. But, as Sunstein acknowledges, Justice Jackson, in his dissent in *Korematsu*, argued that there was no Act of Congress that authorized the evacuation; its sole basis was a military order.[93] Further, in *Endo* the government argued that the same statute authorized detention. The majority of the Court responded

---

[89] *Korematsu* v. *United States*, 323 US 214 (1944).   [90] Sunstein, 'Minimalism at War', 51.
[91] See Samuel Issacharoff and Richard H. Pildes, 'Emergency Contexts Without Emergency Powers: The United States' Constitutional Approach During Wartime' (2004) 2 *International Journal of Constitutional Law* 296–333. Mark V. Tushnet offers not so much a revisionist view as an account of the inevitability of *Korematsu* in 'Defending *Korematsu*? Reflections on Civil Liberties in Wartime' (2003) *Wisconsin Law Review* 273–307.
[92] *Ex parte Endo*, 323 US 283 (1944).
[93] *Korematsu*, at 244. Justice Jackson's dissent has the curious feature that he agreed with the majority that military decisions are not 'susceptible of intelligent judicial appraisal'; (at 245). For this reason, Jonathan Masur argues that Justice Murphy's dissent is to be preferred, since Murphy demonstrated that the military had no reasonable basis for its claims – Masur, 'A Hard Look or a Blind Eye?', 455–6.

that the word detention was not used in the statute and certainly could not be used as a basis for detaining Endo, who had been determined to be loyal.

Sunstein congratulates the Court in *Endo* for avoiding, in minimalist fashion, controversial constitutional issues by confining its analysis to an ordinary exercise in statutory interpretation.[94] But he does not say what is wrong with Justice Jackson's similar point in *Korematsu* that the 1942 statute nowhere explicitly authorized evacuation orders of the sort visited on Japanese Americans.[95] Nor does he mention that in *Endo* Justices Murphy and Roberts in their concurring judgments argued strongly for the necessity for the Court to confront the constitutional issues.

The revival of interest in *Endo* in a bid to sanitize *Korematsu* is troubling. It is true that the majorities in both cases saw them as in some kind of symbiotic relationship. But in the article which first brought this relationship to the attention of the post-9/11 legal public, Patrick O. Gudridge argued that the relationship is far more complex. And this complexity is not acknowledged by the revisionists who subsequently rely on his work.[96]

Gudridge points out that Justice Black, who wrote the majority opinion in *Korematsu* wanted to portray *Korematsu* as addressing an 'already-past short term' – the time of emergency – a term whose closing was marked by *Endo*.[97] Black's claim was that exclusion was temporary, a measure responding to the exigencies of the moment. He wanted to resist the argument put by one of the dissenting judges in *Korematsu*, Justice Roberts, that the exclusion order had to be seen as part of a package meant as whole to accomplish long-term detention.[98] In addition, Gudridge points out that it is misleading to characterize Justice Douglas' majority opinion in *Endo* as an ordinary exercise in statutory, in contrast to constitutional, interpretation, despite Justice Douglas' own less than whole-hearted attempt to portray the opinion in this fashion.[99]

Indeed, in explicit reference to Sunstein's first development of the theory of constitutional minimalism, Gudridge rejects outright the thought that *Endo* is a version of constitutional minimalism.[100] Rather, Justice Douglas used the Constitution to set the stage for the exercise in statutory

---

[94] Sunstein, 'Minimalism at War', 92–3.   [95] *Korematsu*, at 244.

[96] Patrick O. Gudridge, 'Remember Endo?' (2003) 116 *Harvard Law Review* 1933–70.

[97] *Ibid.*, 1934.   [98] *Ibid.*, 1942.

[99] *Ibid.*, 1938–9. Less than whole-hearted because Justice Douglas later said that he wished to write the opinion as a constitutional one, but other Justices, including Black, refused (at 1953). And see the text of Justice Douglas' draft opinion with the constitutional assumptions crossed out (at 1955).

[100] *Ibid.*, 1959.

interpretation.[101] Moreover, Gudridge suggests that even were there no explicit signals in the text of the majority opinion that indicated that the Constitution sets the stage, the use of a doctrine of authorization in this kind of context presupposes constitutional premises, whether these are articulated or not.[102] The issue is not then, as Sunstein would have it, that there are incompletely theorized disagreements, but that the judges prefer for strategic reasons to keep their principles below the surface.[103]

The conclusion to be drawn from the combination of *Korematsu* and *Endo* is not then that the conjunction of the two legitimizes *Korematsu*. Rather, together they raise a puzzle, whether, as Gudridge puts it, it is 'possible for constitutional law to be *both* intermittent and organizational?'[104] *Korematsu*, a decision which bows to an executive claim of necessity, and *Endo*, a decision which affirms constitutional values, are, Gudridge says, 'mutually repelling perspectives'.[105]

In other words, *Korematsu*, on its most charitable reading, held that a state of emergency is a grey hole and that such holes have to be properly created, that is, created by the legislature. It stands not for minimalism but for the grand constitutional claim that in times of emergency judges must blindly defer to the executive. And such deference means that the judges themselves created a situation in which there is the façade of judicial review of the executive, and thus of the rule of law, while in effect they gave the executive a black hole, a situation in which it could operate free of rule-of-law constraints. In contrast, *Endo* held that statutes that respond to emergency situations have to be read down in order to comply with constitutional values because judges should assume to the extent possible that an emergency situation is governed by constitutional values.

It is troubling enough that Sunstein and other revisionists think that such a black hole is legitimized by the fact that it was created by a statute. But it is more troubling that they are willing to relax, with the majority in *Korematsu*, the conditions for telling when a statute in fact authorizes the executive to create a black hole. Most troubling of all is that the revisionist interpretation of *Korematsu* is used to prepare the way for vindicating positions taken by the Bush administration after 9/11.

The revisionists do not support the completely naked assertions of executive authority that the Bush administration initially made, but the more moderate claims it has made as it has tested both public and judicial

---

[101] *Ibid.*, 1947–53.   [102] *Ibid.*, 1953 and 1964.
[103] For a more cautious appraisal of *Endo*, see Masur, 'A Hard Look or a Blind Eye?', 456.
[104] Gudrige, 'Remember Endo?', 1967. (Author's emphasis.)   [105] *Ibid.*

opinion. For example, Sunstein is enthusiastic about the decision of the plurality in *Hamdi*, the 2004 US Supreme Court's decision on enemy combatants.[106]

In *Hamdi*, the plurality held that the detention of such combatants was authorized by the Congressional Order which gave the President authority to 'use all necessary and appropriate force' to respond to terrorism.[107] And it held that while the detainees were entitled to contest their detention orders, a military tribunal would be an appropriate forum for this contest to take place with its procedures determined in accordance with a cost-benefit calculation, that is, one which weights security and rights considerations together.[108]

Sunstein endorses both of these holdings because the first recognizes the need for congressional authorization[109] while the second exhibits the requisite degree of self-discipline.[110] But in endorsing this decision, he also endorses the claim that a delegation of authority in general terms necessarily includes the delegation of authority to detain, and that the executive is entitled to stipulate due process rights that will not afford a detainee a real opportunity to contest his detention. Concerns about the first issue were raised by Justices Scalia and Stevens in dissent[111] and by Justices Souter and Ginsburg in a judgment which concurred reluctantly with the plurality, in order to give the decision of the plurality practical effect by making it into a majority decision.[112] Justices Souter and Ginsburg also expressed grave doubts about the plurality's views about adequate due process.[113]

My concern is that Sunstein's minimalism is committed to a view of legality which not only permits the executive to claim that a system of arbitrary detention is one which operates under the rule of law, but also requires judges to endorse that claim. As long as there is a hint of legislative authorization in the air, judges should accept that the legislature has authorized the measures the executive chooses to take. And when it comes to the question of the compliance of those measures with the rule of law, judges should let the executive decide how best to comply as long as it does put in place some procedures.

Indeed, a truly minimalist court would not have told the executive what sort of measures were minimally appropriate. I will argue later that this aspect of minimalism is unobjectionable as it puts the executive on

---

[106] *Hamdi* v. *Rumsfeld*, 124 S. Ct. 2633 (2004).   [107] *Ibid.*, at 2637–43.
[108] *Ibid.*, at 2643–52.   [109] Sunstein, 'Minimalism at War', 94–5.   [110] *Ibid.*, 102.
[111] *Hamdi*, at 2651–66.   [112] *Ibid.*, at 2653–6.   [113] *Ibid.*, at 2659.

notice that what they do decide will be vulnerable to further judicial scrutiny instead of telling the legislature what it needs to do to achieve a bare constitutional pass.[114] Moreover, the message should have been delivered not to the executive but to the legislature, if minimalism was to do its job of forcing 'democracy-promoting' decisions. But Sunstein is precluded from making this point because his clear statement rule turns out to allow vague authorizations. Indeed, as I will argue in chapter 2, an authentic clear statement rule works only when judges reject the first aspect of minimalism – the avoidance of full justifications for results that seek to preserve the rule of law.

From the perspective of the rule of law, minimalism does more damage than the strategy Sunstein terms National Security Maximalism, which was the strategy adopted by Justice Thomas in *Hamdi*. Thomas accepted the government's main argument – that the executive had a blank cheque to detain even without Congressional authorization since Article II of the Constitution provides that the President is 'Commander in Chief of the Armed Forces'.[115] And he put forward a basically Schmittian argument to the effect that it is necessary that the executive have the authority to respond to exceptional situations unconstrained by legality. This strategy does less damage to the rule-of-law project than Sunstein's approach because it accepts that the government is acting in a space outside of law, ungoverned, that is, by the rule of law.

Now Justice Thomas' strategy is politically unacceptable because it strips from government the basis to claim that the executive's response to the emergency is a legal one. But that is precisely why it is better from the perspective of the rule of law than Sunstein's minimalism, which permits the government to have its cake and eat it too by endorsing an equation of the façade of the rule of law with its substance. In addition Sunstein's minimalism is also worse than Justice Scalia's dissent, which reads like the dissent of a civil libertarian until one realizes that what he objected to was not the executive's decision to dump those it deemed enemy combatants into a legal black hole, but to the fact that the executive has not obtained the proper authorization to do so. That is, Justice Scalia required an explicit Congressional suspension of habeas corpus, an authentically clear statement rather than the vague statement which Sunstein and the plurality find acceptable. But once there is such a clear statement he is prepared to

[114] Kent Roach and Gary Trotter, 'Miscarriages of Justice in the War Against Terror' (2005) 109 *Penn State Law Review* 967–1041, at 1018.
[115] *Hamdi*, at 2674–7.

give the stamp of legality to the legal black hole.[116] Blank cheques are fine as long as they are properly certified. Justice Scalia's approach is problematic in that he sees no problem from the perspective of the rule of law as long as the black hole is legally created. But it is preferable to Sunstein's in two respects. Justice Scalia requires the legislature to make clear its intention to create a legal black hole and does not attempt to shade its blackness, to pretend that it is anything other than a legal void.

Another way of making my point is to say that grey holes cause more harm to the rule of law than black holes. Recall that a grey hole is a space in which the detainee has some procedural rights but not sufficient for him effectively to contest the executive's case for his detention. It is in substance a legal black hole but worse because the procedural rights available to the detainee cloak the lack of substance. As we will see, it is a delicate matter to decide when the blackness shades through grey into something which provides a detainee with adequate rule-of-law protection, when, that is, on the continuum of legality, the void fills up with rule-of-law content. But for the moment I want simply to establish that minimalism is too close to the black hole end of the continuum for comfort. A little bit of legality can be more lethal to the rule of law than none.

It might seem, then, that the only conclusion to be drawn by someone committed to a substantive conception of the rule of law is Schmitt's. One should concede that, in the state of exception or emergency, law recedes leaving the state to act unconstrained by law. Just this conclusion is reached in a fascinating article by Oren Gross. Gross sketches two traditional models which are adopted to respond to emergency situations. The first is the 'Business as Usual' model, which holds that the legal order as it stands has the resources to deal with the state of emergency and so no substantive change in the law is required. The second model is one of 'accommodation', which argues for some significant changes to the existing order so as to accommodate security considerations, while keeping the ordinary system intact to the greatest extent possible. The principal criticism of the Business as Usual model is that it is naïve or even hypocritical, as it either ignores or hides the necessities of the exercise of government power in an emergency. The Accommodation model, in contrast, risks undermining the ordinary system because it imports into it the measures devised to deal with the emergency.[117]

---

[116] *Ibid.*, at 2665–6: 'When the writ is suspended, the Government is entirely free from judicial oversight'.

[117] Gross, 'Chaos and Rules', 1021–2. Gross finds several different models within the accommodation camp, but for the sake of simplicity I will talk about one model.

Gross argues that two basic assumptions dominate debates about the state of emergency and thus underpin the models. The first is the assumption of separation between the normal and the exceptional which is 'defined by the belief in our ability to separate emergencies and crises from normalcy, counterterrorism measures from ordinary legal rules and norms'.[118] This assumption makes it easier for us to accept expanded government powers and extraordinary measures, since we suppose both that once the threat has gone, so we can return to normal, and that the powers and measures will be deployed against the enemy, not us. The second assumption is of constitutionality: 'whatever responses are made to the challenges of a particular exigency, such responses are to be found and limited within the confines of the constitution'.[119] Gross supports the critiques of both models and he also calls into question both assumptions.

The assumption of separation between the normal and the exceptional ignores the way in which emergency government has become the norm, a trend which has only gathered strength since the US administration's reaction to 9/11, a reaction which has been widely copied. And the assumption of constitutionality, whether it is made by claiming business as usual or that the accommodations made conform to constitutional values, risks undermining the legal order.

Thus Gross puts forward a new model, the 'Extra-Legal Measures model'. This model tells public officials that they may respond extralegally when they 'believe that such action is necessary for protecting the nation and the public in the face of calamity, provided that they openly and publicly acknowledge the nature of their actions'.[120] Gross' claim is that this model is best suited to preserving the 'fundamental principles and tenets' of the constitutional order.[121] In addition, public officials will have to disclose the nature of their activities and hope for 'direct or indirect ex post ratification', either through the courts, the executive or the legislature. The process involved will promote both popular deliberation and individual accountability, while the uncertain outcomes will provide a brake on public officials' temptation to rush into action.[122]

In order to persuade us to accept the Extra-Legal Measures model, Gross suggests that we should agree on three points: '(1) Emergencies call for extraordinary governmental responses, (2) constitutional arguments have not greatly constrained any government faced with the need to respond to such emergencies, and (3) there is a strong probability that measures used

[118] *Ibid.*, 1022, footnote omitted.   [119] *Ibid.*, 1023.
[120] *Ibid.*   [121] *Ibid.*, 1023–4.   [122] *Ibid.*

by the government in emergencies will eventually seep into the legal system after the government has ended.'[123] The model, in his view, recognizes the force of all three points, but by rejecting the naïvety of the Business as Usual model at the same time as requiring that exceptional government responses happen outside of law, it greatly, Gross claims, diminishes the probability of seepage.

Gross relies in his argument on two main sources: Locke's account of the prerogative and Schmitt's argument that legal norms cannot apply to exceptions. He has also more recently enlisted A. V. Dicey in his theoretical armoury. He finds support for the Extra-Legal Measures model in Dicey's recognition that officials might have to resort to illegal action in an emergency and that, if they acted in good faith, they should be entitled to an Act of Indemnity to 'legalise their illegality'.[124]

But this enlistment of Dicey comes with costs. It shows that, despite the boldness of his argument, Gross is unable to stick to the claim that drives both Locke and Schmitt that a state of emergency is a lawless void. Law still plays a significant role for Gross after the fact, since it is through law that the public will react to official lawlessness, either by permitting the officials to be punished for their crimes or by using law to exempt or indemnify the officials from punishment. As I have argued elsewhere, a significant problem for the Extra-Legal Measures model is that if it is adopted as a model, as a prescriptive set of considerations for officials who face or think they face an emergency, it is likely that they will come to anticipate and anticipate correctly that the legal response to their extra-legal activity will be an Act of Indemnity or its equivalent.[125] The difference between a statutory creation of a legal black hole in anticipation of officials acting in violation of the law and one which, to use Dicey's phrase, 'legalises illegality' retrospectively, is not merely a question of timing.

Moreover, Gross has also come to suggest that perhaps the better interpretation of Locke, and it seems of his own position, is that the prerogative of the executive to act outside of the law might be located within the constitution.[126] He immediately notes the dilemma that arises – the claim that the power to act outside of law is itself a legal power, indeed, one

---

[123] *Ibid.*, 1097.

[124] A. V. Dicey, *Introduction to the Study of the Law of the Constitution* (10th edn, London: MacMillan, 1959), pp. 412–13.

[125] David Dyzenhaus, 'The State of Emergency in Legal Theory' in Victor Ramraj, Michael Hor and Kent Roach (eds.), *Global Anti-terrorism Law* (Cambridge: Cambridge University Press, 2005) pp. 65–89.

[126] See Oren Gross, 'Stability and Flexibility: A Dicey Business' in Victor Ramraj, Michael Hor and Kent Roach (eds.), *Global Anti-terrorism Law*, pp. 90–106 at p. 97. He relies here on Carl J. Friedrich, *Constitutional Reason of State: The Survival of the Constitutional*

inscribed in the constitutional order whether this is explicitly stated or not, seems to permit the holder of that power to exercise it 'in violation of the prescribed legal limitations on the use of that very power, turning it into an unlimited power, constrained neither by legal norms nor by principles and rules of the constitutional order'.

In recognizing this dilemma, Gross acknowledges precisely the point that Agamben makes in his critique of Rossiter and other theorists of constitutional dictatorship. To concede to Schmitt the claim that emergencies are a black hole is to give up on the idea that law can control emergencies, however the controls are conceived. Further, as I have argued, to try to maintain that law does play a role risks legitimizing whatever steps the executive takes. Even the barest forms of rule by law seem to evoke the idea that the rule is legitimate because it is in accordance with the law, that is, the rule of law.

However, I do not think we should resist the temptation to bring law into the picture. If we are to answer Schmitt's challenge, we have to be able to show that contrary to his claims the exception can be banished from legal order. We also have to be able to show that one can respond through law to emergencies without creating an exceptional legal regime alongside the ordinary one which will permit government to claim that it is acting according to law when it in effect has a free hand and which will, the longer the exceptional regime lasts, create the problem of seepage of rule of lawlessness into the ordinary legal order. States of emergency can be governed by the rule of law. Here it is significant that Dicey, though he recognized that officials might resort, and might even be justified in so doing, to illegal action in response to an emergency, did not contemplate anything like Gross' Extra-Legal Measures model. He did not, that is, recommend extra-legal action as the way in which public officials should respond. Rather, he emphasized the importance of responses being governed by the rule of law which would require a statute that made it possible for judges to supervise public officials in order to check that the officials had acted in a 'spirit of legality'.[127] Such legislation would be legitimate not only because it emanated from Parliament but also because it could be implemented in accordance with the rule of law. It did not get rid totally of official arbitrariness but cut it down to an acceptable degree.

However, if the legislature is able, whether prospectively or retrospectively to legalize illegality in the sense that judges can no longer enforce

---

Order (Providence: Brown University Press, 1957), pp.110–11. Friedrich does not quite say what Gross takes him to say but the more interesting issue for my argument is Gross' temptation to constitutionalize the prerogative.

[127] Dicey, *Law of the Constitution*, pp. 412–13.

the spirit of legality, it might seem that Dicey's aspiration is naïve. This book argues that such an assumption is not naïve, indeed, that it should be seen as one of the most important assumptions of legal theory. And I will show that Dicey's account of the rule of law in fact contains rich, albeit somewhat problematic, resources both for the philosophy of law and for the practice of the rule of law. So I will now set out some of the main features of Dicey's theory in order to frame that argument.

Parliamentary or judicial supremacy?

Dicey's account of the rule of law has two features: the 'omnipotence or undisputed supremacy' of Parliament and the 'rule or supremacy of law'.[128] The supremacy of law is said to require in the first place that:

> no man is punishable or can be lawfully made to suffer in body or goods except for a distinct breach of law established in the ordinary manner before the ordinary courts of the land. In this sense the rule of law is contrasted with every system of government based on the exercise by persons in authority of wide, arbitrary, or discretionary powers of constraint.[129]

In the second place, supremacy requires not only that 'no man is above the law', but also that 'every man, whatever be his rank or condition, is subject to the ordinary law of the realm and amenable to the jurisdiction of the ordinary tribunals'.[130] In the third place, it means that 'the constitution is pervaded by the rule of law on the ground that the general principles of the constitution (as, for example, the right to personal liberty, or the right of public meeting) are with us the result of judicial decisions determining the rights of private persons in particular cases brought before the courts'.[131]

The problem with this set of resources is that it creates the potential for what Murray Hunt has aptly called a contest of 'competing supremacies', between the legislative monopoly on making law and the judicial monopoly on interpreting the law.[132] Dicey is clear that if these supremacies should come into conflict, Parliament will win. Parliament he said has 'the right to make or unmake any law whatsoever . . . and no person or body is recognised by the law of England as having the right to override or set aside the legislation of Parliament'.[133] Thus there is 'no legal basis for the theory that judges, as exponents of morality, may overrule Acts of Parliament'.[134] Judicial dicta which seem to suggest there is such

---

[128] *Ibid.*, pp. 183–4.   [129] *Ibid.*, p. 188.   [130] *Ibid.*, p. 193.
[131] *Ibid.*, p. 195.   [132] Murray Hunt, 'Sovereignty's Blight'.
[133] Dicey, *Law of the Constitution*, p. 40.   [134] *Ibid.*, p. 62.

a basis merely assert that judges when interpreting statutes will presume that Parliament did not intend to violate morality or international law.[135]

Dicey is often placed within the positivist camp in legal theory because he asserts that in a legal order where there is no bill of rights, a statute that explicitly violates morality is no less valid for that reason. He is also often taken as an apologist for parliamentary supremacy, which is why he and John Austin are credited with putting forward the view of public law which gives rise to the doctrine I called earlier constitutional positivism – the doctrine that regards the legislature as the sole legitimate source of legal norms. Hence the fame of Dicey's example of a statute which decreed that all blue-eyed babies should be put to death. Dicey said that 'legislators must go mad before they could pass such a law, and subjects be idiotic before they could submit to it'. This showed that there are 'internal' and 'external' limits on what Parliament can do. But Dicey's point is that a law that goes beyond those limits is still a law.[136] He also offered as proof of the 'highest exertion and crowning proof of sovereign power' the validity of Acts of Indemnity, statutes which make legal 'transactions which when they took place were illegal' just because such statutes bring about the 'legalisation of illegality'.[137]

However, the idea that the very existence of a statute makes possible its supervision by judges in a spirit of legality indicates that Dicey cannot be taken as a simple apologist for parliamentary supremacy. To revert to terms used in the Introduction, it seems that rule by law, by statute, presupposes the rule of law. And Dicey in his treatment of parliamentary sovereignty defines a law as 'any rule which will be enforced by the courts',[138] which might seem to suggest that the judges could simply say that a statute that offends the rule of law does not count as law, and hence does not have to be enforced. The intuition here is that there is a difference between a statute that violates a moral principle which is also a principle of the rule of law and a statute that violates a moral principle which, no matter how important it is, is not a principle of the rule of law. While the latter kind of violation might be much more heinous than the former, the former has for a judge a special quality to it. It introduces a tension or even a contradiction into the judge's attempt to make sense of his legal duty – his obligation of fidelity to law.

---

[135] *Ibid.*, pp. 62–3.

[136] *Ibid.*, pp. 81–2. Dicey took the example and the quotation from Leslie Stephen, *Science of Ethics* (London: Smith, Elder, 1882).

[137] Dicey, *Law of the Constitution*, pp. 49–50.   [138] *Ibid.*, p. 40.

Armed with this intuition, we can note that Dicey's blue-eyed baby example was likely to be problematic from the perspective of both legality and morality. A statute which required the execution would be a bill of attainder, a law which attempts to declare guilt and stipulate punishment in the same breath, thus bypassing the courts which are supposed to ensure that no one is punished who had not been fairly determined to be guilty of a pre-existing crime. I will come back to the interesting topic of bills of attainder in later chapters. But it is probably the case that Dicey supposed that if the supremacies come into conflict, Parliament must win, whatever the nature of the conflict.[139] So the first major problem with Dicey's account of the rule of law is that it depends on Parliament choosing to cooperate with judges, which is why it seems naïve.

A second problem is that Dicey did not contemplate how a statute might prospectively provide for an executive response to a state of emergency in a fashion that preserved the rule of law.[140] His stance had a lot, perhaps everything, to do with the fact that he was averse to any legislative delegation to the executive of an authority that would amount to a discretion which could be exercised free of judicial control. Dicey thought that the administrative state is an affront to the rule of law precisely because he considered that a state in which officials were given vast discretionary powers to implement legislative programmes necessarily placed such officials beyond the reach of the rule of law. Put more generally, Dicey was deeply opposed to the administrative state,[141] as were Lord Hewart[142] and F. A. Hayek[143] after him.

There is no doubt that all three of these figures were opposed to the administrative state for an additional reason: as proponents of laisser-faire, they disliked the socially progressive programmes in whose cause the administrative state was constructed. But whatever one's views on this second issue, it would be a mistake to neglect their concern about the rule of law and unfettered official discretion, a concern which is in principle independent of one's opposition or support for the policies which the officials are supposed to implement. It is this concern which also motivates Dicey's opposition to the claims of the royal prerogative,

---

[139] See the discussion in *ibid.*, note 1, pp. 68–70.

[140] I misinterpreted Dicey on this issue in Dyzenhaus, 'The State of Emergency in Legal Theory' in that I claimed that Dicey clearly expresses a preference that Parliament gives to officials in advance resources to deal with emergencies in accordance with the rule of law. The correct interpretation follows this note in the text.

[141] See for instance, Dicey, *Law of the Constitution*, pp. 227–8.

[142] Lord Hewart, *The New Despotism* (London: Ernest Benn Ltd, 1929).

[143] F. A. Hayek, *The Road to Serfdom* (Chicago: University of Chicago Press, 1994).

just because those claims purport to stand above or beyond the law.[144] His view can be summed up by saying that the difference between the royal prerogative and a statutory discretion is only a matter of form. While the latter is created by law, both are black holes from the perspective of the rule of law.

Dicey thus claimed that the English constitution made no place for martial law in the sense of the French state of siege, where civil liberties are suspended for a period with power over life, death and detention granted to military tribunals.[145] In other words, his conception of constitutional order rejects the idea that the state can operate qua state in a legal black hole and so does not tolerate a constitutional or legal power to create such a black hole.

In making this claim, Dicey suggested that he was merely describing the constitution. But the better view is that he rejects for normative reasons the Schmittian claim that in an emergency the state perforce acts in a black hole. As Schmitt rightly saw, the Kelsenian idea that the state is completely constructed by law, so that officials act illegitimately when they step outside of the law, starts to look less like (as Hans Kelsen claimed it was) an epistemological hypothesis and more like the expression of a normative even natural law aspiration.[146]

Dicey was drawn to that same kind of idea and thus to that same aspiration, despite his own claims to be engaged in mere description. And from that aspiration it follows that it is not sufficient that there is clear legislative authorization for officials; what they do in the name of the law must also comply with the rule of law. Rule by law and the rule of law are for Dicey two sides of the same coin so that when the rule of law is under stress, a question is raised about whether we even have rule by law. We might have, that is, the true legalization of illegality, a state of affairs brought about by law but one in which there is neither the rule of law nor rule by law.

As I will argue, Dicey's position contains the resources for a sophisticated account of the role of Parliament in legal order which helps us to avoid what I will call the validity trap – the trap we fall into if we think that a sufficient condition for the authority of particular laws is that they meet the formal criteria of validity specified by a legal order. It follows from the trap that if the legal order provides no institutional channel to invalidate a law, then no matter how repugnant we might think its

---

[144] Dicey, *Law of the Constitution*, pp. 63–70.
[145] *Ibid.*, pp. 287–8.   [146] Schmitt, *Political Theology*, pp. 40–2.

content, it has complete legal authority. The better position, I will argue, is to see that a law might be both valid and yet have only a doubtful claim to legal authority because it overrides explicitly fundamental principles of the rule of law.

In other words, I think it is important to see that Sir Edward Coke might have drawn the wrong conclusion from a correct claim in his dictum in *Dr Bonham's Case*: 'the common law will controul Acts of Parliament, and sometimes adjudge them to be utterly void: for when an Act of Parliament is against common right and reason, or repugnant, or impossible to be performed, the common law will controul it, and adjudge such act to be void.'[147] That is, while Coke was right to say that the common law constitution will control Acts of Parliament, he was wrong to suppose that it necessarily can void Acts that violate the constitution. However, it does follow from Coke's correct claim that the legal authority of such Acts is in doubt.

But for the moment, I want only to point out that an answer to Schmitt need not accept the terms of his challenge. Indeed, my critique of the positions I have sketched in this section can be summed up in just this fashion. One succumbs to that challenge when one accepts that a sub-stantive conception of the rule of law has no place in a state of emergency, whether this is because one thinks that it is appropriate only for ordinary times or because one thinks that a thin conception is appropriate across the board. To answer that challenge one needs to show that there is a sub-stantive conception of the rule of law that is appropriate at all times. The issue is not how governments and officials should react to an emergency situation for which there is no legislative provision. Rather, it is whether when there is the opportunity to contemplate how the law should be used to react to emergencies, it is possible to react in a way that maintains what I called earlier the rule-of-law project, an enterprise in which the legislature, the government and judges cooperate in ensuring that official responses to the emergency comply with the rule of law. Such reactions will, as we will see, draw on the way in which common law judges have found, contrary to the gloomy predictions of Dicey, Hewart and Hayek, not only that the administrative state is controllable by the rule of law, but also that it has a legitimate role in maintaining the constitutional order.

It is thus a mistake to take regimes of constitutional dictatorship as a test for a substantive conception of the rule of law, for such regimes have already conceded defeat to Schmitt by embedding a black hole in

---

[147] *Dr Bonham's Case* (1610) 8 Co Rep 114.

the constitution even as they try to confine it. Similarly, it is a mistake to take legislative regimes which explicitly announce an intention that officials may do more or less as they please in responding to an emergency. Such regimes establish a dual state in a sense analogous to that used by Ernst Fraenkel when he described the Nazi state as dual, because, while in many respects it continued to govern through the rule of law, in others it established rule by prerogative or legally unchecked power.[148] But it does not follow from the fact that such dualism has existed that it is necessarily the case that emergencies require the establishment of an exceptional legal order alongside the ordinary one, and hence that Schmitt's challenge is unanswerable.[149]

The real test for Schmitt's challenge is whether legislative responses to emergencies necessarily create black holes or grey holes which are in substance black but, as we have seen, in effect worse because they give to official lawlessness the façade of legality. A crucial part of meeting that test is the demonstration that judges can play a meaningful role in keeping legislatures and governments within the rule-of-law project. Moreover, judges can play this role both when the legislature and the executive are cooperating and in keeping them within the project when the legislature and executive seem to indicate that they wish to avoid control by the rule of law.

The rest of this book undertakes that task. It has a normative and theoretical dimension – the account of the substantive conception of the rule of law – and a practical one – an inquiry into the complex nature of adjudication when the rule of law is under stress. Both dimensions come into view at the same time, in seeing how best to understand judicial

---

[148] Ernest Fraenkel, *The Dual State: A Contribution to the Theory of Dictatorship* (New York: Octagon Books, 1969). I am not following Fraenkel's sense precisely because the dualism of the Nazi state for him was not between the prerogative state and the rule-of-law state, but between what he called the Prerogative State and the Normative State. The Normative State is what remains of the rule-of-law state when the legal order has deteriorated to the point where the executive can set aside any legal rule whenever this seems convenient. In this situation the Prerogative State can claim jurisdiction and hence unlimited power over any matter. Fraenkel did not argue that a constitution which allows for the suspension of the rule of law necessarily leads to the creation of legal black holes but simply emphasized how the Nazis had abused the Weimar Constitution to create the prerogative state. See for example, at pp. 9–10. He regarded Schmitt as the chief theorist of the prerogative state.

[149] John Ferejohn and Pasquale Pasquino claim that dualism is a universal feature of the 'non-absolutist western legal tradition' in 'The Law of the Exception: A Typology of Emergency Powers' (2004) 2 *International Journal of Constitutional Law* 210–39 at 239. In order to make this claim, they argue that Dicey recognized the necessity of martial law. I will respond to their claim in ch. 4.

reactions to such stress. But first it is important to sketch the basis for undertaking this task.

The moral resources of law

In his critique of the idea of constitutional dictatorship, Agamben shrewdly picks up on the fact that Schmitt's claim that legal norms have no application to an exceptional situation depends on his position in general legal theory – that in cases where an answer to a question about the law cannot be derived directly from relevant legal norms, the official – that is, the judge – charged with answering that question has to make a quasi-sovereign or legislative decision, one that is ultimately unconstrained by legal norms.[150]

In other words, the claim about the state of exception is a claim about discretion writ large, but it depends on a claim about discretion in ordinary situations. For Schmitt also thought that less dramatic examples of exceptions could be found throughout liberal legal orders, in all those situations where legal officials have to exercise a discretion because the positive law does not dictate an answer. While such situations did not always or even often involve existential decisions, they reveal the incompetence of the rule of law to address even mundane instances of public decision-making that is based on political considerations. Liberals, Schmitt said, attempt to address the exception either by marginalizing it or by attempting to expel it from legal order. But neither tactic works, a fact revealed when an exceptional situation is especially fraught or intense because it involves authentically political or existential considerations, considerations to do with what Schmitt took as the principal mark of the political – the distinction between friend and enemy.

Agamben accepts this view of general legal theory, a view which, shorn of Schmitt's political baggage, is also shared by H. L. A. Hart, with Kelsen, the last century's most eminent legal positivists. For Hart the situation in which a judge has to decide what he called a penumbral case, a case where the determinate content of legal rules does not dictate a result, is exceptional in the sense that the result is not controlled by law, but reached through an extra-legal, quasi-legislative exercise of judicial discretion.[151]

It is not, I think, too much of an exaggeration to say that for Hart and for many other legal positivists the moment of discretionary judgment in a penumbral case is a kind of mini state of emergency or exception.

[150] Agamben, 'State of Exception', pp. 47–8.   [151] Hart, Positivism, pp. 62–4.

If one takes the function of law to be to provide a framework of rules of sufficiently determinate content such that legal subjects are able to plan their lives securely, then that function is undermined on those occasions when it is not clear what the law requires of the subject. However, the emergency is mini as long as the core of settled law is considerably larger than the penumbra of uncertainty. If that is the case, the stability of legal order is not undermined and the emergency is containable in that it is brought to an end authoritatively by the judge's act of discretion.

In other words, the normal situation of law, where positive law provides clear, determinate answers to questions about what the law requires of its subjects, dominates over the exception and that dominance is constantly shored up by judges.[152] The problem posed by the state of emergency is that the exception puts the core of law in doubt by suspending its application. And that problem becomes worse in the post-9/11 world, because the legislative response to emergencies does not create one vast black hole for a limited time, but rather a multitude of black (or grey) holes within the ordinary law of the land. Ackerman's attempt to revive the institution of constitutional dictatorship and Gross' advocacy of an Extra-Legal measures model react precisely to the concern that that this kind of response is likely to become a permanent feature of legal order and to spread.

Since Agamben accepts that Schmitt's general position is right, he does not address the kind of legal theory that tries to show that it does not follow from the fact that a problem is ungovernable by rules, that is, by highly determinate legal norms, that necessarily a decision about its solution takes place in a legal void.[153] For example, Lon L. Fuller argued that positivists failed to appreciate that legal order must aspire to realize principles of an 'inner morality of law', principles on which judges should draw in answering legal questions.[154] And Ronald Dworkin argues that a judge who approaches even the hardest of hard cases with the right

---

[152] In fact, Schmitt adopted just this solution to the exception in his earliest work. See Carl Schmitt, *Gesetz und Urteil: Eine Untersuchung zum Problem der Rechtspraxis* (Munich: CH Beck, 1969, first published in 1912). For a more detailed discussion, see David Dyzenhaus, 'Holmes and Carl Schmitt: An Unlikely Pair' (1997) 63 *Brooklyn Law Review* 165–88 at 180–6.

[153] Strangely, Agamben relies on Hans-Georg Gadamer's theory of interpretation to support his claim, despite the fact that Gadamer's theory is very close to Dworkin's; Agamben, '*State of Exception*', p. 40, referring to H. G. Gadamer, *Truth and Method* (London: Sheed & Ward, 1979). It is Agamben's neglect of such responses that permits him to proceed to his dramatic and utterly opaque conclusions about not-law and pure violence.

[154] Fuller, *Morality of Law.*

interpretative attitude will find that he does not have discretion in any strong sense of that term. Rather, the judge will find that the law provides principled answers to legal questions which show the law in its best light, by which Dworkin means best moral light.[155]

I will come back to the debate between positivists and their critics later in this book. For the moment, I want to note that, as we have seen, when it comes to the issue of legal control over states of emergency, many scholars who are well acquainted with the Anglo–American debate seem to think that it has scant relevance. Even if, like Ackerman and Gross, they accept that a substantive conception is appropriate for ordinary times, they generally suppose that it has little or no purchase during a state of emergency. Indeed, it is because they think that history teaches that judges are incapable of playing a role in enforcing the rule of law during states of emergency that they conclude that the rule of law has little or no purchase.

In other words, even if these scholars suppose that during normal times government can and should be subject to a substantive, principled conception of the rule of law, something blocks the conclusion that the same conception should prevail during an emergency. For them, the historical record of judicial failure to uphold the rule of law during emergencies figures prominently in their explanation of the block.

In contrast, as we also have seen, some scholars, for example, Sunstein, start from the position that a much thinner conception of the rule of law is appropriate for all times, ordinary as well exceptional, so for them it is no surprise that the substantive conception is inappropriate for emergencies. For this second group, our understanding of the historical record has to be revised so that we can appreciate that decisions which were traditionally regarded as badges of shame, as examples of judicial spinelessness in the face of executive assertions, were in fact properly decided.

In my view, it is important to keep a grip on the fact that at one level the debate about the rule of law is a theoretical and normative one and as much about what is appropriate during ordinary or normal times as it is about the kind of test that emergency situations pose for different conceptions of the rule of law. For if we can keep that grip, we keep alive the possibility that a substantive conception of the rule of law has a role to play in legal responses to emergencies. And with that possibility vivid, we maintain a critical resource for evaluating the legal responses to emergencies as well as the judicial decisions about the legality of those responses.

---

[155] Dworkin, *Law's Empire*.

I cannot deny the fact that the record of the judiciary is a problem. But imagine making a decision in a class on the rule of law to teach *Halliday* or *Liversidge* or *Korematsu* without paying any attention to the dissents. Such a class would take as exemplary of the rule of law and of the judicial role in upholding it the reasoning of the majorities in those cases. Consistent sceptics about judicial review would not be bothered by this point because their scepticism about judges is matched by their scepticism about any attempt to understand the rule of law as anything more than the rule by law, which is to say the rule of statutes understood as the rule by the commands of the uncommanded commander. For these sceptics, the slogan 'the rule of law rather than the rule of men' is the slogan of those who want rule by judges.[156]

But for those who think that the dissents are important these judgments are at the same time a record of failure and success. They are a record of failure but the failure that is recorded is that of the majority. We look back on these dissents with approval, and on the majority with disapproval, because the dissents show us that it was open to the majority to decide differently. And because we have the benefit today of understanding why the majority should have decided differently, the dissents point to the moral resources of the law that judges and lawyers can draw upon when the rule of law is again put under stress, as it has been since 9/11. That judges in the United Kingdom, Australia, and Canada are showing that they too are capable of folding under stress, that they do not have the nerve of Lord Shaw, Lord Atkin, and Justice Jackson, does nothing by itself to undermine my claim about the moral resources of the law.

Indeed, the very fact that some judges and academics are tempted to rewrite history to support a continuation of the dismal judicial record might show us that law's potential to provide us with moral resources in times of stress is inexhaustible. One day, and I hope the day is not too far off, judges will have to reckon with the fact that when they had the opportunity to stand up for the rule of law, they decided to take the path of South Africa's Appellate Division during apartheid, or of the majority of the House of Lords during the two world wars, or the American Supreme Court in *Korematsu*. Prominent in their number will be Lord Woolf, for his own decision in *Rehman* as well as in *Belmarsh*, the judges of the House of Lords who decided *Rheman* and the judges who have decided equivalent cases in Australia and Canada.

---

[156] See for example Conor Gearty, *Principles of Human Rights Adjudication* (Oxford: Oxford University Press, 2004), pp. 67–8.

Even worse, these judges have made their decisions in full awareness of the past, so with the complete benefit of foresight. And they have done so at a time when, in Canada and the United Kingdom, their jurisdictions had either enacted or entrenched legal protections for human rights and at a time when in all three jurisdictions judges had gone a long way in developing the common law understanding of the rule of law in ways consistent with the postwar drive to protect human rights.

I do want to sound one very necessary cautionary note. I just spoke about law's potential to provide us with moral resources in times of stress. In making that claim, it is important to put the emphasis on 'us' and not 'law'. It would be a mistake to think that judges or the law can save us in times of stress. The first president of postwar Germany made the point that the collapse of the Weimar Republic took place not because of flaws in the Weimar Constitution, but because in Germany's first experiment with democracy there were not enough democrats. Similarly, without enough believers in the rule of law, law cannot deliver its resources to us. Moreover, it is not enough that many lawyers and judges are committed to the rule of law. It is important, indeed much more important, that politicians, public officials, journalists and plain 'we the people' share this commitment. But to say that public opinion is the ultimate basis of the rule of law does not make its principles contingent on what the public thinks.

Towards the end of his dissent in *Korematsu*, Justice Jackson said that that the courts 'wield no power equal to' restraining the command of the war power, should the people let it 'fall into irresponsible and unscrupulous hands'. Thus he concluded that the 'chief restraint upon those who command the physical forces of the country, in the future as in the past, must be their responsibility to the political judgments of their contemporaries and to the moral judgments of history'. But prior to reaching this conclusion, Justice Jackson warned against the danger of a court upholding the constitutionality of the evacuation order after the alleged emergency was over, especially when the order was based on the principle of racial discrimination in criminal procedure:

> The principle then lies about like a loaded weapon ready for the hand of any authority that can bring forward a plausible claim of an urgent need. . . A military commander may overstep the bounds of constitutionality, and it is an incident. But if we review and approve, that passing incident becomes the doctrine of the Constitution. There it has a generative power of its own, and all that it creates will be in its own image.[157]

---

[157] *Korematsu*, at 246.

Taken together these remarks make the point that even though judges cannot restrain power when it is in the wrong hands, so that it is ultimately up to the people to exercise that restraint, judges must nevertheless carry out their duty to uphold the rule of law. If the judges fail to carry out their duty, they will also fail to clarify to the people what constitutes responsible government – government in compliance with the rule of law. I will now turn to my defence of the claim that judges have such a duty and, moreover, one to uphold a substantive conception of the rule of law.

2

Constituting the legislature

Constitutional positivism

It is conventional to speak of the legislature as constituted by rules that
speak to the number of members, their regional distribution, the way in
which bills become statutes, and so on. But I mean by the constitution of
the legislature the fundamental legal values that constitute its authority,
whether or not there is a written constitution. I will start with the dramatic
example of an alleged state of emergency. We saw in chapter 1 that Carl
Schmitt argued that legal norms cannot apply to exceptional situations.
He thus claimed that in a state of exception or emergency the writ of the
rule of law does not run. I will show that contrary to Schmitt there is
a genuine choice in any real or alleged emergency whether to respond
to the emergency through the rule of law. I will also argue that where
judges are involved in making that choice clear to a government that
controls the legislature, they should articulate fully the basis for their
decision.

It is a mistake then for judges to adopt the stance of judicial minimalism
we saw Cass Sunstein outline in chapter 1. That stance requires judges to
say as little as possible about the justification for the result they reach and it
also asks them to intrude as little as possible into the work of the legislature
by confining the scope of what they order. They should, that is, prescribe as
little as possible to the legislature. My quarrel with minimalism is not with
its second requirement. As I indicated in chapter 1, for judges to identify
a constitutional problem and then leave it to the legislature to decide how
to respond to it is not to write the legislature a blank cheque. Rather, it
tells the legislature both that if it wishes to continue the constitutionally
problematic practice it must find a way of making that practice comply
with the constitution and also that the court, if called upon, will check to
see that the reforms do comply. It is far better to give the legislature that
message than to tell it what it needs to do to achieve a bare passing grade,
as we saw the plurality of the Supreme Court of the United States did in

Hamdi.[1] So my quarrel is with the first requirement of minimalism – the restriction on justification.

Recall that Sunstein argues that judges should avoid taking stands on the most deeply contested questions of constitutional law, preferring to leave the most fundamental questions – 'incompletely theorized disagreements' – undecided. His hope is that such judicial 'shallowness' can attract support from people with a wide range of theoretical positions or who are undecided about answers to the deep questions.[2] I agree that judges will sometimes reach results in politically contentious matters by avoiding giving the full justification for the result. But I will argue that such avoidance is counterproductive.

I pointed out in the Introduction that the cases I will deal with fall into three categories. First, there are judges who think that they have a duty to uphold the rule of law in the sense of fundamental principles only when there is a bill of rights that imposes such a duty. They also tend to think that in an emergency situation legal rights, including entrenched constitutional rights, have no or little application. Second, there are judges who articulate and follow through on such a duty, despite the fact that they have no bill of rights to rely on, and despite the fact that the legislature and or the executive claims that there is an emergency situation. Third, there are judges who reach the same conclusions as judges in the second category, but who avoid making explicit their constitutional commitments. They are not quite Sunstein's minimalists because they do not accept that they should always aim for the narrowest result. But they do accept they should give the most minimal justification for the result they reach, thus avoiding controversy about constitutional fundamentals.

I will contend that it is important for judges in the third category to make their commitments explicit. Only then can we see why it makes sense to say that judges are under a constitutional duty to uphold the rule of law, despite the fact that they might not always be able to fulfil that duty in the face of an executive and legislature determined to operate without the rule of law. Moreover, there is more than a theoretical point riding on the claim that judges should reach their rule-of-law preserving conclusions by articulating fully the theory that sustains those conclusions. As we will see, judges who avoid making their commitments explicit risk lending support to judges in the first category as well as to future legislative and executive departures from the rule of law.

---

[1] *Hamdi* v. *Rumsfeld*, 124 S. Ct. 2633 (2004).
[2] Sunstein, *One Case at a Time* and Sunstein, 'Minimalism at War', 47–109.

Indeed, minimalism turns out to be more of an explanation for what judges in the second category do than a justification. They say as little as possible lest they be accused of activism and injudicious meddling in politics. And the real justification is not so much incompletely theorized as Sunstein would put it, but hidden, and the way in which it is hidden is what makes minimalism counterproductive.

As we will see, deciding on the most minimal possible basis usually means resorting to the rhetoric of the position I call constitutional positivism, a rhetoric that presumes that all that matters is the plain meaning of authoritative constitutional or statutory text. But that rhetoric is the surface manifestation of a position that if consistently followed does not lead to results consistent with a position that aspires to uphold fundamental principles of legality. So it is a mistake for judges who adopt an aspirational conception of the rule of law to take refuge in the rhetoric of constitutional positivism. Rather, they should stick to their common law guns and hold that legislation necessarily seeks to realize certain principles, because without compliance with those principles, statutes not only lack legitimacy, but also legal authority. So, before I discuss the constitution of the legislature, it is important to put in place some of the features of constitutional positivism.

Constitutional positivism is a particular practical expression of the positivist tradition, though it has a rather complex relationship with it. Traditionally, positivism is hostile to judicial review for political reasons to do with ensuring that the law is made by the legislature, since it is in the legislature that collective judgments about the common good are most appropriately made. Thus positivists wish to avoid any device which will allow judges to claim that they are interpreting the law when in fact what they are doing is substituting their own judgment about the good for the legislative one. I will call this tradition political positivism, to distinguish it from its conceptual relation in the work of H. L. A. Hart and Joseph Raz. And I call it political rather than democratic positivism because, as its founder Jeremy Bentham showed, its opposition to bills of rights can only be consistently maintained if one supposes that the decision to entrench a bill of rights is a mistake, even when it is taken by the democratically elected representatives of the people who have the overwhelming support of their electorate. When Bentham said that rights talk is nonsense upon stilts he did not mean only that it is politically dangerous because it gives to judges the opportunity to grab legislative power. He also meant that to adopt a bill of rights is a grave political mistake, no matter how much popular support it has.

The difference between political positivism and constitutional positivism comes about because constitutional positivism is a practical stance – the stance of judges who try to follow a positivist ideal of fidelity to law despite the fact that they work within legal orders in which the Benthamite dream of a completely codified legal order, one in which all law is positive law with a determinate content, was not realized. They are thus forced to try to make the legal order in which they find themselves conform as far as possible to their understanding of law and the rule of law.[3]

These judges are committed by their understanding of the doctrine of legislative supremacy to applying the law enacted by their legislatures in a manner true to the idea that the legislature has a monopoly on making law, so that judges should seek to understand statutes as providing rules with determinate content. But as judges in a common law legal order, they have to contend with the fact that they have an interpretative role which goes far beyond what political positivism considers ideal, a role premised on the idea that their judgments are authoritative expositions of the law. They do their best to make sense of that role through the rigid doctrine of the separation of powers. While the legislature has a monopoly on law making, they have a monopoly on law interpretation. But they exercise their monopoly by seeking to be true to their understanding of law and so seek to resolve the tension between the competing supremacies of Parliament and the judiciary by tethering the judiciary to the legislature's commands. The judicial task to determine the content that the legislature in fact intended requires negatively that judges avoid relying on arguments about what moral ideals they think the legislature ought to be trying to achieve. For if they so rely, they will end up imposing their moral views on the statutes and thus usurping the law-making role of the legislature.

At best, such judges will have a profound ambivalence to the common law, something nowhere better illustrated than in Justice Antonin Scalia's *A Matter of Interpretation: Federal Courts and the Law.*[4] Thus while Scalia is willing to have the writ of the common law run in private law, he is hostile to the idea that the common law should form an interpretative backdrop to the interpretation of statutes. Here he exemplifies the classic hostility of positivism to the common law tradition. He also displays the

---

[3] See David Dyzenhaus, 'The Genealogy of Legal Positivism' (2004) 24 *Oxford Journal of Legal Studies* 39–67.

[4] (Princeton: Princeton University Press, 1997). I deal with Scalia's position in more detail in David Dyzenhaus, 'The Unwritten Constitution and the Rule of Law' in Grant Huscroft and Ian Brodie (eds.), *Constitutionalism in the Charter Era* (Markham, Ontario: LexisNexis Butterworths, 2004), pp. 383–412.

concern that common law judges will say that they are simply deciding in accordance with the reason of the law in order to bootstrap themselves into an increasingly powerful position in their relationship with the legislature.

Matters become worse for positivist judges when they are required to apply a bill of rights. They will experience at least some dissonance because they desire to avoid the kind of moral deliberation required by the duty to apply their bill of rights. As Scalia's work demonstrates, such judges cope with the dissonance by confining the scope of their interpretations to various proxies for factual legislative intention – what the founding fathers, or ratifiers of the constitution in fact had in mind, what their immediate audience would have taken them to have in mind, and so on. These interpretative techniques are rife with well-known problems. But the problems are serious only if one regards the techniques as genuine attempts to legitimate constitutional interpretation. If instead they are seen as techniques or holding actions, designed to limit the scope of an illegitimate activity in which judges have no choice but to engage, the techniques are a lot more plausible. It follows that any interpretative activity that goes beyond these techniques is even more illegitimate. Claiming that constitutional values can be inferred from the text of a division of powers or federal constitution is more illegitimate, while a claim that the values float free of any text, and thus that there is an unwritten constitution, is even worse.

Constitutional positivism is then not then so much a way of legitimating an approach to interpretation, but a compromise positivist judges make in order to prevent a bad situation from getting worse. It is much the same approach that is advocated for interpreting the text of ordinary statutes when these incorporate open-textured value terms like fairness or reasonableness. These terms should not be treated by judges as invitations to engage in deliberation about their meaning, but as landmines which the judges should try to defuse by confining their scope to the smallest extent possible. Similarly, the common law is to be treated as far as possible as a system of determinate rules whose content does not form a backdrop for interpretation of general law, but rather as rules which apply only within particular areas of private law. Thus positivist judges will try hard to 'hedge' themselves in by 'announcing rules' in their judgments.[5]

When lawyers and academics use the label 'positivist' to describe judges it is this position they have in mind and we will see it exemplified in many of the cases discussed below. I cannot go into much detail here about the

---

[5] Antonin Scalia, 'The Rule of Law as a Rule of Rules' (1989) 56 *University of Chicago Law Review* 1175–88 at 1180.

intellectual genealogy of the position. But I do want to note that in the legal orders on which I focus it comes about through a combination of John Austin and A. V. Dicey.

Austin is perhaps the principal intellectual influence on Dicey which is one of the reasons why Dicey is often regarded as falling within the positivist tradition. But those who think of Dicey as a positivist neglect to notice that Austin made a significant break with Bentham when he argued that judges were not only in the business of making law, but that they did not do enough of this. He made that break because he thought that Bentham had not foreseen the dangers of concentrating a monopoly of law-making power in a legislature that would be captured by the ignorant masses. In other words, Austin wished to carve out a space in positivist legal theory for a judicial elite which could counter a legislature controlled by the masses.[6] But, as I have argued elsewhere, this move threatens to subvert positivism. The subversion becomes even worse when Dicey takes from Austin the idea of a supreme legislature and combines it with an account of how judges in interpreting legislation legitimately draw on the values of the common law to make it conform with what he calls 'the spirit of legality'.[7] In making this move, Dicey seems to jettison the political positivist idea that judges have a quasi-legislative role in a common law legal order, a role which Bentham despised and Austin welcomed. For on Dicey's account, much like Dworkin's, judges when they interpret statutes in the light of common law principles are merely applying the law – the values of the common law. And in this role they have their own monopoly – a monopoly on interpretation of the law.[8] So it is Dicey who articulates the rigid doctrine of the separation of powers.

Dicey's legal theory is not then positivist. Rather, it is a radically unstable mixture of political positivism and a common law, aspirational conception of law – and it this instability that leads to the idea that a common law legal order is a contest between the competing supremacies of the legislature and the judiciary. Judges who accept the rigid doctrine of the separation of powers can attempt to stabilize things in one of two ways. They can adopt constitutional positivism and seek to subordinate their interpretations to

[6] John Austin, *Lectures on Jurisprudence* (5th edn, London: John Murray, 1885), vol. II, pp. 532–3.

[7] Dicey, *Law of the Constitution*, pp. 412–13.

[8] A. V. Dicey in *Lectures on the Relationship Between Law and Public Opinion in England During the Nineteenth Century* (1st edn, London: MacMillan and Co., 1905), at Note IV, pp. 481–93 talks of judge-made law. But he does not mean by this anything more that creative judicial interpretation in which all the reasons given are legal reasons.

facts about legislative intention or, if there is a written constitution, to facts about the intentions of the drafters. Alternatively, they can seek to show that judges are entitled to uphold the aspirational conception whatever the facts about legislative intention.

As I will now show, a division of powers constitution offers an opportunity to judges minded to adopt an aspirational conception to hide that conception behind constitutional text. But, I will argue, it would be better for them to articulate their common law constitutionalism fully whether or not they have the resources to invalidate statutes which override fundamental legal values. Indeed, the point of this chapter is not so much to resolve as to explore a set of puzzles. As we will see more clearly in chapters 3 and 4, the puzzles arise when we fail to see that there is an essential continuity between the situation where judges interpret a statute in the light of their understanding of the common law constitution and when they seek to understand the provisions of a division of powers constitution in the same way. The only difference a division of powers constitution makes from the perspective of the rule of law is that it might afford to judges the authority to invalidate a statute that explicitly overrides the rule of law.

The *Communist Party* case[9]

> History and not only ancient history, shows that in countries where democratic institutions have been unconstitutionally superseded, it has been done not seldom by those holding the executive power. Forms of government may need protection from dangers likely to arise from within the institutions to be protected. In point of constitutional theory the power to legislate for the protection of an existing form of government ought not to be based on a conception, if otherwise adequate, adequate only to assist those holding power to resist or suppress obstruction or opposition or attempts to displace them or the form of government they defend.[10]
>
> Dixon J

[9] Throughout this section, I rely heavily on George Winterton, 'The Communist Party Case' in H. P. Lee and George Winterton (eds.), *Australian Constitutional Landmarks* (Cambridge: Cambridge University Press, 2003), pp. 108–44 at p. 108. This is a revised version of his 'The Significance of the Communist Party Case' (1992) 18 *Melbourne Law Review* 630–58. All references below are to the essay in the book. My discussion of the case is based on my earlier treatment, 'Constituting the Enemy: A Response to Carl Schmitt' in Andras Sajo (ed.), *Militant Democracy* (Utrecht: Eleven International Publishing, 2004), pp. 15–45.

[10] *Australian Communist Party* v. *Commonwealth* (the '*Communist Party* case') (1951) 83 CLR 1 at 187–8.

In 1949, a government was elected in Australia which had as part of its platform a ban on the Australian Communist Party. In 1950 it secured passage of the Communist Party Dissolution Act, which declared the Australian Communist Party to be dissolved and forfeited its property to the Commonwealth (s. 4). The Act also made other bodies of persons who were (or had been in the period since the establishment of the Australian Communist Party) likely to be under the influence of communists liable to be dissolved and their property forfeited to the Commonwealth, upon the Governor-General's being satisfied that they fell within the legislation (ss. 5–8), and made persons who were (or had been since the establishment of the Party) communists liable to being banned from Commonwealth public service employment, holding offices in Commonwealth bodies corporate or unions that were declared to have substantial membership in vital industries, also upon the Governor-General's being satisfied that they fell within the legislation (ss. 10–11). The only safeguards were, first, that the Governor-General could not make a declaration before an executive committee had considered the evidence, but his declaration did not depend on its approval. Second, judicial review was available on the question of whether a body was affiliated. But the body had the onus of proving that it was not affiliated and the declaration that the body was prejudicial to defence and security was not open to review. Finally, the Act made it an offence, punishable by five years' imprisonment, for a person knowingly to be an officer or a member of an unlawful association (s. 7).

The Act commenced with nine recitals, indicating 'facts' that purported to bring the Communist Party within the reach of Commonwealth legislative power, and specifically its power to legislate with respect to matters incidental to national defence (s. 51(xxxix) of the Constitution in its operation on s. 51(vi)), and the execution or maintenance of the Constitution and Commonwealth laws (s. 51(xxxix) of the Constitution in its operation on s. 61). Draconian as the substantive provisions of the statute were, its most remarkable feature consisted in these lengthy preambular recitals. For besides enumerating the provisions of the Constitution which were claimed to be the basis of the statute, the recitals also deemed certain facts to be true. Thus the preamble stated that the Communist Party aimed to seize power and was engaged in activities, including espionage, sabotage, and treason, to achieve that end and asserted that the statute was necessary for Australia's defence and security and the execution and maintenance of its Constitution and laws. In other words, the recitals were a kind of legislative fiat, which purported to provide the constitutional basis for the statute together with the evidence that the objectives of the statute were not only consistent with the Constitution, but indeed required if the legislature and government were to fulfil their constitutional responsibilities. In addition, as we have seen, the statute gave to the executive the authority to make the same kind of fiats in respect of other association and individuals.

Governments had advocated banning the Party before and it had been banned from 1940 until 1942 in terms of wartime regulations. On the day of the Communist Party Dissolution Act's enactment, the Australian Communist Party, ten unions and several union officials challenged the constitutional validity of the statute, asking the High Court for an injunction to restrain the government from enforcing the Act. Dixon J refused to issue such an injunction. Instead, he stated two questions for the High Court: first, did the validity of the Act depend upon proof in court of the facts recited in the Act's preamble, facts which the plaintiffs could contest, and, if not, second, was the Act invalid?

The case was politically charged, to say the least. The majority of Australians, as many as 80 per cent according to one poll, supported the ban and at the time Australia was participating in the Korean War. As a Bill, the measure had been bitterly contested in Parliament by the Opposition Labor Party and it had drawn the unfavourable attention of the international press. The Chief Justice, Sir John Latham, had been Attorney-General in one of the earlier governments that supported such a ban, a fact which would have supported a demand that he recuse himself, though the plaintiffs decided against making that demand. Finally, prominent among the plaintiffs' lawyers was H. V. Evatt, Deputy Leader of the Labor Party, who had been vociferous in his opposition to the Bill. When his participation in the case was announced, he was immediately subjected to a government smear that he was a communist sympathizer.

In what is regarded as a significant victory for constitutionalism and the rule of law, five of the seven judges while answering 'no' to the first question answered 'yes' to the second, thus invalidating the statute. Of the other two, one – the Chief Justice – answered 'no' to both questions. The remaining judge answered 'yes' to both.

Australia then as now has no entrenched bill of rights, but only what I have called a division of powers constitution, a constitutional division of authority between the federal government and the governments of the Australian states, including provisions for the separation of federal judicial power. And we will soon see that for the six judges who answered 'yes' to the second question, that answer was put on the basis that the federal legislature had no authority to enact this particular statute. For them, the main question was framed in the following way. Federal legislative powers are enumerated in the Australian Constitution, so that federal legislation must be grounded by a positive source of authority for an enactment, and, where it regulates matters that are incidental to the main power, the legislation must be reasonably incidental to that power. That requirement, together with the constitutional provisions which give the High Court jurisdiction to determine constitutional questions, is the textual peg on which the reasoning is hung.

Thus while the case did not turn on an interpretation of a bill of rights, it did turn on the existence of a written division of powers constitution. Hence, it might well seem that the case is hardly fertile ground for the argument I have advertised about the common law constitution of the legislature and the executive. I will argue, however, that judges who are minded to uphold the common law constitution often find that a federal constitution offers them convenient pegs on which to hang their reasoning. They can read into the text of the federal constitution the normative controls they think are required by the rule of law. But as I will show by contrasting Latham CJ's somewhat neglected dissent with the majority judgments, if judges take too seriously the pegs, regarding these as the essential elements of their reasoning, they weaken their reasoning and undermine the rule of law. The real basis of their reasoning is not the text but the values for which they take the text to be evidence.

None of the majority judges disputed the authority of the Commonwealth to legislate against subversion, whether they derived this authority from the explicit powers of the Commonwealth or reasoned, as Dixon J did, that it is an authority which inheres in every polity – the existential necessity for self-protection. Rather, they trained their fire on the preambular recital of powers, which they regarded as an illegitimate exercise in constitutional bootstrapping. As Dixon put it, 'The difficulty which exists in referring the leading provisions of the Act to the defence power and the power to make laws against subversive action evidently did not escape the notice of the legislature. For that and perhaps other reasons the Act is prefaced with an elaborate preamble'.[11]

At one level, the majority's objection to the preamble is a formal one – the claim that judges almost always make that it is an axiom of the rule of law that legal authority is constituted by law, hence it must be exercised within the limits of the law, which requires that the body purporting to have authority cannot itself decide what those limits are. As Dixon J

[11] *Ibid.*, at 189.

said, government is government under the Constitution, 'an instrument framed in accordance with many traditional conceptions, to some of which it gives effect, as, for example, in separating the judicial power from other functions of government others of which are simply assumed. Among these I think it might fairly be said that the rule of law forms an assumption'.[12]

A corollary is that some other body must have the task of policing the limits. And judges understand their role as interpreters of the law independent of other branches of government in constitutional terms, as vesting in them the authority to decide on the limits. Indeed, in the Australian Constitution, s. 71 entrenches the separation of federal judicial power and s. 75(iii) and (v) entrench the original jurisdiction of the High Court in all matters in which 'the Commonwealth, or a person . . . being sued on behalf of the Commonwealth, is a party' and 'a writ of Mandamus or prohibition or an injunction is sought against an officer of the Commonwealth'.

On the basis of this assumption, the majority judges constructed a doctrine of constitutional fact: whether the Commonwealth had authority to enact the statute depended on whether as a matter of fact the Constitution gave it authority and this fact could not be brought into existence by the very law which required such authority to be valid. As Fullagar J put it, it is 'an elementary rule of constitutional law . . . that a stream cannot rise higher than its source' and, he went on to say, 'Parliament cannot recite itself into a field the gates of which are locked against it by superior law'.[13]

There is, however, an important ambiguity in the idea of 'superior law'. Does it mean simply the explicit text of the division of powers constitution or does it mean the text read against a backdrop of the fundamental values of the common law constitution? The majority judges preferred for the most part to style their reasoning as if all that they had to do was interpret explicit text. With the exception of the claim that the Court has a role as guardian of constitutional validity, they suggest that the explicit terms of the Constitution gave them the entire basis for the conclusion that the statute was invalid.

Their option for a kind of constitutional positivism is understandable because their Constitution could be understood as a mere division of powers constitution – one which protected no substantive values – and still deliver that conclusion. And in the charged political climate in which they were deciding the case, they could claim that they were simply doing

---

[12] *Ibid.*, at 193.   [13] *Ibid.*, at 263.

their job and not presuming to second-guess Parliament's judgment about political policy. Their task was made easy in this regard by the fact that the Australian Constitution allocated to the states the power to legislate over areas which were not reserved to the Commonwealth, which meant that the states, but not the federal Parliament, had power to regulate voluntary associations. Some of the majority judges thus reasoned that the states had authority to do what the Commonwealth could not.[14]

This suggestion created some serious tensions in the majority's reasoning. One was that the majority was committed to accepting that had the states enacted legislation banning the Communist Party, that legislation would have been perfectly valid, and thus that the constitutional validity of the statute depended on the contingent fact of where particular powers had been distributed. At least two of the majority judges explicitly, and the others more or less implicitly, subscribed to the positivist view that the difference between a common law legal order without a division of powers constitution and one with such a constitution is as follows. Where there is no division of powers constitution, there is no legal limit on the power of the unitary legislature other than the limits of manner and form – the procedures the legislature has to follow to enact valid law. Where there is a division of powers constitution, there is the further set of limits because of the explicit distribution of power. But this further set of limits is to be understood much like the limits of manner and form. It does not impose any moral or substantive limit on what the legislatures of the federation may do, but simply adds a question to the list of questions that the courts are entitled to answer about the technical validity of statutes. Courts might ask not only whether the legislature followed the prescribed steps in enacting legislation, but also whether that kind of legislation fell within its constitutionally prescribed jurisdiction. It follows that whether and to what extent the rule of law controls either the legislature or the executive depends on the contingencies of history, in the case of the legislature whether there exists an entrenched constitution and in the case of the executive whether the authority it wields is subject to explicit controls, whether statutory or constitutional. This understanding of division of powers constitutionalism is then the ultra vires rule of administrative

---

[14] Fullagar and Kitto JJ, at 262 and 271 respectively expressly said that the states would be able to legislate in the form the Commonwealth had. Dixon J said the legislation was within the 'prima facie' competence of the States, at 200; Williams and Webb JJ confined themselves to saying that the power to legislate on the subject matter of voluntary associations is reserved to the States, at 226 and 243 respectively. McTiernan J made no reference to the states' capacity to legislate on the matter.

law writ large. No body which has delegated authority may act beyond its powers, where beyond powers or ultra vires means outside the explicitly stated limits of its authority.

So the conception of the rule of law entailed by constitutional positivism is one where the content of the rule of law is contingent, in that how the rule of law applies depends on the particular history of a legal order, as manifested in its positive law. That the law delegates virtually uncontrolled or arbitrary power to an official to ban a political party, or that the law in itself is an exercise of such power, is not considered problematic from constitutional positivism's perspective on the rule of law, since that exercise is, on its terms, according to law.

But of the judges, the only consistent constitutional positivist was Latham CJ. He reasoned that the defence power of the Constitution included the power to protect against subversion, because the defence power is the power to protect the state against enemies and enemies are not found only without a country's borders, a claim he seemed to think was recognized in the fact that the defence power was not limited by the Constitution to dealing with the external enemy. As he put things:

> The exercise of these powers to protect the community and to preserve the government of the country under the Constitution is a matter of the greatest moment. Their exercise from time to time must necessarily depend upon the circumstances of the time as viewed by some authority. The question is – 'By what authority – by Parliament or by a court?'[15]

His answer was that just as the decision as to who is an external enemy and by what legal means that enemy is to be combated is a quintessentially political decision to be made by government and the legislature, so the government and legislature must decide who is an internal enemy and how he is to be combated. Moreover, the actual combating of the enemy is a task which government is best suited to perform unhindered by judges, though Latham CJ indignantly rejected the proposition to which the majority seemed committed – that in times of war the legislature could give to government the power to act outside of the law. According to him, 'they can act within the law to meet the crisis without being subject to the risk of being told by a court that they were acting illegally. In such a case, the Government and parliament are not left by the Constitution to action under a cloud of legal doubt'.[16] Influential in his reasoning here were both wartime decisions of his own Court and the House of Lords'

---

[15] *Ibid.*, at 142.   [16] *Ibid.*, at 164.

decision during the First World War in *Halliday*, decisions which upheld what these courts understood as unreviewable delegations of authority to the executive.[17]

In Latham CJ's view, there was no middle ground on this question, so that it was the case that:

> [a]ll the arguments for the plaintiffs upon this question depended upon the acceptance of a principle that it was for a court and not for a Government or a Parliament to determine whether interference with, resistance to, and undermining of a defence policy approved by a Government and by the Parliament to which it was responsible was proved to exist by admissible evidence of actual happenings and whether it was sufficiently dangerous to the community to justify an exercise of the defence power for the purpose of destroying what the Government and Parliament regarded as a hostile and traitorous organization.[18]

He also suggested that the majority, since they found the statute invalid accepted the same principle, whether or not they answered 'no' to the question whether the validity of the Act depended upon proof in court of the facts recited in the Act's preamble.

Latham CJ was, in my opinion, right to impute this principle to the majority. But what he failed to see is that the principle depends on the assumption that there is no middle ground between a Parliament and government having the power to make the final determination whether there is an emergency and a court having that same power. But there is a middle ground – the ground of legality – which requires that when Parliament and government make such a determination they make it in a way that respects the requirements of the rule of law. Hence courts must ask what the legal limits are on the power of Parliament, whatever the nature of the emergency.

We have already seen one answer to that question – that the power to ban the Communist Party belonged to the states not the Commonwealth. But that is an odd answer since it seems to attribute unlimited or arbitrary power to another part of the federation, an issue I will come back to below. A second answer offered by the majority was that, while it was acceptable for the legislature and the executive to be unconstrained by law when the country is on a war footing because it faces an external enemy, this is unacceptable when the threat comes during peacetime from within. But

---

[17] *Lloyd* v. *Wallach* (1915) 20 CLR 299; *Ex Parte Walsh* [1942] ALR 359; *R* v. *Halliday, ex parte Zadig* [1917] AC 260. See *Communist Party* case at 158–65.

[18] *Ibid.*, at 146.

then they were, as Latham CJ pointed out, taking judicial notice of the nature of the emergency. Moreover, to take such notice required the judges to second-guess the government and the legislature about the judgment that there was an emergency, despite the fact that they claimed, with one exception, not to be answering the question whether the validity of the Act depended upon proof in court of the facts recited in the Act's preamble. In addition, this answer seemed to commit them to the proposition that if there were a genuine emergency, one occasioned by an external enemy, then the legislature had a free hand or could give the executive a free hand, that is, the freedom to act arbitrarily or outside of the law.[19]

The majority was, however, uneasy with the thought that the executive might be given this arbitrary power. In a fascinating study of the transcript of the trial, George Williams shows that much of the action in Court was taken up with exchanges between the leading counsel for the Commonwealth, Garfield Barwick, and the majority judges on the topic of the power the statute granted the executive.[20] Williams suggests that the concern of the majority that the statute, if upheld, gave the Governor-General an unreviewable discretion was crucial to the Court's conclusion that the statute was invalid.[21] As he points out, Evatt argued that the discretion was in fact unreviewable, an argument which had its risks. For if the High Court had gone on to find that the statute was nevertheless valid, the result would have been that Evatt and the other lawyers for the plaintiffs would seem to have conceded that the statute validly delegated an unfettered discretion to the executive.

This line of reasoning creates the second major tension for the majority. While uneasy with the thought that the executive might wield arbitrary power, they are nevertheless committed to the proposition that a constitutionally uncontrolled or plenary legislature is entitled to delegate such power to the executive and, moreover, they seem to think that such a delegation is appropriate, whether or not there is a unitary Parliament, in a situation of wartime emergency. They thus accept the majority of the House of Lords' stance in the Second World War detention decision,

---

[19] See McTiernan J, at 206 and Fullagar J, at 258. Dixon J pointed to examples of wartime legislation that were held by the Court to be not incidental to defence, at 185, and remarked on the differences between the National Defence legislation and the statute at 186. Webb J insisted that the actual exercise of the power (legislative or executive) was reviewable on constitutional grounds in any particular case, at 239–42, and Kitto J seemed to hold the same view, at 281–2.

[20] George Williams, 'Reading the Judicial Mind: Appellate Argument in the Communist Party Case' (1993) 15 *Sydney Law Review* 3–29.

[21] *Ibid.*, 11–14.

Liversidge v. *Anderson.*[22] It seems then that the only difference between them and Latham CJ is that while they describe such a delegation as one of power to act outside of the law or arbitrarily, Latham CJ does not think that government is left to act 'under a cloud of legal doubt'. Indeed, it is a striking feature of the case that two of the most famous quotations from the majority's judgments – Dixon J's discourse on history in the epigraph to this section and Fullagar J's assertion that the constitutional stream cannot rise higher than its source – occur within passages in which these two judges accepted Evatt's argument that the Communist Party Dissolution Act delegated virtually unreviewable authority to the executive to deal with the enemy. Indeed, Fullagar J's assertion follows hard on the heels of his perhaps reluctant acceptance of the Australian authority on this point as well as of the English authority, exemplified for him in *Liversidge.*

In my view, where Dixon and Fullagar JJ go wrong is in their insistence that the invalidity of the statute had its entire basis in the explicit text of the Constitution. Rather, its basis was in the text of the Constitution understood in the light of a highly normative understanding of the rule of law. Their invocation of the constitutional fact doctrine is only superficially the formal argument that delegated authority, whether parliamentary or administrative, is an authority which is inherently limited by the explicit text of the delegation. Their deeper argument is that the delegates are bound by both the formal limits and by a commitment to the rule of law which does not have to be explicitly stated.

One can in this regard glean from Williams' account of the trial that Evatt thought that the attack on the legislation and the attack on the power given to the executive by the legislation were one and the same. Both were premised on the assumption that the government could not usurp powers that properly belonged to the judiciary, whether this was by government-initiated legislative fiat or by giving the power to make such fiats to the executive. And prior to the enactment of the statute, Evatt had argued in public debate that it was in the nature of an Act of Attainder since it imposed, or authorized the executive to impose, penalties on individuals without those individuals being able to protest their innocence to a court of law. He thus regarded the statute as a denial of basic principles of British justice, that is, the justice of the common law.[23]

I will later return to the subject of an Act of Attainder because, with Trevor Allan, I regard the constellation of concepts which this idea

---

[22] *Liversidge* v. *Anderson* [1942] AC 206.
[23] Winterton, 'The Communist Party Case', p. 118.

encompasses to be of the utmost importance to our understanding of the rule of law.[24] For the moment, I will refer briefly to the explanation of that idea by the author of the Note in 1962 in the *Yale Law Journal*, that the term Act or Bill of Attainder comes from the practice in sixteenth, seventeenth and eighteenth century England of using statutes to sentence 'to death, without a conviction in the ordinary course of judicial trial, named or described persons or groups'.[25] In addition, the term came to be used for 'bills of pains and penalties', statutes that imposed sanctions less than capital.[26] Both sorts of statute were aimed at revolutionaries and were considered contrary to the spirit of the common law because they attempted to bypass the courts by establishing a system of either legislative or administrative conviction and punishment. The offence is then to an idea of the separation of powers, where the role of the judiciary in determining in an open trial both guilt and appropriate punishment is considered a constitutional fundamental. Thus the framers of the American Constitution, in reaction to the use of similar instruments during the revolutionary era, inserted into the Constitution, Article I, Section 9: 'No Bill of Attainder or ex post facto law shall be passed'.

Latham CJ alone of the judges was required to confront directly Evatt's argument on this score, which I will refer to as the attainder argument. The others could avoid it – or at least pretend to avoid it – since they rested their reasoning on the text – positivistically construed – of the Constitution. But Latham CJ denied that an attainder argument had either purchase or application in the Australian context. He said that the argument had no purchase because protection against such statutes had not been elevated to the constitutional level, as it had in the United States. It had no application because the Communist Party Dissolution Act did not have the effects of either an Act of Attainder or of Pains and Penalties. In his view, the statute did not convict or purport to convict any person of any act, nor did it 'subject him to any penalty. He may be convicted of an offence against the Act if he is prosecuted before a court, but the Act itself does not produce any of the results of an Act of Attainder or of an Act of Pains and Penalties'.[27]

This last claim is technical and formal to the point of absurdity. It relies on a distinction between preventive and punitive measures which says that

---

[24] T. R. S. Allan, *Constitutional Justice: A Liberal Theory of the Rule of Law* (Oxford: Oxford University Press, 2001).

[25] See 'Notes and Comments, The Bounds of Legislative Specification: A Suggested Approach to the Bill of Attainder Clause' (1962) 72 *Yale Law Journal* 330–67 at 330.

[26] *Ibid.*, 330, 331.   [27] *Communist Party* case, at 172–3.

legislation is not punitive even when it permits detention, imprisonment, as well as other measures which severely impact on the rights and liberties of individuals, as long as the measures are not the point of the administrative scheme but incidental to it.[28] For example, if controlling immigration is the scheme, the fact that the detention of those awaiting refugee status determinations is incidental to controlling immigration makes a provision permitting such detention not punitive in the context of an immigration statute. Similarly, if the objective of the scheme is national security, the fact that the executive is given authority to ban or detain people is incidental to that objective.

This version of the theological doctrine of double effect is no more convincing here than it is elsewhere. It is a form of double speak, which is completely exposed by the preambular recitals of the statute, since these revealed that the government had decided that the Communist Party was guilty of treason and subversion and the statute implemented its judgment on this issue. Further, the statute gave to the executive the authority to make similar determinations about 'affiliated' individuals and groups and thus made the executive the effective judge of the guilt of the groups and individuals, Finally, the statute created an offence, punishable by imprisonment, of knowingly being an officer or a member of an unlawful association.

This absurdity is, in my view, evidence of a significant moment of dissonance for Latham CJ.[29] He could have rested his case on the no purchase basis – the thought, consistent with the rest of his judgment, that even if the statute were an Act of Attainder or of Pains and Penalties, a judge needed explicit constitutional authority before he could find that such a statute is invalid. His problems at this point surely arise from the fact that he knew that there was something awry with the statute from the perspective of the rule of law and that it had to do with the substantive issue addressed by the common law tradition's aversion to these bills. As he said, although he tried to put things as impersonally as possible, 'Such legislation is always unpopular with those against whom it is directed and in general is detested'.[30] It is then part of his attempt to minimize the

---

[28] This distinction is explored in detail by Webb J, who supported it (see especially, *ibid.*, at 240), only to find that the Court was entitled to test the factual basis of the preambular recitals and he found that the facts did not support the recitals. He did seem to suggest that if the statute were punitive in nature, it would constitute a usurpation of judicial power.

[29] Latham failed to mention this penalty in his summary of the statute's provisions at the beginning of his judgment.

[30] *Communist Party* case, at 172.

dissonance caused by his awareness of the substance of the argument that he alleges that the statute was not in fact an Act of Attainder or of Pains and Penalties.

It might seem that the majority judges should not be subject to the same kind of dissonance. Not only did they find the statute invalid; they were able to do so on a basis which allowed them to stop short of confronting squarely the attainder argument, although Fullagar J did address some remarks to this issue. That is, they upheld the rule of law through striking down the statute on a different ground. But they did not avoid dissonance. Their articulation of that ground meant that, no less than Latham CJ, they accepted that claims about the separation of powers cannot in the absence of explicit constitutional text be used against either a unitary or a federal legislature to defeat legislation which usurps the judicial function. As we have seen, they explicitly or implicitly accepted that the Australian states could enact the Communist Party Dissolution Act, indeed enact it without taking the trouble to recite themselves into power, since the states by definition had the residual powers; powers left over from the specific allocations to the Commonwealth. Moreover, they also accepted that, as long as any power fell within the explicit jurisdiction of the Commonwealth, the federal Parliament could enact a statute which had exactly the effects of the Communist Party Dissolution Act. Finally, several among them seemed to accept that the statute was preventive rather than punitive in nature.

Here I want to quote at some length from Fullagar J's judgment, since he spoke very fully to some of these points. He said:

> I come now to the Act itself. The most conspicuous feature of the Act is s. 4, and the most conspicuous feature of s. 4 is that it does not purport to impose duties or confer rights or prohibit acts or omissions, but purports simply to declare a particular unincorporated voluntary association unlawful and to dissolve it. It is, one supposes, to be classed as a public enactment as distinct from a private enactment, but it is, or at least is extremely like, what the Romans would have called a privilegium. Such a law (for I would not deny to it the character of a law) may well be within the competence of the Commonwealth legislative power, which is, within its constitutional limits, plenary . . . It would be impossible, I should think, to challenge s. 4 if the Parliament had power to make laws with respect to voluntary associations or with respect to communists. It would be a law 'with respect to' each of those 'matters'. So an Act of the Parliament dissolving the marriage of A with B would be a law with respect to divorce. It would be a privilegium, but what the Act actually did would be a thing which fell within a class of

subject matter on which the Parliament was authorized to legislate. The Parliament has power to make laws with respect to divorce, and the Act is a law which effects a divorce. It is a privilegium, but it is a good law.[31]

And he went on:

It should be observed at this stage that nothing depends on the justice or injustice of the law in question. If the language of an Act of Parliament is clear, its merits and demerits are alike beside the point. It is the law, and that is all. Such a law as the Communist Party Dissolution Act could clearly be passed by the Parliament of the United Kingdom or of any of the Australian States. It is only because the legislative power of the Commonwealth Parliament is limited by an instrument emanating from a superior authority that it arises in the case of the Commonwealth Parliament. If the great case of *Marbury v. Madison* (1803) 1 Cr 137 (2 Law Ed 118) had pronounced a different view, it might perhaps not arise even in the case of the Commonwealth Parliament; and there are those, even to-day, who disapprove of the doctrine of *Marbury v. Madison* (1803) 1 Cr 137 (2 Law Ed 118), and who do not see why the courts, rather than the legislature itself, should have the function of finally deciding whether an Act of a legislature in a Federal system is or is not within power. But in our system the principle of *Marbury v. Madison* (1803) 1 Cr 137 (2 Law Ed 118) is accepted as axiomatic, modified in varying degree in various cases (but never excluded) by the respect which the judicial organ must accord to opinions of the legislative and executive organs.[32]

These passages are rife with dissonance. Fullagar J expresses both doubt and certainty about the legal character of such a law and his remarks about the privilegium indicate his concern that the legislature is using a public power to bring about some goal that does not belong properly in the public domain. In addition, he wishes both to assert that there is unquestionable authority for the majority's division of powers argument – the text of the Constitution – and that there is an alternative view of legality in which courts are not the final judges of the limits of legality, exactly the view that we saw Latham CJ express when he chided his colleagues for thinking that the state may act outside of the law when it confronts an external enemy. Moreover, Fullagar J's reference to *Marbury* v. *Madison* is of a piece with Dixon J's claim about the role of the Court as arbiter of constitutional validity. These judicial references are to something extra-textual, in that they find the basis for their constitutional review authority

---

[31] *Ibid.*, at 261.   [32] *Ibid.*, at 262–3.

in an understanding of the proper place of the judiciary as guardians of a substantive conception of the rule of law.[33]

For Fullagar J, like the other majority judges, dissonance arises because the resource offered them by the text of the division of powers constitution enabled them to avoid confronting the real basis of their argument. They thus avoided the basis for the only solid answer to the question of the legal limits on the power of both Parliament and the executive, which is that the source of these limits is to be found in the common law, which supports both a constitutional doctrine of judicial independence and a sense of the fundamental values which that independence is supposed to serve. More accurately, they were willing to accept one part of that basis, the claim about independence, but were not prepared to articulate the values to which independence is instrumental. Moreover, even that claim could be put on those parts of the Constitution which protected the High Court's jurisdiction.[34] But, as I have shown, in avoiding that other part, they adopted significant chunks of Latham CJ's positivist view and moreover then showed themselves to be inconsistent in a way that Latham CJ was not.

The difficulty in asserting this basis is illustrated by the fact that, in the classic article about the case, George Winterton, while hailing the case as a significant victory for the rule of law and constitutionalism, also cautioned against reading too much into the decision. He even suggested that the case 'fits squarely within this tradition of judicial self-preservation', a suggestion which chimes with the point we saw Brian Simpson make about the dissent in *Liversidge* in chapter 1. It was not 'primarily about civil liberties, but about the limits of legislative and executive power and the supremacy of the judiciary in deciding such questions.'[35] But Winterton also argued that the 'fundamental constitutional flaw of the legislation

---

[33] See further Dixon J's recognition of the manner in which the statute denied due process (at 196–8) as well as his sense that the 'substantial nature and effect' of the statute posed problems from the perspective of the separation of powers, at 200. He also observes, at 193, that even if the Parliament has power on the direct subject matter, it is required to legislate consistently with Chapter III and express constitutional rights. Fullagar J refers to the role of the Court as arbiter of constitutional validity at 262–3, although he clearly does not buy the argument that the Act defeats due process. So they both look to extra-textual norms, although arguably Dixon J draws in more norms than Fullagar J allows are relevant in assessing the Act. See also McTiernan J's opening statement, at 206.

[34] See *Polyukhovich* v. *Commonwealth* (1991) 172 CLR 501; *Chu Kheng Lim* v. *Minister for Immigration* (1992) 176 CLR 1; *Kable* v. *DPP* (*NSW*) (1996) 189 CLR 51.

[35] Winterton, 'The Communist Party Case', p. 133, quoting from Brian Galligan, *Politics of the High Court* (Brisbane, Queensland University Press, 1967), p. 203; Simpson, *In the Highest Degree Odious*, p. 363.

proved to be its nature as an Act of Pains and Penalties (or "bill of attainder" in its generic sense) . . . .'[36]

The difficulty which both judges and lawyers face here stems from the assumption that the unitary Parliament of the United Kingdom, and thus of the legal order in which their common law tradition was developed, is not subject to the constraints of any fundamental or constitutional values, because such a Parliament can always override these values by explicit statutory statement. I do not wish to contest the claim that such a Parliament can in the absence of a written constitution explicitly override the values. Rather, my argument is that this claim fails to prove the assumption that such a Parliament is not subject to the constraints of these values.

As I will now show in a discussion of a case from another common law jurisdiction, what matters at the level of theory is not the presence of a written constitution, whether in the form of a bill of rights or a division of powers constitution, but a judicial understanding of the unwritten, common law constitution of legality. It of course makes a difference at the level of remedy what the explicit institutional arrangements are for enforcing the rule of law. But even where a written constitution seems to provide judges with the remedial tools they need for enforcement, as did the Australian Constitution in the *Communist Party* case, judges should avoid relying on the tools alone. If they fail to bring the theory underpinning the tools into play, they assume at least at a rhetorical level the truth of constitutional positivism, and that assumption not only creates dissonance for them, but commits them to conclusions on other facts which contradict their commitment to the rule of law.

Canada's common law bill of rights

In the 1950s, the same era in which the *Communist Party* case was decided, Canada's Supreme Court delivered a string of judgments which are often regarded as articulating a theory of implied or common law rights in Canada's federal or division of powers Constitution, the British North America Act 1867,[37] that is, as cases in which judges read into the terms of the division of powers constitution rights such as the right to free speech. But these cases are, in my view, better understood as being about the common law constitution in the sense explored in this book.

---

[36] Winterton, 'The Communist Party Case', p. 127.
[37] Since 1982, this statute is referred to as 'The Constitution Act 1867'.

For our purposes, the most significant of this string of cases is the 1957 decision in *Switzman* v. *Elbling*.[38] The Province of Quebec had enacted an Act to Protect the Province against Communistic Propaganda 1941. This statute was known colloquially as the Padlock Act, since it made it illegal to use any 'house' to 'propagate communism or bolshevism by any means whatsoever' and gave to the Attorney-General the authority to place a padlock order of up to one year on such a house. While the Attorney-General had to have 'satisfactory proof' that the house was being used in this way, he was made the sole judge of that issue. The majority of the Supreme Court held that the Act was invalid because under Canada's division of powers Constitution the federal Parliament had sole authority to criminalize activity.

Quebec argued that its authority stemmed from its power to regulate property and the lone dissenter, Taschereau J, held that the impact of the statute on individuals was incidental to a scheme of regulating property and such schemes fell within the authority of provinces.[39] Kerwin CJ for the plurality said that 'in cases where constitutional issues are involved, it is important that nothing be said that is unnecessary'[40] and he stuck resolutely to the division of powers basis, a stance in which he was joined by Locke, Nolan and Cartwright JJ. However, Rand and Abbott JJ gave much fuller reasons and Kellock J concurred in Rand J's judgment.

Both Abbott and Rand JJ stressed that the British North America Act had to be seen as part of a constitutional tradition, something expressly recognized in its preamble, which stated that the four provinces desired to be united in a federal union with a constitution 'similar in principle to that of the United Kingdom'. Rand J took that statement to embody the 'political theory . . . of parliamentary government . . . This means ultimately government by the free public opinion of an open society . . .'[41] 'But', he went on, 'public opinion, in order to meet such a responsibility, demands the condition of a virtually unobstructed access to and diffusion of ideas'. And this led to what he termed a 'constitutional fact' that freedom of expression 'has a unity of interest and significance extending to every part of the Dominion'. This fact, he said, is the 'political expression of the primary condition of social life, thought and its communication by language . . . As such an inherence in the individual it is embodied in his status of citizenship'.[42] On this basis, he denied that any province had the authority to regulate free speech using the mechanisms of the criminal

---

[38] [1957] SCR 285. The best discussion of these cases is to be found in David Mullan, 'The Role for Underlying Constitutional Principles in a Bill of Rights World' (2004) *New Zealand Law Review* 9–38.

[39] *Switzman*, at 299.   [40] *Ibid.*, at 288.   [41] *Ibid.*, at 306.   [42] *Ibid.*, at 306–7.

law, though he expressly declined to comment on whether the federal Parliament would have such authority.[43] Abbott J, however, ran with this argument. He said that, while it was not necessary to determine the question, his view was that under the Constitution as it stood, 'Parliament itself could not abrogate this right of discussion and debate. The power of Parliament to limit is . . . restricted to such powers as may be exercisable under its exclusive jurisdiction with respect to criminal law and to make laws for the peace, order and good government of the nation'.[44]

As we can see, the premise of both Rand J's and Abbott J's judgments is not that the federal Constitution is a text into which judges may read or imply rights. Rather, they start from the premise that their division of powers constitution is a continuation of a tradition in which Parliament is seen as the guardian of these rights and so can be called to account by judges when it seems to stray from this role. Their reliance on the preamble to the British North America Act is in substance an invocation of the idea that the values of the common law constitution are part of the inheritance of all common law legal orders. It is fairly remarkable in this era to find judges prepared to articulate this premise so openly.

Of course, the fact that judges are prepared to articulate this as their premise will seem to many just another flagrant example of judicial arrogation of power. And here we should note that in these cases the premise was often articulated by Rand J alone, with most of the majority preferring to stick to an allegedly literal reading of the division of powers constitution, that in each case there was at least one dissent, and that the Supreme Court in the 1970s rejected the premise.[45] In addition, while the Supreme Court has revived the premise more recently, its revival has been greeted with some anxiety despite the fact that the revival happened after the Court had developed a large body of jurisprudence on Canada's Charter of Rights and Freedoms. Indeed, as I will now show, it might be more accurate to say that the anxiety arises not despite but because of the fact that the revival happened after the Court had developed a large body of jurisprudence on the Charter.

Anxiety about judicial review of legislation

One of the Supreme Court's revivalist decisions upheld an attack on the legislation of three provinces which reduced the salaries of provincial court judges on the basis that the unwritten constitution contains a

---

[43] *Ibid.*, at 307.   [44] *Ibid.*, at 328.
[45] See Mullan, 'The Role for Underlying Constitutional Principles'.

principle of judicial independence, essential to maintaining the rule of law.[46] Lamer CJ reasoned that the independence of the judiciary is 'definitional to the Canadian understanding of constitutionalism'[47] and that such independence 'reflects a deeper commitment to the separation of powers':[48]

> [J]udicial independence is at root an unwritten constitutional principle, in the sense that it is exterior to the particular sections of the *Constitution Acts*. The existence of that principle, whose origins can be traced to the *Act of Settlement* of 1701, is recognized and affirmed by the preamble to the *Constitution Act, 1867*. The specific provisions of the *Constitution Acts, 1867 to 1982*, merely 'elaborate that principle in the institutional apparatus which they create or contemplate': *Switzman* v. *Elbling* [1957] S.C.R. 285, at p. 306, *per* Rand J.[49]

Here the anxiety focuses understandably on the fact that judges appear to wax most lyrical about the rule of law when in issue is their status in the order of things, and, in this context, they could be seen as even crasser in their motivation, since the issue was judicial salary. Moreover, while one explanation for the revival is that judges used to interpreting a bill of rights will be more comfortable with the idea that there are implied or unwritten rights, that explanation is not a justification. For one can reason from the fact that judges have an explicit mandate to protect entrenched rights to the conclusion that those are the only rights which they are entitled to suppose are constitutionally protected, as did La Forest J in dissent in that case. 'The consequence of parliamentary supremacy', he said, is that 'judicial review of legislation is not possible.'[50] Such review is legitimate only when it 'involves the interpretation of an authoritative constitutional instrument'[51] and its legitimacy is 'imperiled . . . when courts attempt to limit the power of legislatures without recourse to express textual authority'.[52]

It is helpful to an understanding of La Forest J's anxiety to see that the term 'implied Bill of Rights' was not coined as one of endearment. It was first used by John Willis in order to make the claim that the rights amounted to a 'Pseudo Bill of Rights', that is, rights asserted by judges in their continued attempt to thwart the intention of the legislature.[53] Such

---

[46] *Reference re Remuneration of Judges* [1997] 3 SCR 3.   [47] *Ibid.*, at 77.
[48] *Ibid.*, at 85.   [49] *Ibid.*, at 63–4, emphasis in the original.
[50] *Ibid.*, at 178.   [51] *Ibid.*, at 181.   [52] *Ibid.*
[53] John Willis, 'Administrative Law and the British North America Act' (1939–40) 53 *Harvard Law Review* 251–81 at 274 and 281.

judges, said Willis, invoke their preferred maxims of statutory interpretation 'not as a means of discovering an unexpressed intent but as a means of controlling an expressed intent of which they happen to disapprove'.[54]

I do not wish to deny that these dangers lurk in any aspirational account of the rule of law, especially one which asserts that there are unwritten constitutional values which the legislature must respect. However, there are dangers which lurk in the judicial stance which I have called constitutional positivism, as well as in the position taken by Willis and those who follow him in the family of positions that make up the positivist tradition, one which we have seen is deeply sceptical of judicial review, and which has powerful torch bearers today in all three of the Commonwealth jurisdictions on which I am focusing.

The dangers should be obvious. Whether such judges operate within a common law or division of powers constitutional order, they cannot qua judge distinguish between a statute that permits arbitrary detention and a statute that regulates the most banal activity one can imagine. They might bleat about how they love rights as much as the next man, but when push comes to shove it is the rights of the detainee that are shoved.

But there is worse to come. It is one thing for judges to shy away from invalidating a statute when they have no explicit textual authority to do so. But it is quite another for them to refuse to interpret a statute in the light of unwritten constitutional values because, as Willis suggested, such interpretation is a means of controlling rather than determining intent. But this is precisely where constitutional positivism leads, something well illustrated by the recent decision of the Australian High Court in *Al-Kateb* v. *Godwin*,[55] a decision which though not about emergency legislation or national security is clearly one of a number of decisions by judges in the Commonwealth which are profoundly shaped by judicial sensitivity to the world after 9/11.

The appellant, Ahmed Al-Kateb, was a stateless person. Section 189 of the Migration Act 1958 requires the compulsory administrative detention of unlawful non-citizens; s. 198 provides that an officer must remove an unlawful non-citizen 'as soon as reasonably practicable'; s. 196 stipulates that an unlawful non-citizen detained under s. 189 must be detained until removed, deported or granted a visa. Section 196(3) prevents the release even by a court of an unlawfully detained non-citizen except for removal or deportation (unless the person has been granted a visa). *Al-Kateb's* case raises the issue that this scheme presumes the compliance of

[54] *Ibid.*, 276.   [55] *Al-Kateb* v. *Godwin* (2004) 208 ALR 124.

another state (in most cases, obviously, the person's home state) willing to take such a person. Diplomatic channels had failed to find another state willing to accept Al-Kateb, and the question then became whether the legislation requires his permanent detention given the absence of hope that his removal will ever be 'reasonably practicable'. Al-Kateb had lost in the courts below.

The majority – McHugh, Hayne, Callinan and Heydon JJ – dismissed the appeal. Separate dissents were written by Gleeson CJ, Gummow and Kirby JJ. While the judgments are quite different, the majority and the dissents, as least those of Gleeson CJ and Kirby J,[56] divide roughly along the following fault line. The dissenters tend to see the question as one of statutory interpretation, an enterprise arguably engaging interpretative presumptions along the lines of common law rights and compliance with international law. The majority, for the most part, saw two main questions: first, the construction of the statute and, second, a constitutional question: did the legislation correctly construed run afoul of the Constitution's Chapter III constitutional protection of judicial power because it conferred a punitive function on the executive? At its most profound, though, the difference between the two sets of judges boils down to a view of legal authority, constructed around a view of who is the proper subject of the law's protection, who is in the legal community and who is out. For Kirby J and Gleeson CJ, it is sufficient that an individual is subject to the law for him to get the protection of the rule of law. For the majority, a non-citizen is an alien who, depending on his status, will get something less, and in a case like Al-Kateb's something far less, than the full protection of the law.

Gleeson CJ read the provisions of the Act as creating a gap since they made no express provision for indefinite or permanent detention where the assumption of the reasonable practicability of removal is false. 'The possibility that a person, regardless of personal circumstances, regardless of whether he or she is a danger to the community, and regardless of whether he or she might abscond, can be subjected to indefinite, and perhaps permanent, administrative detention is not one to be dealt with by implication.'[57] Thus he reasoned that one had to resort 'to a fundamental principle of interpretation':[58]

---

[56] The third dissenting judge, Gummow J, sought for the most part to put his dissent on a purely textual basis, thus evidencing the same urge to take refuge in constitutional positivism that we saw in the majority judgments in the *Communist Party* case.

[57] *Ibid.*, at 130.   [58] *Ibid.*, at 129.

Where what is involved is the interpretation of legislation said to confer upon the Executive a power of administrative detention that is indefinite in duration, and that may be permanent, there comes into play a principle of legality, which governs both Parliament and the courts. In exercising their judicial function, courts seek to give effect to the will of Parliament by declaring the meaning of what Parliament has enacted. Courts do not impute to the legislature an intention to abrogate or curtail certain human rights or freedoms (of which personal liberty is the most basic) unless such an intention is clearly manifested by unambiguous language, which indicates that the legislature has directed its attention to the rights or freedoms in question, and has consciously decided upon abrogation or curtailment. That principle has been re-affirmed by this Court in recent cases.[59] It is not new. In 1908, in this Court, O'Connor J referred to a passage from the fourth edition of *Maxwell on Statutes* which stated that '[i]t is in the last degree improbable that the legislature would overthrow fundamental principles, infringe rights, or depart from the general system of law, without expressing its intention with irresistible clearness'.[60]

And he added that this stance is an aspirational one:

A statement concerning the improbability that Parliament would abrogate fundamental rights by the use of general or ambiguous words is not a factual prediction, capable of being verified or falsified by a survey of public opinion. In a free society, under the rule of law, it is an expression of a legal value, respected by the courts, and acknowledged by the courts to be respected by Parliament.[61]

Kirby J shared this view, saying:

[T]he *Communist Party Case* . . . is of substantial assistance to Mr Al-Kateb. It is inconsistent with a basic proposition of Australian constitutional doctrine, at least since 1951, that the validity of a law or of an act of the Executive should depend on the conclusive assertion or opinion of the Parliament (eg expressed in recitals to an Act) or the assertion or opinion of an officer of the Executive (eg that the preconditions for the exercise of power have been satisfied). This is why the *Communist Party Case* is such an important statement of the rule of law as it operates in Australia. It remains

---

[59] Referring to *Coco* v. *R* (1994) 179 CLR 427; *Plaintiff S157/2002* v. *Commonwealth* (2003) 195 ALR 24 at 36.

[60] *Al-Kateb*, at 130. Referring to *Potter* v. *Minahan* (1908) 7 CLR 277 at 304; *R* v. *Secretary of State for the Home Department, ex parte Pierson* [1998] AC 539 at 587–9, per Lord Steyn; *R* v. *Secretary of State for the Home Department, ex parte Simms* [2000] 2 AC 115 at 131, per Lord Hoffmann.

[61] *Al-Kateb*, at 130.

for the judiciary in each contested case to interpret the applicable law. As in the *Communist Party Case*, this requirement has proved an important, even vital, protection for individual liberty . . .[62]

In his judgment, McHugh J expressly rejected the relevance of the *Communist Party* case. However, in order to reject it he found himself compelled to affirm Latham CJ's dissent:

> In that case, this Court held that the law in question was not supported by s 51(xxxix) ('the incidental power') in conjunction with s 61 ('the executive power') of the Constitution or s 51(vi) ('the defence power') of the Constitution. The *Communist Party Case* had nothing to do with aliens, and no Justice found that the law infringed Ch III of the Constitution. Latham CJ, who dissented and upheld the validity of the law, expressly held that it did not contravene Ch III of the Constitution.[63]

Following the logic of this affirmation, McHugh J went on to affirm the correctness of the High Court's wartime decisions which had adopted the same stance as the majority of the House of Lords in *Halliday* and *Liversidge*.[64]

Kirby J in response said these cases 'hardly amount to a proud moment in Australian law. Nor are they ones that should be propounded as a precedent and statement of contemporary legal authority'.[65] Indeed he likened the cases to *Korematsu*,[66] the US wartime decision on the internment of Japanese-Americans, saying that just as such cases 'are now viewed with embarrassment in the United States and generally regarded as incorrect . . . we should be no less embarrassed by the local equivalents'.[67]

At many places in his judgment, Kirby J was able to refer to either extra-curial writing by McHugh J or to his judgments which were at odds with the constitutional positivism of McHugh's judgment in *Al Kateb*, which Kirby J claimed to be not 'too dissimilar' to the interpretative views of Justice Scalia.[68] There is much to this claim; indeed, it is remarkably understated against the backdrop of the outright hostility between Kirby J and McHugh J that is manifested in their judgments. For McHugh J's judgment pivots on the claims that if there is a written constitution, its meaning is frozen at the moment it comes into force with the result that judges are not entitled to interpret it in light of legal norms which

---

[62] *Ibid.*, at 164, footnotes omitted.   [63] *Ibid.*, at 138, footnotes omitted.

[64] See *ibid.*, at 139–40 referring to *Lloyd* v. *Wallach* (1915) 20 CLR 299 and *Ex Parte Walsh* [1942] ALR 359.

[65] *Al-Kateb*, at 166.   [66] *Korematsu* v. *United States*, 323 US 214 (1944).

[67] *Al-Kateb*, at 165.   [68] *Ibid.*, at 172.

postdate the constitution. In particular, against Kirby J he argues that it is 'heretical' to suppose that the Constitution should be interpreted in light of international legal norms that postdate it.[69] At most, he is prepared to concede that if a statute is ambiguous, a court is entitled to interpret it consistently with 'rules' of international law that existed at the time the statute was enacted.[70]

I will later discuss in detail this kind of disagreement between the two judges about the relationship between domestic and international law. For the moment I want to note that McHugh J's position is the classic dualist one with a twist. Dualism is the direct result of constitutional positivism. It argues that since the only legitimate source of legal norms within a legal order is the legislature, international legal norms may have force domestically only when the legislature has explicitly incorporated them by statute. Executive ratification of a treaty is a signal to the outside world but not to the subjects of the domestic legal order. To allow such norms any force would be to permit the executive to usurp legislative power, though the instrument of usurpation would not be the executive itself, but the judges, who would in substance have incorporated the norms through the back door. When a domestic statute is in conflict with an international norm, even if it is a norm of customary international law, the domestic norm must prevail. The only port of entry for international law into domestic law is via the maxim that judges should deal with statutory ambiguity by resolving it in favour of international law and via the claim that customary international law applies unless a domestic statute is clearly inconsistent with it. The twist McHugh adds is that the international norms which legitimately influence the interpretation of domestic law must have existed at the time the statute was enacted, but this twist is perfectly consistent with the general drive in constitutional positivism to understand law as a matter of rules with a determinate content, fixed in time at the moment of their enactment.

Kirby J in contrast is clear that his view of the appropriateness of drawing on international law norms has much to do with the fact that his conception of law is not limited to rules but includes principles,[71] and that all those who are subject to law are entitled to the protection of the principles. So, as I suggested earlier, the disagreement between the judges is a deep one, not only about the authority of law, but also about the subject of the protection of the rule of law.

---

[69] *Ibid.*, at 140.   [70] *Ibid.*   [71] *Ibid.*, at 168.

McHugh J said in this regard:

> where a non-citizen has entered or attempted to enter Australia without a visa, detention of that person excludes that person from the community which he or she sought to enter. Only in the most general sense would it be said that preventing a non-citizen making landfall in Australia is punitive. Segregating those who make landfall, without permission to do so, is not readily seen as bearing a substantially different character. Yet the argument alleging invalidity would suggest that deprivation of freedom will *after a time* or in some circumstances *become* punitive . . . Only if it is said that there is an immunity from detention does it become right to equate detention with punishment that can validly be exacted only in exercise of the judicial power.[72]

With this appreciation of the source of the judges' disagreement, one must view with great suspicion McHugh J's claim that the statute unambiguously provides for open-ended detention until deportation is practicable and that it was also constitutional because the purpose of the detention is non-punitive, that is, is not detention for the sake of punishment but pending deportation. In support of this proposition, he argues that if Parliament were unable to provide for potentially indefinite detention through the Migration Act, it could create a criminal offence of being a prohibited immigrant in Australia, which would have exactly the same result:

> If Parliament were forced to achieve its object of preventing entry by enacting such laws, form would triumph over substance. The unlawful non-citizen would still be detained in custody. The only difference between detention under such a law and the present legislation would be that the detention would be the result of a judicial order upon a finding that the person was a prohibited immigrant. In substance, the position under that hypothesis would be no different in terms of liberty from what it is under ss. 189, 196 and 198. Under the hypothesis, the only issue for the court would be whether the person was a prohibited immigrant. Under the present legislation, the issue for the courts is whether the person is an unlawful non-citizen. A finding of being a prohibited immigrant or an unlawful non-citizen produces the same result – detention. The only difference is that in one case the detention flows by the court applying the legislation and making an order and in the other it flows from the direct operation of the Act.[73]

---

[72] *Ibid.*, at 190, emphasis in original. Compare Hayne J at 188, and Callinan J at 196.
[73] *Ibid.*, at 136.

In making this argument, McHugh J seems unaware that the point he makes about not letting form triumph over substance in fact undermines his whole judgment. Even if it were right that the Commonwealth could achieve by constitutional means the purpose of indefinite detention by making it an offence to be a prohibited immigrant in Australia, we do not know from the Act that was its purpose. Further, the decision to make such a purpose explicit within a statute creating a new criminal offence, and reducing the courts to a role of merely checking whether an individual fell into the category of prohibited agreement, might well raise constitutional questions since the executive would be given a role that might be regarded as constitutionally suspect, in light of the *Communist Party* case. Finally, any reasonable conception of democratic politics must ascribe value to the fact that a provision which trenches on human rights is introduced and debated in the legislature and scrutinized by the media and public. McHugh J overlooks the value in demanding that the legislature be explicit about its ends. In so doing, he shows the inaptness of using the label democratic to describe his positivism, since the procedures of democratic deliberation as well as the claim that it is important for participants to face up to the consequences of their decisions, have no importance for him qua judge.

That McHugh J's judgment is driven by constitutional positivism does not however show that he was wrong. Recall that the majority in the *Communist Party* case accepted the distinction between punitive and other sorts of detention, did not dispute the authority of the cases which upheld wartime detention powers, and avoided articulating an explicitly normative basis for their conception of the rule of law and constitutionalism. Thus, I argued that in many respects Latham CJ was more consistent than were they. And one might thus think the conclusion is warranted that the costs of constitutional positivism are outweighed by its benefits; not only does it preserve judges within the legitimate bounds of their role, but also it exhibits a more coherent stance.

Notice in this regard that McHugh J said both that if Australia were to have a bill of rights, 'it must be done in the constitutional way – hard though its achievement may be – by persuading the people to amend the Constitution by inserting such a Bill'[74] and that the doctrine of the separation of powers does 'more than prohibit the Parliament and the Executive from exercising the judicial power of the Commonwealth. It

---

[74] *Ibid.*, at 144.

prohibits the Ch III courts from amending the Constitution under the guise of interpretation'.[75]

I have already suggested, however, that constitutional positivism is not a coherent stance. Rather, it is a compromise positivist judges are forced to make with what we might think of as authoritative sources of moral value within the law, whether a bill of rights, the common law, or even international law. Take, for example, the situation where there is a unitary Parliament which is not subject to any written constitution and which delegates a very wide discretion to the executive to detain perceived enemies. In a common law legal order, judges who are asked to review the executive's decisions are faced with a clear choice. They can adopt the stance of constitutional positivism and say that, because the legislature did not stipulate any controls on the exercise of discretion, there are none. And they can call in support the existential nature of the situation. Or they can adopt the stance of common law constitutionalism and say that it is their duty to interpret the grant of discretion in the light of the fundamental values of legal order, values which are nowhere more important than at a time when the legal order is under severe political stress. If they take the latter course, the legislature may respond by re-enacting the statute and making it clear that the legislative intention is that the executive is permitted to violate such values. Such a reaction raises the stakes to the point where judges must consider whether they will take literally Coke's thought in *Dr Bonham's case* that judges can void statutes.

But the claim that there is a common law constitution which controls Parliament does not depend on whether judges will in fact decide they have the authority to resist such an explicit override. As I will argue more fully in chapter 4, all it depends on is the insight that when a Parliament has explicitly declared that it does not want the executive to be bound by fundamental legal values, that declaration comes with a political cost. The people to whom the government is accountable will be able to judge whether they want a government that is not committed to the rule of law. This cost is exactly analogous to that associated with the s. 33 override of Canada's Charter of Rights and Freedoms, which permits the federal and provincial legislatures to override certain judicial determinations of constitutional invalidity.

The difference a division of powers constitution makes is then that, like a statute which delegates authority to the executive, it supplies text which delegates authority to legislatures. Judges who adopt the stance of

---

[75] *Ibid.*, at 145.

common law constitutionalism will find that the text is evidence of the fundamental values of their legal order, in so far as it can be rendered consistent with such values. That there is such a text makes a difference. Judges do not have to assert an authority against the legislature, since the legislature has authority only in virtue of the federal constitution. The only override available in these circumstances is likely to be the process of constitutional amendment set out in the constitution. But even if the government of the day successfully procures such an amendment, one should not conclude from that fact that the legislature was unconstrained by the constitution. As before, the government minded to break free of constitutional constraints has to be willing to do so in way that makes public its unwillingness to be constrained by the fundamental values of its legal order.

Here it is worth noting the reaction of the Australian people to the decision in the *Communist Party* case. In the wake of that decision the government, buoyed by the knowledge that the Communist Party Dissolution Act had enjoyed popular support, sought to amend the Constitution in order to give the Commonwealth the explicit authority to re-enact the statute. Such an amendment required the approval of the electorate in a referendum and they rejected the government's attempt. But if all that the Australian people cared about was that formal legal limits were respected, then, given their initial support for getting rid of communism, they should have supported the amendment to the Constitution. Thus, one can attribute to them a sense, derived from the High Court's decision, that there was more wrong with the statute than that it had transgressed the formal limits of the Constitution. Similarly, it would be important to present to Parliament, and thus to the people, a proposal to make indefinite detention by executive fiat part of the 'ordinary law' of Australia.

What constitutional positivists fail to see, but what one can interpret Australians as having seen in the 1950s, is that a federal constitution is not merely a blueprint for dividing powers.[76] In order to divide the powers, its drafters will be forced to confront the question of how to articulate some of the constitutional presuppositions of legal order in general, whether in a unitary or a federal system. What can be left unsaid over the centuries might have to be said as politicians and lawyers struggle to articulate their own understanding of how to take the project of legal order forward in

---

[76] Unfortunately, in the present political climate, it is likely that that the Australian people would accept a proposal for indefinite detention with enthusiasm. But even if that is the case, it is important that that acceptance be public and explicit.

their particular federal context, even if they seek to avoid saying anything very explicit. Moreover, the general and usually quite laconic propositions used to express their understanding in legal form are in a common law legal order open for interpretation, as judges and others take the project forward, unless one seeks to understand, as constitutional positivists do, the meaning of all law, including constitutional law, as frozen at the point of its making.

There is therefore a political necessity in the design of a federal state to divide powers between the federal power and the states or provinces and that necessity requires an explicit attempt to designate which powers will reside in the federal entity and which in the others. It also requires that the drafters of the constitution put their minds to the question of the unity of the legal order – the extent to which a unitary legal order is required – and that will require them among other things to answer explicitly the question of how to secure the place of the highest court in the general court structure. As long as some significant degree of unity is required, a unity which will be overseen by the highest federal court, text will exist that permits judges to read into the actual words used an intention to provide the normative safeguards often associated with a doctrine of the separation of powers.

But while the text provides comfort to judges, it cannot provide the basis for the claim that these normative safeguards exist. The thought that there should be a unity to legal order, tailored to the particular circumstances of politics which make a federal structure appropriate, and that independent judges should preside over that unity, is the bequest of a constitutional tradition which provides the unwritten assumptions of that legal order. So in a federal constitution, it is likely that a textual basis will exist for judges to assert a constitutional guarantee of their independence. But independence, whatever the nature of the constitution, is not an intrinsic value. Rather, it is instrumental in that is secures a place for judges in constitutional order in order to serve other values, for example, the right to have determinations of guilt decided in open court.

Their duty as judges is to the rule of law or legality, a rule which includes both procedural and substantive values. We have seen that submerged in the majority's judgments in the *Communist Party* case but wholly explicit in Rand J's judgment in *Switzman* is the claim that there is a connection between the rule of law and equal citizenship. And in Kirby J's dissent in *Al-Kateb* the rights-bearing individual, the legal subject who gets the equal protection of the law, is not limited to the category of citizen but is anyone who is subject to the law of the land. It is sufficient that an individual is the object of an exercise of state power for that individual to be entitled to the protection of the rule of law.

Of course, as I have indicated, a legislature might explicitly command that public officials are beyond the reach of the rule of law. Such a command attempts to create a legal black hole, a space within legal order which produces a different kind of dualism from that supposed to exist between international and domestic legal orders. This is the dualism analogous to the one we encountered in chapter 1, in Ernst Fraenkel's description of the Nazi legal order, a situation where the legal order is divided into two, one which regulates the ordinary situation in accordance with the rule of law, while the other gives officials an unlimited discretion, what Fraenkel referred to as prerogative powers.

These dualisms refer to distinctions between different entities – the dualism between the international legal order and the domestic legal order, on the one hand, and, on the other, a dualism within the domestic order between, the prerogative state and the rule-of-law state. But, as Fraenkel points out, those like Schmitt who supported the idea in Weimar Germany that the state is a pre-legal political entity which might need to act decisively outside the limits of the rule of law took their inspiration from the first distinction between international legal order and domestic legal order. They argued that because a state may repudiate international legal norms if its security is threatened, so it may repudiate domestic legal norms. Fraenkel says that 'the concept which permitted an unlimited sovereignty to ignore international law is the source of the theory that political activity is not subject to legal regulation. This was the presupposition for the theory of the Prerogative State'.[77]

My claim here is not that constitutional positivism causes legislatures to create the legal black holes that amount to the Prerogative State. Rather, a judge who subscribes to the tenets of constitutional positivism will generally find that there is nothing legally amiss with statutes that put public officials beyond the reach of the rule of law. And that is because the constitutional positivist does not really regard those officials as beyond the reach of rule of law as long as their power is delegated to them by statute. As long, that is, as there is rule by law, constitutional positivists will tend to think that there is the rule of law. It is this feature of constitutional positivism which distinguishes it from the political theories of those like Schmitt who argue on political grounds for the claim that the state is a pre-legal entity, which will manifest itself as such in times of exception

---

[77] Fraenkel, *The Dual State*, pp. 65–6.

or emergency. That constitutional positivists suppose that the state is still subject to the rule of law when in fact it is acting as a prerogative or legally unlimited state is, according to Schmitt, symptomatic of a theory which cannot bear to confront the reality of the political.

But there are points where even constitutional positivism finds that rule by statute law puts officials so far beyond the reach of the rule of law that judges should not take explicit expressions of legislative intent seriously. And as I will now show, one way in which constitutional positivism is tested it in this way is by legislative reliance on privative or ouster clauses, legislative provisions which seek to exclude judges from review of the question whether officials have acted within the limits of their statutory authority. In the remaining part of this chapter, I will discuss three approaches to privative clauses, and the third of these will take us into chapter 3, a chapter which shifts focus from the legislature to the executive.

Disobeying Parliament[78]

> Although in theory perhaps, it may be possible for Parliament to set up a tribunal which has full autonomous powers to fix its own area of operation, that, so far, has not been done in this country. The question, what is the tribunal's proper area, is one which it has always been permitted to ask and to answer, and it must follow that examination of its extent is not precluded by a clause conferring conclusiveness, finality, or unquestionability upon its decisions . . . In each task [the courts] are carrying out the intention of the legislature, and it would be misdescription to state it in terms of a struggle between the courts and the executive. What would be the purpose of defining by statute the limit of the tribunal's powers, if, by means of a clause inserted in the instrument of definition, those limits could be safely passed? Lord Wilberforce[79]

> The judges appreciate, much more than does Parliament, that to exempt any public authority from judicial control is to give it dictatorial power, and this is so fundamentally objectionable that Parliament cannot really intend it . . . [C]lauses excluding the courts [are] left with no meaning at all and . . . judges will be unable to deny that they are flatly disobeying Parliament . . . All law students are taught that Parliamentary sovereignty is

---

[78] This section is based on my discussion in 'Disobeying Parliament: Privative Clauses and the Rule of Law' in Tsvi Kahana (ed.), *Legislatures and Constitutionalism: The Role of Legislatures in the Constitutional State* (Cambridge: Cambridge University Press, forthcoming).
[79] *Anisminic Ltd* v. *Foreign Compensation Commission* [1969] 2 AC 147 at 207–8.

absolute. But it is judges who have the last word. If they interpret an Act to mean the opposite of what it says, it is their view which represents the law. Parliament may of course retaliate . . .' Sir William Wade, *Constitutional Fundamentals*[80]

The privative clause, otherwise known as an ouster or preclusive clause, is a statutory provision to which Commonwealth Parliaments have resorted in order to protect public officials from judicial review. Judges in the Commonwealth have not found it easy to make sense of these provisions. They work within a tradition of public law, whose classical expression is still to be found in Dicey,[81] in which, as we saw in chapter 1, two assumptions are taken for granted.

First, there is the assumption of legislative supremacy, or what William Wade in the second epigraph to this section calls 'absolute', parliamentary sovereignty. Second, there is the assumption that judges should have, as Wade says, the 'last word' when it comes to interpretation of the law. On Dicey's and Wade's conception of the rule of law, judges enforce that rule by seeing to it that public officials stay within the limits of the law, where law means both the law of the constitutive statute – the statute which delegates authority to the officials – and the common law. Moreover, both Dicey and Wade are firmly within the common law tradition which, as we have seen, regards the influence of the common law as morally beneficial. The common law contains moral principles, for example, presumptions about liberty and the principles of natural justice or fairness – the right to a hearing and the right to an unbiased adjudication. Judges, on their view, are entitled to interpret the law of the constitutive statute as if the legislature intended its delegates to exercise their authority in compliance with these principles.

The privative clause radically subverts this conception of the rule of law by driving a wedge between these two assumptions. It goes further than telling judges that they do not enjoy the last word; it tells them that they have no say at all. For example, the privative clause in *Anisminic* provided that a determination by the Foreign Compensation Commission 'shall not be called in question in any court of law'. Moreover, the issue goes beyond the fact that the principles of the common law cannot play their allegedly beneficial role in disciplining official authority. The statute which delegates authority will prescribe the mandate the officials are to carry

---

[80] Sir William Wade, *Constitutional Fundamentals* (The Hamlyn Lectures) (London: Stevens & Sons, 1989), p. 82.
[81] Dicey, *Law of the Constitution*.

out. If that mandate is protected by a privative clause, it will seem that the officials may do as they please, that they are, in the phrase adopted by judges from the New Testament, 'a law unto themselves'. So the problem can be seen as internal to the first assumption. A Parliament is supreme only if its laws prescribe limits on the authority of public officials. Hence, a law which at one and the same time prescribes limits on authority and gives to the officials the authority to decide on those limits sets up an internal contradiction. At least, there is a contradiction if one assumes that it is of the essence of there being legal limits that these limits are enforceable by judges.

As we can see from the first epigraph, judges can then claim that the statute presents them with a puzzle which they are entitled to solve. They do so by subordinating Parliament's alleged particular intention to make the official a law unto himself through the privative clause to its abstract intention, contained in every statute, to prescribe a necessarily limited authority, the latter manifesting itself in those particular provisions of the statute which set out the official's mandate.

The tension between the privative clause and the other provisions of the statute, a clash between particular expressions of intent, can then be deployed by judges to sustain a claim that there is a further component to Parliament's abstract intention that officials have a legally limited authority. As already suggested, the idea of legal limits can be claimed to include the limits set by common law principles. Parliament is said to have the abstract intention that officials should abide by the relevant principles of the common law as well as the terms of the statute. The difference is that while Parliament seems constitutionally disabled from contradicting the abstract intention to prescribe a limited authority in the sense of statutory limits on authority, it is hardly obvious that it cannot oust review on the basis of common law principles just by, for example, saying clearly that officials do not have to give the subjects of their decisions a hearing.

Put differently, if common law principles operate as a kind of implied statutory condition on administrative authority, then it might seem that all Parliament has to do to get rid of that condition is to remove any basis for the implication. Moreover, it might seem that all Parliament has to do to get rid of the problem of a tension between, on the one hand, the abstract intention to delegate a limited authority coupled with particular limiting provisions and, on the other, a privative clause, is to refrain from stating any limiting provisions. In other words, Parliament simply delegates an unfettered discretion. And, as we will see, there is yet another possibility –

Parliament might be understood to have prescribed limits but also to have made it optional for the officials to decide whether or not to accept these. In other words, what seem at first sight like mandatory limits might turn out to be more in the nature of guidelines.

However, if the principles of the common law are constitutional in nature, and so operate directly on administrative authority without requiring the medium of intention, implied or express, it might seem that Parliament is constitutionally disabled from contradicting the abstract intention that administrative authority be limited by the common law.[82] That would still leave it up to Parliament to decide whether to pre-scribe any limits beyond the common law, and thus to that extent to give the officials an unfettered discretion, as well as to decide whether to indi-cate limits but to put observance of the limits within the discretion of the officials. It might then also seem that in respect of the common law we are stuck with the choice between what I referred to earlier as competing supremacies – the supremacy of judges and the supremacy of Parliament, exactly the problem that Dicey bequeathed to the common law.

In my view, it is this deep issue that lies behind the disagreement between Wade and Wilberforce in the epigraphs to this section. Wilber-force says of the judicial solution that 'it would be misdescription to state it in terms of a struggle between the courts and the executive', while Wade portrays the issue as a struggle, albeit between judges and Parliament. Wade does propose that the judges are completely justified in resisting Parliament's attempt to create 'pockets of uncontrollable power in vio-lation of the rule of law'. But they are not, he thinks, justified in a 'legal sense', only in a 'distinct constitutional sense', 'as for example is the case if Parliament were to legislate to establish one-party government, or a dictatorship, or in some other way to attack the fundamentals of democ-racy'.[83] Indeed, Wade even seems unsure of the import of his claim about constitutionality. He goes on to say that 'judges have almost given us a constitution, establishing a kind of entrenched provision to the effect that even Parliament cannot deprive them of their proper function. They may be discovering a deeper constitutional logic than the crude absolute of statutory omnipotence'.[84]

The difference between Wilberforce's confident assertion that all he is doing is applying the law and Wade's more nuanced and tentative account

---

[82] These issues are at the heart of the 'ultra vires' debate in the United Kingdom; see Christo-pher Forsyth (ed.), *Judicial Review and the Constitution* (Oxford: Hart Publishing, 2000).

[83] Wade, *Constitutional Fundamentals*, p. 83.   [84] *Ibid.*, p. 87.

could be explained in terms of perspective. On the one hand, there is the judicial perspective – the perspective of the engaged participant in legal practice who to preserve his sense of role, whether or not he believes this, has to claim that he is not engaged in a political battle. He is simply carrying out Parliament's intention. On the other hand, there is the academic commentator who can give a realistic account of what the participant is up to.

Wade's account is, however, no less engaged than Wilberforce's. He does not, for example, rely on what one might think of as a standard legal realist account of adjudication in a politically fraught matter where there are serious legal arguments on both sides. On such an account, the most one can say is that the judges had discretion and had to take a stand determined by their political convictions and thus not by the law.[85] But Wade clearly supposes that the judges were doing their duty by preserving the rule of law, even though he is unwilling to categorize that duty as legal, preferring to think of it as constitutional, or quasi-constitutional.

In my view, any claim about realism is premature without investigating further the disagreement between Wilberforce and Wade. As I hope to show, that disagreement, provoked by the perplexing legal character of the privative clause, provides insights into the content of the rule of law or legality, which in turn helps us to grasp better the relationship between Parliament, the judiciary, and also the executive.

I will discuss below three approaches that Commonwealth judges have taken to the privative clause: the English or 'evisceration' approach, one which empties the privative clause of all meaning, thus giving rise to Wade's charge of flat or outright disobedience; the Australian or 'reconciliation' approach, which seeks to give effect to Parliament's intention while preserving judicial control over the executive; and the Canadian or 'deferential' approach, which understands the privative clause as just one kind of signal Parliament can send judges about the appropriate standard judges should adopt when it comes to reviewing administrative decisions.

The evisceration approach is on its face the most dramatic of the three reactions, though, as we will see, there is a genuine question about whether the differences are more rhetorical than substantial. It is, however, worth noting right now that one curious aspect of the differences is that the least dramatic approach is adopted by the judges who have the surest

---

[85] See H. L. A Hart, *The Concept of Law* (2nd edn, Oxford: Clarendon Press, 1994), p. 153: 'Here all that succeeds is success'. Perhaps Wade and Hart are closer here than I suggest in the text; see David Dyzenhaus, 'Form and Substance in the Rule of Law: A Democratic Justification for Judicial Review' in Forsyth, *Judicial Review*, pp. 141–67 at pp. 153–60.

ground for a constitutional stand against Parliament, in that, as we have seen, the Australian Constitution very explicitly protects the High Court's jurisdiction, though not by entrenching specific grounds of review. Put differently, it is the case that counter to intuition the more judges have to rely on an implicit or common law understanding of constitutionality in responding to privative clauses, the more vigorous, at least at the level of rhetoric, their response seems likely to be.

Evisceration

Anisminic Ltd was a British corporation which sought compensation for property damage caused to its mines in Egypt during the Suez crisis. The British government had set up a fund for this purpose, administered by the Foreign Compensation Commission, in terms of the Foreign Compensation Act 1950. As we have seen, s. 4(4) of that Act provided that any 'determination by the commission of any application made to them . . . shall not be called into question in any court of law'. The Commission largely rejected Anisminic's claim on the basis that it had sold its operation to the United Arab Republic before 1959, the date when the treaty establishing the Commission had been concluded. The Commission thus held that Anisminic had not shown that in 1959 it or its successors in title were British nationals, a requirement set out in an Order in Council, made under the Act. The House of Lords declared that the Commission's decision was void, because it considered that the requirement about 'successors in title' did not apply when the original owner was the claimant.

Wade points out that the important holding in the case is not that a privative clause cannot protect jurisdictional errors, but the Court's claim that the Commission's decision on this issue was a jurisdictional error, rather than an error of law within jurisdiction. While the judges in *Anisminic* purported to maintain the distinction between these two kinds of error, it is not clear that they provide any principled basis for doing so. And since subsequent decisions have explicitly confirmed that a privative clause does not protect errors of law of any kind, it might well seem that there is no such basis.[86] Put differently, once judges assert that they are still entitled to review for jurisdictional error in the face of a privative

---

[86] See H. W. R Wade and C. F. Forsyth, *Administrative Law* (7th edn, Oxford: Oxford University Press, 1994), pp. 735–6, 737–9. And see the discussion at pp. 302–5 of *Pearlman v. Harrow School Governors* [1979] QB 56; *Re Racal Communications Ltd* [1981] AC 374; *O'Reilly v. Mackman* [1983] 2 AC 237 and *R v. Hull University Visitor, ex parte Page* [1993] AC 682.

clause, there is no principled way of stopping them from eviscerating the privative clause to the point where they have in effect read it out of the statute.

Reconciliation

In *R v. Hickman; ex parte Fox and Clinton*,[87] the Australian High Court had to interpret regulation 17 of mining regulations made under the National Security Act 1939. A Local Reference Board had a general power to settle disputes in the coal mining industry in any local matter likely to affect amicable relations between employers and employees. Regulation 17 provided that its decisions should 'not be challenged, appealed against, quashed or called into question, or be subject to prohibition, mandamus or injunction, in any court whatever'. The Board decided that lorry drivers, employed by independent hauling contractors and whose work was not confined to transporting coal, fell within their jurisdiction.

The High Court held that this decision was invalid. The privative clause could neither protect decisions which went beyond jurisdiction, which the Court concluded this decision did, nor could it protect decisions which violated constitutional requirements. Nevertheless, Dixon J's judgment for the High Court is considered to have put forward a reconciliation approach, one which tries to give genuine effect to the privative clause instead of reading it out of the statute. He said:

> [a privative clause] is interpreted as meaning that no decision which is in fact given by the body concerned shall be invalidated on the ground that it has not conformed to the requirements governing its proceedings or the exercise of its authority or has not confined its acts within the limits laid down by the instrument giving it authority, provided always that its decision is a bona fide attempt to exercise the power, that it relates to the subject-matter of the legislation, and that it is reasonably capable of reference to the power given to the body.[88]

The clauses that followed 'provided' became known as the *Hickman* provisos. While they were of course subject to the principle that no privative clause can be understood to transgress the Constitution, they were also understood to expand the jurisdiction of the tribunal or official by protecting a class of decisions which would otherwise be considered reviewable errors of law. In subsequent cases, Dixon J complicated matters by adding

---

[87] *R v. Hickman, ex parte Fox and Clinton* (1945) 70 CLR 598.   [88] *Ibid.*, at 615.

one more proviso: that no decision could be valid when it breached an 'inviolable limit' – a statutory constraint which was so important that the legislature must have intended it to be supreme.[89]

Section 474 of Australia's Migration Act 1958 was first tabled in Parliament in 1997, but was enacted finally together with various statutory measures in September 2001, as Australia reacted to the events of 9/11. We have already encountered the privative clause in *Anisminic*, which stated that no court could call 'into question' a determination of the administrative body. We can think of such clauses as finality clauses, since they deem that an administrative decision is final either by saying just that or by declaring that the decision is not reviewable by a court. Section 474 combined a finality clause with what I will call a 'no jurisdictional review clause', since it also prohibited the courts from granting the traditional remedies of judicial review for jurisdictional error: it told the court that it may not review even when the administration has done something outside of its authority.

There was no doubt about the authority of the Commonwealth Parliament to regulate immigration, as in Chapter I, Part V of the Constitution, 'Powers of the Parliament', s. 51 says:

> The Parliament shall, subject to this Constitution, have power to make laws for the peace, order, and good government of the Commonwealth with respect to:-
>
> (xix)   Naturalization and aliens . . .

The privative clause in the Migration Act 1958, s. 474(1), stated:

1. A privative clause decision:
   (a) is final and conclusive; and
   (b) must not be challenged, appealed against, reviewed, quashed or called in question in any court; and
   (c) is not subject to prohibition, mandamus, injunction, declaration or certiorari in any court on any account.

Section 474(2) defined a 'privative clause decision' as 'a decision of an administrative character made, proposed to be made, or required to be made, as the case may be, under this Act or under a regulation or other

---

[89] See Mark Aronson, Bruce Dyer, and Matthew Groves, *Judicial Review of Administrative Action* (3rd edn, Sydney: Lawbook Co., 2004), pp. 852–7.

instrument made under this Act . . .' The term 'decision' is defined broadly in s. 474(3) and includes a reference to the grant or refusal of a visa.[90]

In *Plaintiff S157 of 2002* v. *Commonwealth*,[91] the plaintiff argued that s. 474 of the Migration Act 1958 was invalid because it violated the separation of powers in Chapter III of the Constitution and s. 75(5), which entrench the original jurisdiction of the High Court in all matters in which 'the Commonwealth, or a person . . . being sued on behalf of the Commonwealth, is a party' and 'a writ of Mandamus or prohibition or an injunction is sought against an officer of the Commonwealth'.[92]

The plaintiff had been refused a protection visa and he claimed that this refusal had denied him natural justice, since the tribunal had taken into account material adverse to his claim for refugee status without giving him notice of the material or any opportunity to address it.

The Court rejected this challenge because it read down s. 474 by reasoning that the section did not violate s. 75(5) of the Constitution; that is, the High Court was not deprived of its jurisdiction to review for jurisdictional error. Gleeson CJ and Callinan J[93] gave separate reasons while Gaudron, McHugh, Gummow, Kirby and Hayne JJ delivered a joint judgment.

In his reasons for judgment, Gleeson CJ said that 'Parliament has legislated in the light' of its acceptance of *Hickman* and so s. 474 could not be read literally as an attempted ouster of the Court's jurisdiction.[94] In his view, Parliament had accepted that a provision like s. 474 had to be read so as to avoid violating not only the Constitution, but also the judicial controls articulated in *Hickman*, including the added proviso about inviolable statutory limits. It was then a matter of ordinary statutory interpretation how to understand the section, which meant that it had to be understood in a general context as part of a statute that 'affects fundamental human rights and involves Australia's international obligations'. This, Gleeson CJ said, had the result of making certain 'established principles' relevant.[95]

First, in the case of an ambiguity the Court should favour a construction which accords with Australia's international obligations. Second, the Court should not 'impute to the legislature an intention to abrogate or

---

[90] It also includes a decision on merits review of a decision – by the Refugee Review Tribunal (protection visas), Migration Review Tribunal (other visa categories), or Administrative Appeals Tribunal (particular questions arising in review proceedings).

[91] (2003) 195 ALR 24.

[92] The plaintiff also argued that s. 486A – which set a thirty-five-day time limit on application to the High Court for review of 'privative clause' decisions – was invalid. I will not deal with this aspect of the case.

[93] Callinan J's reasons add little to those given by Gleeson CJ.   [94] *Plaintiff S157*, at 32.

[95] *Ibid.*, at 26. The principles are set out, one per paragraph, in paras. 29–33.

curtail fundamental rights or freedoms unless such an interest is clearly manifested by unmistakable and unambiguous language'. Third, the Australian Constitution is, following Dixon J in the *Communist Party* case, 'framed upon the assumption of the rule of law'.[96] Fourth, and 'as a specific application of the second and third principles', privative clauses are construed by reference to a presumption that the legislature does not intend to deprive the citizen of access to the courts, other than to the extent expressly stated or necessarily to be implied. Fifth,

> a principle of relevance to *Hickman* is that what is required is a consideration of the whole Act, and an attempt to achieve a reconciliation between the privative clause and the rest of the legislation . . . There may not be a single answer to that question. But the task is not to be performed by reading the rest of the Act as subject to s. 474, or by making s. 474 the central and controlling provision of the Act.

Now Gleeson CJ reasoned that the Commonwealth's argument was inconsistent with these principles, since it supposed that the effect of s. 474 was radically to transform the pre-existing conditions, so that they were no longer 'imperative duties' or 'inviolable limitations' on decision-makers. It followed, the Commonwealth had concluded, that as long as a decision satisfies '*Hickman* conditions' in the sense that it is a bona fide decision about whether to grant a protection visa, it will then be valid.[97]

Gleeson CJ responded that the principles of statutory construction did not lead to the conclusion that Parliament had evinced an attention that an unfair decision could stand as long as it was bona fide:

> People whose fundamental rights are at stake are ordinarily entitled to expect more than good faith. They are ordinarily entitled to expect fairness. If Parliament intends to provide that decisions of the Tribunal, although reached by an unfair procedure, are valid and binding, and that the law does not require fairness on the part of the Tribunal in order for its decisions to be effective under the Act, then s 474 does not suffice to manifest such an intention.[98]

In evaluating Gleeson CJ's response, it is helpful to know that the Commonwealth also argued that Parliament could delegate to the minister 'the power to exercise a totally open-ended discretion as to what aliens can

---

[96] *Ibid.*, citing as authority Dixon J's well known dictum in *Australian Communist Party Case* v. *Commonwealth* (1951) 83 CLR 1 at 193.

[97] *Plaintiff S157*, at 35.   [98] *Ibid.*, at 36.

and what aliens cannot come to and stay in Australia'.[99] Alternatively, it was suggested that the statute could be redrafted so as to say in effect '[h]ere are some non-binding guidelines which should be applied' with the 'guidelines' being the balance of the statute.[100] These arguments tell us that the Commonwealth did not so much ignore the proviso about inviolable limits, as take literally the thought that the issue was whether any particular statutory constraint was so important that the legislature must have intended it to be supreme.

Put differently, the Commonwealth's argument was that it is the task of the legislature to determine how to structure the discretionary authority of its delegates. It can choose to give them an unfettered discretion or a very narrowly confined discretion. Given that, it can also set out criteria for the exercise of discretion and make it clear that these criteria are not mandatory. Section 474 is then arguably consistent with *Hickman* in that does not deprive the High Court of jurisdiction but simply makes it clear that that the criteria set out in the statute are not mandatory.[101]

Gleeson CJ did not respond directly to the Commonwealth's claims that Parliament could delegate an unfettered discretion and so could also stipulate that statutory criteria are not mandatory. However, it is easily inferable from his reasoning, in particular the passage quoted above in which he says that s. 474 'did not suffice to manifest [an] . . . intention' to exclude natural justice, that his view was that if Parliament were to exclude with complete clarity particular grounds of review, the High Court would have to defer to that exclusion, with the exception naturally that the

---

[99] Subject only to the Court's jurisdiction to decide any dispute as to the 'constitutional fact' of alien status; *ibid.*, at 51.

[100] *Ibid.*, at 36.

[101] Note that in his reasons for judgment, at 62, Callinan J quoted from the Minister's second reading speech in 1997:

> The legal advice I received was that a privative clause would have the effect of narrowing the scope of judicial review by the High Court, and of course the Federal Court. That advice was largely based on the High Court's own interpretation of such clauses in cases such as Hickman's case, as long ago as 1945 . . .
>
> Members may be aware that the effect of a privative clause such as that used in Hickman's case is to expand the legal validity of the acts done and the decisions made by decision makers. The result is to give decision makers wider lawful operation for their decisions and this means that the grounds on which those decisions can be challenged in the Federal and High Courts are narrower than currently.
>
> In practice, the decision is lawful provided the decision maker: was acting in good faith; had been given the authority to make the decision concerned – for example, had the authority delegated to him or her by me, or had been properly appointed as a tribunal member – and did not exceed constitutional limits.

officials would have to stay within limits set by the Constitution. It is this feature of Gleeson CJ's judgment, his adherence to what can be thought of as a clear statement rule when it comes to an override of principles of statutory interpretation, that distinguishes his reasoning from that in the joint judgment.[102]

His reasoning here, as one year later in *Al Kateb*, does not rely on the division of powers Constitution unless there is a clear violation of its provisions, and so stakes its claim on a common law doctrine of legislative intent. In the Australian context such a stance has the advantage of including statutes enacted by the states within its scope, since, as we saw in the *Australian Communist Party* case, a stance which roots itself wholly in the division of powers Constitution can have the effect of permitting the states to do what is constitutionally barred to the federal Parliament. Moreover, by treating the privative clause to the extent possible as expanding jurisdiction, but not to the point where the clause violates either the values of the common law or the Constitution, the stance avoids eviscerating the clause and thus avoids forcing Parliament to consider whether or not to challenge the judicial assertion of supremacy.

In contrast, the joint judgment adopts the evisceration approach while purporting to follow the reconciliation approach.[103] The judges deny that s. 474 is a literal privative clause. But they are unprepared to find that any result follows from it, so that they read it not so much down as out of the statute, in effect invalidating it because it is a privative clause.

In addition, the joint judges responded directly to the Commonwealth's claims about Parliament's authority either to delegate an unfettered discretion or to convert all the statutory provisions into permissive considerations in the following way:

---

[102] See Sir Anthony Mason, 'The Foundations and Limitations of Judicial Review' (2002) 31 *Australian Institute of Administrative Law Quarterly Forum* 1 at 17:

> No encouragement should be given to attempts to restrict access to the courts for the determination of rights by converting provisions restricting access into provisions having substantive validity. If the legislature intends to treat non-compliance with its prescribed limitations as not resulting in invalidity, it should be encouraged to say so without achieving that result indirectly through the operation of an ouster clause. The efficacy of the legislative process will be enhanced if statutory provisions are expressed in a way that captures their intended operation.

See further Leslie Zines, 'Constitutional Aspects of Judicial Review of Administrative Action' (1998) 1 *Constitutional Law and Policy Review* 50–4.

[103] Contrast in this regard, *Plaintiff S157*, at 45–6.

> The inclusion in the *Act* of such provisions to the effect that, notwith-
> standing anything contained in the specific provisions of that statute, the
> Minister was empowered to make any decision respecting visas, provided
> it was with respect to aliens, might well be ineffective. It is well settled that
> the structure of the *Constitution* does not preclude the Parliament from
> authorising in wide and general terms subordinate legislation under any
> of the heads of its legislative power . . . But what may be 'delegated' is the
> power to make laws with respect to a particular head in s 51 of the *Consti-
> tution*. The provisions canvassed by the Commonwealth would appear to
> lack that hallmark of the exercise of legislative power identified by Latham
> CJ in *The Commonwealth* v. *Grunseit*,[104] namely, the determination of 'the
> content of a law as a rule of conduct or a declaration as to power, right or
> duty'. Moreover, there would be delineated by the Parliament no factual
> requirements to connect any given state of affairs with the constitutional
> head of power . . . Nor could it be for a court exercising the judicial power
> of the Commonwealth to supply this connection in deciding litigation said
> to arise under that law. That would involve the court in the rewriting of the
> statute, the function of the Parliament, not a Ch III court . . .[105]

And the judges went on to say:

> [T]he issues decided in these proceedings are not merely issues of a technical
> kind involving the interpretation of the contested provisions of the *Act*. The
> Act must be read in the context of the operation of s 75 of the *Constitution*.
> That section, and specifically s 75(v), introduces into the *Constitution* of
> the Commonwealth an entrenched minimum provision of judicial review.
> There was no precise equivalent to s 75(v) in either of the Constitutions of
> the United States of America or Canada. The provision of the constitutional
> writs and the conferral upon this Court of an irremovable jurisdiction to
> issue them to an officer of the Commonwealth constitutes a textual rein-
> forcement for what Dixon J said about the significance of the rule of law for
> the *Constitution* in *Australian Communist Party* v. *The Commonwealth*.[106]
> In that case, his Honour stated that the *Constitution*: 'is an instrument
> framed in accordance with many traditional conceptions, to some of which
> it gives effect, as, for example, in separating the judicial power from other
> functions of government, others of which are simply assumed. Among these
> I think that it may fairly be said that the rule of law forms an assumption'.[107]

The joint judges thus seem also to suggest not only that they might
find unconstitutional a grant of unfettered discretion but also a grant
that explicitly excludes grounds of review, for example fairness, from

[104] (1943) 67 CLR 58 at 82.   [105] *Plaintiff S157*, at 51.
[106] (1951) 83 CLR 1 at 193.   [107] *Plaintiff S157*, at 27.

consideration by the High Court. Here we should note that a previous incarnation of the Immigration Act contained a provision which excluded review in this way, though only in respect of the Federal Court. It provided in s. 476 that the Federal Court of Australia has jurisdiction to review decisions made by immigration officials on very specific grounds, set out in subs. (1). Subsection (1)(f) said that the Court can review if 'the decision was induced or affected by fraud or by actual bias'. Subsection (1) was explicitly made subject to subs. (2) which says: 'The following are not grounds upon which an application may be made under subsection (1): (a) that a breach of the rules of natural justice occurred in connection with the making of the decision; (b) that the decision involved an exercise of a power that is so unreasonable that no reasonable person could have so exercised the power'. Subsections (3) and (4) sought to specify and narrow some of the grounds of review listed. Thus, subs. (1)(d) permitted review for an 'improper exercise of power' but subs. (3)(f) said that this did not permit review for 'an exercise of power in bad faith'.[108]

I will call this kind of privative clause a 'substantive' privative clause, because it does not say 'no review' nor purport to confer finality on decisions, but seeks to remove particular grounds of review from the jurisdiction of the courts. So the joint judgment suggests that at least some members of the High Court might invalidate such a clause, and they would do so on the basis of the way in which the text of their Constitution differs from that of both Canada and the United States. It is this emphasis on text which explains how McHugh J could join Kirby J in the joint judgment in *Plaintiff S157* but would later so vehemently disagree with him in *Al-Kateb*.

The joint judgment is thus ambiguous between two positions, between Kirby J's common law constitutionalism and McHugh J's constitutional positivism. The contradictions in McHugh J's general stance stem from the instability of the rigid doctrine of the separation of powers that is part of the constitutional positivist package. Because constitutional

---

[108] Section 474(1) reacted to the fact that although the High Court upheld the validity of s. 476 on the basis that the Commonwealth Parliament was entitled to restrict the jurisdiction of the Federal Court, in *Abebe* v. *Commonwealth* (1999) 197 CLR 510 it subsequently held that an error might give rise to several of the grounds of review specified in s. 476(1) by reason of their protean nature, and that where this was the case, review would not be made unavailable by reason of the limitations set out in s. 476(3). That is, because the limitations in s. 476(3) only referred to specific grounds and did not have a global operation, there was no reason to give any other available grounds a narrower meaning than conveyed by the ordinary usage: see *Minister for Immigration and Multicultural Affairs* v. *Yusuf* (2001) 206 CLR 323.

positivism holds that the legislature has a monopoly on law making and that judges have a monopoly on interpretation of the law, a general privative clauses forces positivist judges to choose between submitting to legislative supremacy or asserting their own.[109] Since a legal order in which they have no interpretative role is unimaginable to them, they will pretend that a general privative clause was not intended to do what it states.

A substantive privative clause poses an even harder problem for judges who have an aspirational conception of the rule of law but who also adopt or purport to adopt the rigid doctrine of the separation of powers. Such a clause leaves them with their review authority but deprives them of its point – the protection of the rule-of-law principles developed by the common law. When such judges have a division of powers constitution, one which will almost of necessity protect to some extent their review jurisdiction or at the least contain provisions which can be so interpreted, they might be tempted to read into the text an intention to protect these principles. That allows them to pit text against text – the constitutional text against the text of the statute – and intention against intention, that is the intention of the founders of the constitution against the intention of the legislature. The text offers them the luxury of a prop to avoid the charge of judicial activism, while elevating rule-of-law values to a level where the values seem entrenched, not overridable even by the most determined legislature.

These judges then find themselves tempted in the direction of constitutional positivism, as long as they have a written constitution that is capable of being interpreted as preserving the separation of powers in a way that gives to them the role they want. They adopt the rigid doctrine of the separation of powers because it is convenient for them but that then creates tensions when they have to deal with situations in which all they have to rely on is the common law.

In contrast, Gleeson CJ in both cases relies exclusively on a common law method of interpretation. It might be that he is keeping his constitutional powder dry for the appropriate occasion. But I think his stance has much more to with the fact that he is not as preoccupied as the other judges with a rigid doctrine of the separation of powers. Thus in *Plaintiff S157*, he suggests that a privative clause protects errors of law that do not go to jurisdiction and, in this way, expands the jurisdiction of a tribunal beyond what it would have been had there been no privative clause. But he is well

---

[109] Hunt, 'Sovereignty's Blight'.

aware that it is in the abstract very difficult to provide any successful test to distinguish between errors of law that go to jurisdiction and errors which do not. Here it is noteworthy that he traces this difficulty back to the source of the reconciliation approach, the fact that in *Hickman* Dixon J found a jurisdictional error when it was clearly arguable that at most the error was one of law.[110] Indeed, it is most likely that the distinction between jurisdictional error and mere error of law is not that important to Gleeson CJ. As we have seen, he advocates interpretation of the alleged privative clause by placing it within the context of the statute as a whole, informed by presumptions of interpretation taken from both the Constitution and the common law. And he suggests at one point that the result of such a process is that the courts will review administrative decisions with different degrees of intensity, rather than by regarding some as totally protected by a privative clause.[111]

In other words, it might not be the case that the reconciliation approach has to collapse into evisceration. Instead, it might collapse into the Canadian deferential approach, which I will shortly sketch. And, as we will see in the next chapter, the deferential approach has a consequence that some judges might find unpalatable. It requires judges not only to accept that they do not have a monopoly on interpretation. It also requires them to make sense of the fact that fundamental or constitutional values can have that status and yet be overridable by the legislature.

---

[110] See *Plaintiff S157*, at 30, where he has this to say about *Hickman*:

> In *Hickman*, it was claimed that a purported decision was beyond power because the dispute in question was between parties who were not in the relevant industry. It might have been thought that the view that they were in the relevant industry was at least fairly open. There was certainly a bona fide attempt by the Board to pursue its powers. Even so, the 'decision' . . . in the Court's opinion, did not on its face appear to be within power. Therefore, it was not protected by reg. 17 from judicial interference.

[111] Compare, *Plaintiff 5157*, at 26 and 28. Sir Anthony Mason has suggested that the High Court together with the House of Lords rejects this deferential approach on the basis that it amounts to an 'abdication of the judicial responsibility to declare and enforce the law'. 'Implicit in this', he says, 'is the assumption that a question of law can be distinguished from a question of fact and a matter of policy. This is one of the great assumptions of Anglo-Australian administrative law. Although the distinction is supported by legislation and by a wealth of judicial authority, it is an assumption which perhaps may be challenged one day, as it has been in the United States and Canada'. He also notes that the approach presents 'more of a challenge to the established distinction between judicial review for illegality and merits review'. Sir Anthony Mason, 'Judicial Review: A View From Constitutional and Other Perspectives' (2000) 28 *Federal Law Review* 331–43 at 339–40.

Deference

The leading case on privative clauses in Canada is *CUPE: Canadian Union of Public Employees, Local 963* v. *New Brunswick Liquor Corporation.*[112] Here the tribunal was a Public Service Staff Relations Board, constituted by the Public Service Labour Relations Act 1973 whose decisions were protected by the following privative clauses: section 101(1) reads 'Except as provided in this Act, every order, award, direction, decision, declaration, or ruling of the Board, the Arbitration Tribunal or an adjudicator is final and shall not be questioned or reviewed in any court'; section 102(2) reads: 'No order shall be made or process entered, and no proceedings shall be taken in any court, whether by way of injunction, *certiorari*, prohibition, quo warranto, or otherwise, to question, review, prohibit or restrain the Board, the Arbitration Tribunal or an adjudicator in any of its or his proceedings.'

The Board had to interpret a particularly badly worded provision in its statute on which turned the issue of whether management could do the work of employees during a strike. The New Brunswick Court of Appeal had held that the tribunal's expertise had to do with the application of the law to the particular facts of the dispute, so that the tribunal's interpretation of the provision had to be correct, that is, in accordance with the reviewing judge's understanding.

In the Supreme Court, Dickson J made it clear that judges had to take the privative clause seriously, and hence should not use previously popular devices in an attempt to read it out of the statute. But he was also careful to state the view that it was not only the formal expression of legislative intent in the privative clause that mattered, but also the good reason for that formal expression – that an administrative agency is expert within its specialized area of law:

> Section 101 constitutes a clear statutory direction on the part of the Legis-
> lature that public sector labour matters be promptly and finally decided by
> the Board. Privative clauses of this type are usually found in labour rela-
> tions legislation. The rationale for protection of a labour board's decisions
> within jurisdiction is straightforward and compelling. The labour board is
> a specialized tribunal which administers a comprehensive statute regulat-
> ing labour relations. In the administration of that regime, a board is called
> upon not only to find facts and decide questions of law, but also to exercise

---

[112] *Canadian Union of Public Employees, Local 963* v. *New Brunswick Liquor Corporation*
[1979] 2 SCR 227.

its understanding of the body of jurisprudence that has developed around the collective bargaining system, as understood in Canada, and its labour relations sense acquired from accumulated experience in the area.[113]

One natural way to understand Dickson J's judgment in *CUPE* is as giving rise to two standards for review: correctness for jurisdictional issues and patent unreasonableness for issues that fell within jurisdiction. It seemed to follow from the Supreme Court's subsequent jurisprudence on s. 96 of The Constitution Act 1867, the provision which reserves to the Prime Minister the authority to appoint judges to the superior courts, that administrative decisions about the interpretation of the Constitution, the common law, statutes other than the tribunals' own constitutive statutes, as well as the jurisdictional limits on delegated authority would all count as constitutional.[114] The last category was to be determined by a 'pragmatic and functional' approach to statutory interpretation, one which sought to reconcile the privative clause with the rest of the statute by working out which provisions went to jurisdiction. In short, it might seem the Canadian approach is reconciliation by another name, and, moreover, one might expect the same result – the collapse of reconciliation into evisceration. And, as the Supreme Court developed its jurisprudence on deference, some of the judges made it clear that the collapse into evisceration was exactly their fear.

They saw two causes for alarm. First, Dickson J had warned that judges should be wary of characterizing an error as jurisdictional in order to make it reviewable on the correctness standard. However, it seemed that this warning was not being heeded. Second, recall that on Dickson J's approach errors of law within jurisdiction are not deemed unreviewable: they will be reviewed if they are manifestly or patently unreasonable. The same

---

[113] *Ibid.*, at 235–6.

[114] The leading case is *Crevier* v. *Québec (AG)* [1981] 2 SCR 220. Laskin CJ, writing for the Court, reacted adversely to an attempt by the Quebec Legislature to create a 'Professions Tribunal' with exclusive appellate jurisdiction over the discipline committees of most of the statutory professional bodies in Quebec and to make the decisions of the tribunal 'final' or not subject to judicial review. At 237–8, he held that a provincial legislature is not permitted to create a non-s. 96 court whose main task is to act as a s. 96 court would in reviewing administrative action (sentence construction). He also held that s. 96 provides a constitutional guarantee of judicial – that is, s. 96 court – review of provincial statutory authorities for jurisdictional error. In his view, a privative clause in provincial legislation achieves the right balance between the legislature and the 'Courts as ultimate interpreters' of s. 96 and of the Constitution, as long as 'issues of jurisdiction which are not removed from issues of constitutionality' are not shielded from review.

group of judges thought that when a tribunal or official offered reasons for a decision, judges should refrain from evaluating reasonableness by asking whether the reasons supported the decision. Rather, judges should focus solely on whether an error jumped out at them. Their fear was that an exercise that focuses on the relationship between reasons and results inevitably draws judges closer to the point where the standard they apply is whether they themselves would have made that decision.[115] While these fears cannot be discounted, one has to see that they attach to risks which are inherent in the judicial attempt to take the administrative state seriously, to regard it as a legitimate part of the constitutional order. This is the topic of my third chapter.

[115] For example, Wilson J in *National Corngrowers Association* v. *Canada Import Tribunal* [1990] 2 SCR 1324 and Cory J dissenting in *Dayco (Canada)* v. *CAW – Canada* [1993] 2 SCR 230.

Taking the administrative state seriously

Recognizing rationality

It is still the case today that the most sustained attempt to understand judicial review for jurisdictional error as a legal phenomenon occurred in a series of articles, starting in the 1920s and finishing in the 1970s, by D. M. Gordon, a lawyer who practised in British Columbia.[1] By legal phenomenon, I mean an attempt to understand such review within a coherent account of the rule of law. For it is easy to understand the political and other rationales for delegating authority to officials to implement public programmes – rationales to do with complexity, efficiency, and expertise. It is also easy to understand the reasons why governments think it necessary to protect public officials from the kind of judicial meddling which undermines the delivery of the statutory programmes the officials are charged with administering. In chapter 2, I discussed one of the main vehicles for protection, the privative clause which tells judges to refrain from review.

But as we have seen, there are significant problems from the perspective of the rule of law for understanding the privative clause, which is why the evisceration approach developed in the United Kingdom, the approach which we saw simply empties a privative clause of all meaning. And, as we have also seen, the Australian attempt to take the privative clause seriously, as a legislative expansion of administrative jurisdiction, perches uneasily between evisceration and a rather different approach, the Canadian deferential approach. Finally, I indicated that the deferential approach risks, as it becomes more sophisticated, collapsing back into evisceration.

Gordon did not, however, find the privative clause to be a particular problem because it followed from his theory of jurisdiction that such clauses are redundant. In his 1929 article, 'The Relation of Facts to Jurisdiction', Gordon argued that the way to establish order in the common law

---

[1] I rely here on the study by Kent Roach, 'The Administrative Law Scholarship of D. M. Gordon' (1989) 34 *McGill Law Journal* 1–38.

of judicial review lay in adopting a very formal concept of administrative jurisdiction in which the only question permitted to judges was: 'Was the tribunal that so found the tribunal whose opinion was made the test?'[2] Even if the statute prescribed procedural steps for a tribunal to follow, failure to follow these steps would not constitute jurisdictional error, for, in Gordon's words, such a prescription does 'not make observance a condition of the power, but merely regularity of exercise'.[3] It follows from this formal concept that the privative clause is redundant. All it does is state the obvious fact that the question was made appropriate simply because the legislature had delegated authority to the official, whether this is done by saying that the official has discretion to decide the matter, or by saying that jurisdiction is conferred upon him. Thus when *Anisminic*,[4] the decision of the House of Lords which led to evisceration in the United Kingdom, was decided, Gordon did not criticize the judges who found that there was a reviewable error for their sidestepping of the privative clause.[5] Rather, he criticized them because they had the wrong understanding of jurisdictional error. In contrast, other administrative lawyers have focused almost exclusively on the judicial sidestep.

Gordon's theory of jurisdiction remains illuminating. It illustrates the longevity of a strategy that attempts to preserve the rule of law by dint of a strategic retreat from an area of state activity which might not seem amenable to its control. In the context of states of emergency, we have seen this strategy exemplified in strategies that seek to preserve the law of the rule-of-law state by consigning measures to deal with the emergency either to extra-legal space or to space that is only nominally controlled by law.

Gordon's theory floats free of any ideology. It is consistent with a left-wing ideology that welcomes the idea that judges should understand that they should not interfere with the workings of the administrative state. Not only do the judges come from an elite group that is likely to be opposed to the policies the administrative state seeks to implement but they are also generalists when it comes to the law, and thus ignorant of the highly specialized regimes of the administrative state. But Gordon's theory is also consistent with an ideology that is deeply opposed to the administrative state because it both disapproves of the policies that such a state was set up to implement and despairs of imposing the rule of law on it.

---

[2] D. M. Gordon, 'The Relation of Facts to Jurisdiction' (1929) 45 *Law Quarterly Review* 459–93 at 461–2.
[3] *Ibid.*, 483.   [4] *Anisminic Ltd* v. *Foreign Compensation Commission* [1969] 2 AC 147.
[5] D. M. Gordon, 'What did the Anisminic Case Decide?' (1971) 34 *Modern Law Review* 1–11.

A. V. Dicey and Lord Hewart, the author of a 1929 polemic against the administrative state, *The New Despotism*,[6] are early examples of the latter position, while F. A. Hayek's *The Road to Serfdom*[7] is a mid-twentieth century example. They opposed the administrative state because of their commitments to a free market economy. But they also opposed it because they could not understand how it could be controlled by the rule of law. For them the activities of the administrative state occurred for the most part in a legal black hole, created by the statutes that set up that state. And from that source of opposition often followed the conclusion that judges should take a hands-off stance. This phenomenon is nowhere better illustrated than by the fact that Lord Hewart also wrote one of the judgments that sought to entrench a distinction between quasi-judicial and administrative decisions in the common law of judicial review, which had the result that vast swathes of administrative activity were considered unreviewable.[8] In other words, the very illegitimacy of the administrative state does not make it a fit subject for review because its decisions take place for the most part in a space outside the reach of the rule of law.

The most prominent example in the United Kingdom of the leftwing ideology is the functionalist school of thought associated with the London School of Economics, a school often associated with the work of John Griffith, in particular *The Politics of the Judiciary*.[9] This school is deeply sceptical of judicial review because of judicial lack of expertise in administrative matters. But it also believes that judges will be disposed by their class membership to use any toehold with which the law might provide them to undermine the redistributive programmes of the welfare state.

While it is often difficult to discern the normative theory of particular functionalists, they are in my view best understood as part of the positivist family, because they espouse a kind of leftwing Benthamism, a political positivism which regards law as the necessary instrument for conveying judgments about collective welfare to the officials who will have to implement those judgments. Law is the commands of an elite which makes

[6] Hewart, *The New Despotism*.

[7] F. A. Hayek, *The Road to Serfdom* (Chicago: University of Chicago Press, 1994).

[8] See *R* v. *Legislative Committee of the Church Assembly* [1928] 1 KB 411 at 415: 'In order that a body may satisfy the required test it is not enough that it should have legal authority to determine questions affecting the rights of subjects; there must be super-added to that characteristic the further characteristic that the body has the duty to act judicially'. Hewart claimed that this superadded duty was the correct interpretation of Lord Atkin's remarks in *R* v. *Electricity Commissioners; ex parte London Electricity Joint Comittee Co. (1920) Ltd* [1924] 1 KB 171 at 204–5.

[9] J. A. G. Griffith, *The Politics of the Judiciary* (5th edn, London: Fontana, 1997).

judgments about utility that are then put into practice by expert officials. Official expertise is required because the commands are that mandates be carried out, and that means that expertise is necessary to develop as well as to apply the mandate. Functionalism is then one way in which legal positivism adapts to a world in which the content of the statutory commands of the legislature seems largely to be that the commands will be made determinate by the officials who are delegated the authority to do that task.

It is important to see that it is not only law that has an instrumental role in functionalist theory. The institutions of democracy, including Parliament, also have an instrumental role. Parliament is useful in so far as it provides the forum in which judgments about utility or welfare can be given proper legal form, so that the executive can get on with the job. It follows that legitimacy in a functionalist theory comes from success, from successful delivery of social programmes. Functionalism might not then be best understood as seeking to provide what we might think of as a normative account of law, an account of law's authority, nor even of politics or democracy. Rather, it is a theory that is completely parasitic on the existence of a social democratic programme. If such a programme is in place, functionalists have a theory about how best to deliver it.

It is this feature of functionalism that explains why functionalists found themselves without any resources to deal with the neo-liberal turn in politics, pioneered by Margaret Thatcher, nor more recently with the post-9/11 turn by some liberal democracies away from the rule of law. Their purely instrumental conception of law had the result that they had little to say from the perspective of law or the rule of law about the fact that rule by law was being used to mandate public officials to privatize the state or, more recently, to grant officials wide powers to respond to perceived threats to security. It also explains why those whose basic commitments are the same as those which animate functionalism have now faced up explicitly to the task of constructing a normative theory of law.[10]

I will come back to the topic of what we might think of as the new left legalism in chapter 4. For the moment I want to note that Gordon's theory of jurisdiction provides the only way of making sense of functionalism from within a theory of the rule of law. It is not that Gordon is sympathetic

---

[10] For example, Martin Loughlin, *Public Law and Political Theory* (Oxford: Oxford University Press, 1992); Keith D. Ewing and Conor A. Gearty, *The Struggle for Civil Liberties: Political Freedom and the Rule of Law in Britain, 1914–1945* (Oxford: Oxford University Press, 2000); Adam Tomkins, *Our Republican Constitution* (Oxford: Hart Publishing, 2005).

to the functionalist. Rather, his account can make legal sense of the idea of a binary or dualist state in which the only legal control on officials who wield delegated authority is that, for example, immigration officials do not decide tax matters delegated to tax officials and vice versa. But that legal sense preserves coherence at the cost of accepting that the administrative state is a state in which there is rule by law, but little rule of law.

Functionalists, however, did not want officials to be entirely a law unto themselves. They saw the need to protect individuals against arbitrary decision-making, and thus for an independent check on public officials, whether through internal mechanisms of review, through a specialized administrative court, or through parliamentary oversight. Since they regarded the administrative state as legitimate, they also thought that its power could be exercised legitimately, though the criteria for legitimate exercise would not come from the rule of law. And when they discussed such criteria, they often showed themselves impatient with the very categories that judges had devised as a means of disciplining their own review authority: The distinction between review and appeal, the distinction between procedural review and substantive review, the distinction between review of discretion and review of administrative interpretations of the law, the distinction between merits or correctness review and review on a patent unreasonableness or the *Wednesbury* unreasonableness standard,[11] which says that decisions are reviewable only if they are utterly irrational, and the quasi-judicial/administrative distinction.

Their impatience stemmed from their thought that these distinctions could operate just as well as a smokescreen for judicial expansion of review as for self-discipline. But in addition, the abstract conceptualism of these distinctions got in the way of effective review. Since, on the functionalist understanding, everything that officials did amounted to the implementation of policy, that is, there was no distinction between law and policy in the administrative state, if there were a need for independent review that review should be of everything that public officials did. However,

---

[11] The test developed in *Associated Provincial Picture Houses Ltd* v. *Wednesbury Corporation* [1948] 1 KB 223. Lord Greene MR said that discretions were reviewable when unreasonably exercised, where unreasonableness means that a person 'entrusted with a discretion' fails to 'call his own attention to the matters which he is bound to consider' or fails to 'exclude from his consideration matters which are irrelevant to what he has to consider'. He also said that an act of discretion is also unreasonable when it is 'so absurd that no sensible person could ever dream that it lay within the powers of the authority'. To illustrate what he meant by absurdity, Lord Greene MR used the example of the 'red-haired teacher, dismissed because she has red hair' *ibid.*, at 228–30).

they then hastened to add the injunction against giving such a review authority to the courts.[12]

I mentioned already the problem that arises for functionalism when state institutions become involved in a project that contradicts the social democratic commitments that made them think that the administrative state is legitimate. But, as I also indicated, my concern here is different: it is with the fact that, while Commonwealth countries have experimented with various alternatives to judicial review, the experiments have never gone far enough, or been given sufficient resources, to make judicial review unnecessary. So while judges might justly be charged with at times being motivated to subvert the administrative state, it is also true that they had no option but to try to develop theories of legitimate intervention, given that they had no option but to respond to calls on them to consider reviewing alleged arbitrary exercises of power. Put differently, while functionalists might have wanted a world in which there is administrative law but no judges, the world that would make their utopian vision possible was never properly created. Thus functionalists, either because they from the start saw that the judgeless world would never be created, or because they eventually came to that realization, found themselves arguing for a disciplined or chastened form of judicial review, something like Gordon's theory.

But chastened judicial review does not work, as is illustrated by the story of jurisdictional review in Canada. Recall from chapter 2 that *CUPE*,[13] the Supreme Court's decision that is the basis for the Canadian deferential approach, instructed Canadian courts to take seriously the rationale behind privative clauses – the deliberate legislative decision to delegate interpretative authority to an expert agency. Justice Dickson for the Court said that to respect that decision, courts should refrain from characterizing a tribunal's decision as jurisdictional in nature and should review tribunal decisions within jurisdiction on a patent unreasonableness standard. He thus advocated chastened judicial review, an admonition that was reinforced by the fact that patent unreasonableness seemed akin to *Wednesbury* unreasonableness, that is, a standard which public officials would only rarely fail to meet. I have already indicated that the Supreme

---

[12] See John Willis, 'Three Approaches to Administrative Law: The Judicial, the Conceptual, and the Functional' (1935–6) 1 *University of Toronto Law Journal* 53–81. Compare H. W. Arthurs, 'Rethinking Administrative Law: A Slightly Dicey Business' (1979) 17 *Osgoode Hall Law Journal* 1–45.

[13] *Canadian Union of Public Employees, Local 963 v. New Brunswick Liquor Corporation* [1979] 2 SCR 227.

Court found that it had to move beyond patent unreasonableness and that this move had led to concerns about the re-emergence of triumphalist judicial review masquerading behind deference. But, as I will now argue, the move was inevitable, not because of a judicial drive towards regaining supremacy, but because of the very logic of an account of the rule of law that recognizes the legitimacy of the administrative state.

This logic is illustrated by *Nicholson*,[14] a case decided by the Court in the same year as *CUPE*. In *Nicholson*, the Canadian equivalent of the influential decision of the House of Lords in *Ridge* v. *Baldwin*,[15] the Court scotched the idea that natural justice applied only to quasi-judicial functions, and thus not to administrative functions, and stated that in general a legal authority is one that acts in compliance with a duty of fairness.

These two decisions might seem in combination to have built a paradox into the Canadian common law of judicial review. On the one hand, *CUPE*, in contrast to *Anisminic*, seemed to signal a deferential or non-interventionist stance for judges when it comes to review of the substance of tribunals' decision-making. On the other hand, *Nicholson* signalled that judges should intervene in an area which had been regarded as immune to the requirements of natural justice.

CUPE tells judges that because administrative tribunals can make rational decisions about the law, judges must not assume that the courts should have the last word about what the law is. But *CUPE* also thereby invites judges to intervene when administrative tribunals in fact fail to live up to the standards which in principle make their decisions rational. Even if the standard of review is patent unreasonableness, it is a standard applied within the area of jurisdiction which Gordon and the functionalists wanted kept off limits to judges. Likewise, *Nicholson* tells judges that processes of administrative decision-making are rational, and thus amenable to judicial scrutiny, even where the agency making the decision is not like a court. But *Nicholson* also contains an implicit limitation on judicial review by requiring judicial attention to the particular administrative context in order to determine the appropriate content of fairness. Indeed, *Nicholson* can also be interpreted as suggesting, and I think is

---

[14] *Nicholson* v. *Haldimand-Norfolk Regional Board of Commissioners of Police* [1979] 1 SCR 311. The issue before the Court was whether a probationary police constable could have his employment terminated without a hearing of any sort, when the statute in question explicitly granted hearings in such matters only to police constables who had passed the probationary period.

[15] *Ridge* v. *Baldwin* [1964] AC 40.

rightly so interpreted, that courts should defer to expert determinations of appropriate procedures, just as *CUPE* prescribes deference to official interpretations of the law.

The impulse behind both judgments is, I suggest, the same – the judicial sense of the need for a positive response to the fact that the administrative state is here to stay. The impulse leads to an attempt to put into effect a judicial recognition of the inherent or at least potential rationality of the administrative process, where by rationality I mean that the process is amenable to control by the rule of law. In addition, the recognition, in order to be positive, had also to take into account that the criteria for rationality of the administrative process often are and should be different from the criteria for rationality of the judicial process. In other words, judges had to recognize that tribunals have a deserved claim to at least some autonomy in the legal order and that required judges to recognize the administrative state as legitimate from the perspective of the rule of law.

But for the courts to recognize the administrative process as inherently or at least potentially rational, is also precisely what creates the paradox of the recognition of rationality. To recognize rationality is at the same time to claim a judicial role in supervising the administrative process to ensure that it meets standards of rationality, even if a sincere attempt is made to conceive these differently. We have then the idea that administration is at least in principle and often in practice rational. Taking this to be true leads to paradox because to recognize rationality in practice is always at the same time to begin to measure a practice against standards of rationality. To date the only model of rationality with which the courts have generally been comfortable is one which approximates the way in which judges think decisions should be made. The recognition of the rationality of administration thus seems to carry with it the risk of the imposition of judicial standards of rationality – and that means that a return to intrusive judicial review is an ever present danger.

In the following section I try to show how perhaps the most important administrative law decision in Canada, decided in the 1950s, already contained both that paradox and the basis of solution to it, a basis which it took the Supreme Court of Canada another forty years to articulate. The best known of the majority judgments in that case – *Roncarelli v. Duplessis*[16] – was given by Rand J, whom we have already encountered in chapter 2 as the author of the common law bill of rights cases of the 1950s.

---

[16] *Roncarelli* v. *Duplessis* [1959] SCR 121.

Roncarelli was not however a constitutional challenge, based on the division of powers constitution, the Constitution Act 1867. It was a challenge to the exercise of discretionary authority by a public official. Moreover, it was decided after the string of common law bill of rights cases. As we will see, it and the Supreme Court of Canada's decision in *Baker*[17] in 1999 in an immigration matter form the bookends of an approach to administrative law, which shows how public officials can emerge from the shadows of the prerogative state into the light of the rule of law. And from that perspective, we can productively approach the question whether official decisions about national security can and should likewise emerge from the shadows.

Maintaining the rule of law[18]

Frank Roncarelli owned a successful restaurant in Montreal, but his business was ruined when Edouard Archambault, the Chairman of the Quebec Liquor Commission, cancelled his liquor licence. Roncarelli is portrayed in Rand J's judgment as an upstanding citizen – a man of good education, who ran a superior sort of restaurant in an exemplary fashion. But he was also a Jehovah's Witness during the era when the Premier of Quebec was Maurice Duplessis, and Duplessis, with much popular support, was determined to stamp out the aggressive proselytizing of the Witnesses. Roncarelli drew the attention of the government not because he took any part in missionary activities himself, but because he posted surety bail for around 383 Witnesses in Montreal who had been charged with municipal infractions for distributing and peddling materials without a licence. These infractions were of by-laws passed by the City of Montreal in an attempt to crush Witness missionary activity.

In all of these cases, Roncarelli offered his restaurant as security for the release of a Witness. So trusted was he that he would often sign blank bonds for the Prosecutor's office when he travelled outside of Montreal. On 12 November 1946, the Chief Attorney of the Recorder's Court in Montreal refused to accept Roncarelli's sureties, since a cash bail requirement had been instituted for Witnesses and Roncarelli then ceased to post bail.

The Witnesses responded to this and other signs of government intent to stamp out their activity with a pamphlet entitled 'Quebec's Burning

---

[17] *Baker* v. *Canada (Minister of Immigration)* [1999] 2 SCR 817.
[18] For a much more extensive discussion of the decision, on which this section is based, see David Dyzenhaus, 'The Deep Structure of *Roncarelli v. Duplessis*' (2004) 53 *University of New Brunswick Law Journal* 111–54.

Hate for God and Christ and Freedom is the Shame of all Canada', which Rand J described in his judgment as 'a searing denunciation of what was alleged to be the savage persecution of Christian believers'.[19] The Chief Crown Prosecutor in Montreal decided to take measures to prevent the distribution of the pamphlet, and police seized a cache located in a Witnesses' hall, which Roncarelli had leased to the congregation. Shortly thereafter, the Chief Crown Prosecutor advised Archambault of Roncarelli's 'involvement' with the Witnesses. Archambault phoned Duplessis, who was Attorney-General as well as Premier, to seek advice on the matter. After learning about Roncarelli's 'involvement' with the Witnesses, Duplessis recommended that Roncarelli's existing liquor licence be cancelled forever. On 4 December 1946, Roncarelli was given a copy of the cancellation permit while police raided his restaurant during the lunch hour and seized approximately $5,000 worth of liquor. Six months later, he was forced to close his restaurant.

In the days that followed, Duplessis gave a number of press conferences to explain his decision. He stated that the danger the Witnesses posed was on a par with communism and the Nazis. Indeed, the Witnesses, along with the Communist Party, had been banned under wartime regulations during the war. The Witnesses had been banned because they opposed conscription.[20] But in post-war Quebec they were feared because of their potential to subvert the Roman Catholic religion of the majority of Quebec's inhabitants. It was that hostility which continued to fuel legal and political repression of the Witnesses after the war. Indeed, such repression continues to this day.

Put differently, we have to see that there are two kinds of internal enemy – the enemy, as in the cases discussed at the beginning of chapter 2, who is seen as aiming at subversion of the political status quo and the enemy who aims at subversion of the moral status quo. The Witnesses were clearly engaged in moral subversion as they avoided politics entirely, while communists were engaged in both. For many in Quebec, the government was entitled to use the full force of the law to combat such enemies.

Roncarelli had first tried to sue Archambault in terms of the Liquor Law of Quebec.[21] However, that law required that they obtain the permission

---

[19] *Roncarelli*, at 133.
[20] See William Kaplan, *State and Salvation: The Jehovah's Witnesses and Their Fight for Civil Rights* (Toronto: University of Toronto Press, 1989) for the history of the wartime ban.
[21] The Alcoholic Liquor Act 1941. See the account in Sandra Djwa's biography of Scott, *The Politics of the Imagination: A Life of F. R. Scott* (Vancouver: Douglas & MacIntyre, 1987/ Toronto: McClelland and Stewart, 1987), ch. 18.

of the Chief Justice of the Quebec, a position to which Archambault had been elevated and he refused two petitions. (The second was made because the team had thought from his response to the first that he was willing to entertain a second, which made a clearer case.) The next avenue available was to sue the Liquor Commission as a whole. But here the consent of the Attorney-General was required and Duplessis not only refused to give his consent but indeed gave no response at all, thus delaying the legal process. The team then decided to try relying on the principle of English common law which seemed to allow a suit against Duplessis personally as long as it could be established that he had acted wrongly. The action itself was principally advanced in delict under art. 1053 of the Quebec Civil Code: and here Quebec law seemed to provide an insurmountable obstacle. Article 88 of the Quebec Code of Civil Procedure required that notice was given one month before the issue of a writ of summons against an official for damages 'by reason of any act done by him in the exercise of his functions' and the team had failed to issue such a writ in time because of the delays that had initially plagued them. Notwithstanding these obstacles, Roncarelli not only had his day in court, but won. However, the decision was sharply contested. There were three dissents,[22] and it followed a Court of Appeal decision which went against Roncarelli with only one dissent. As I will now argue, the constitutional significance of Rand J's judgment emerges when we appreciate that the decision was so contested because its jurisprudential basis was the unwritten values of the common law constitution.

The obstacle which art. 88 of the Quebec Civil Code posed did not bother Rand J for more than a moment. He held that the abuse of discretionary authority was such that the act which constituted it so far exceeded the authority of the official that it was 'one done exclusively in a private capacity'.[23] But I do not think that the significance of the case lies in this issue, nor in the interesting issue which I shall not deal with at all – the complexity of the award of damages – nor even in the claim that Duplessis had unlawfully usurped a statutory power. Rather, the judgment's deep significance lies in Rand J's discussion of the 'purposes for which public power or authority may be exercised legitimately'.[24] It is that discussion which reveals Rand J's understanding of the substantive content of the rule of law and thus of what one might call the constitution of legality.

---

[22] In *Roncarelli*, Taschereau, Cartwright, and Fauteux JJ dissented.   [23] *Roncarelli*, at 144.

[24] See David Mullan, 'Mr Justice Rand: Defining the Limits of Court Control of the Administrative and Executive Process' (1979–80) 18 *University of Western Ontario Law Review* 65–114 at 74.

One way of understanding the legal wrong is that Archambault had sought Duplessis' advice and had received what Duplessis regarded, and Archambault accepted, as an order. Since Duplessis, whatever he himself thought, was not entitled to give orders to Archambault, the wrong consisted in the fact that Duplessis acted illegally in applying this pressure on Archambault. Just this understanding is offered by Canada's leading constitutional lawyer, Peter Hogg, who summarizes the holding of the case as 'the principle of validity – that every official act must be justified by law'. Hogg says: 'Duplessis could not rely on his high office, nor his judgment as to the public interest, as justification for his act. Only a statute would suffice to authorize the cancellation of the license, and the statute which did authorize license cancellations gave the power to another official, not the Premier'.[25] A similar view of the case was articulated by Bora Laskin, later Chief Justice of Canada, in 1959.[26]

There are two problems with this view. The first is that it invites disagreement about whether Duplessis had as a matter of fact dictated Archambault's decision. Indeed, at trial Mackinnon J had found that in fact there had been such dictation, while the majority of the Quebec Court of Appeal denied that there had been, as did the dissenters in the Supreme Court. Here it is important to recall that Archambault had asked for Duplessis' advice. Whether or not Duplessis himself regarded what he had said as constituting an order which Archambault had to follow, it was not totally implausible to understand the situation as one in which, from Archambault's perspective, Duplessis had merely strongly confirmed the correctness of a course of action which Archambault was in any case contemplating. Imagine, for example, that Archambault had consulted Duplessis about the propriety of cancelling the licence because diners in Roncarelli's restaurant regularly drank to excess and then created a public nuisance once they left the restaurant. However strongly Duplessis couched his instruction to cancel the licence, I doubt that there would have been a case against either him or Archambault.

The second problem is more significant. Hogg and Laskin, together with the majority of the Quebec Court of Appeal and the dissenters in the Supreme Court, seem committed to the view that had Archambault taken the decision without consulting Duplessis the decision would then have

---

[25] Peter W. Hogg, *Constitutional Law of Canada* (3rd edn, Toronto: Carswell, 1992), pp. 768–9.

[26] B. Laskin, 'An Inquiry into the Diefenbaker Bill of Rights' (1959) 37 *Canadian Bar Review* 77–134 at 99.

satisfied what Hogg calls 'the principle of validity – that every official act must be justified by law'.

Just what goes wrong here is illustrated best by Cartwright J's dissent in *Roncarelli*. While Cartwright J held the view that Duplessis had not influenced the decision to cancel the licence to any great degree, he was prepared to assume that Duplessis' instructions to Archambault constituted a 'determining factor' for the purposes of the legal discussion. But after setting out the statutory framework, he observed:[27]

> On a consideration of these sections and of the remainder of the Act I am unable to find that the Legislature has, either expressly or by necessary implication, laid down any rules to guide the commission as to the circumstances under which it may refuse to grant a permit or may cancel a permit already granted. In my opinion the intention of the legislature, to be gathered from the whole Act, was to enumerate (i) certain cases in which the granting of a permit is forbidden, and (ii) certain cases in which the cancellation of a permit is mandatory, and, in all other cases to commit the decision as to whether a permit should be granted, refused or cancelled to the unfettered discretion of the commission. I conclude that the function of the commission in making that decision is administrative and not judicial or quasi-judicial.

And he invoked Masten JA, speaking in *re Ashby et al.*, saying that the legislature intended such administrative discretion 'to be a law unto itself'.[28]

The second problem is, then, that this view of the rule of law is substantively empty. It holds that if the legislature has delegated authority to an official, the only controls on the official are those controls explicitly stated in the legislation. Of course, an official whose authority is to issue and cancel liquor licences is limited to just those tasks; he cannot start making decisions about immigration matters. But as long as he stays within the limits of his authority he can act as he pleases. For judges to impose controls beyond what the legislature has explicitly stated is for them to usurp the law-making role which in a democracy is reserved to the legislature.

In other words, Cartwright J subscribes to the ultra vires doctrine as the legitimating basis of judicial review. That doctrine holds that the rule of law is maintained by judges seeing to it that the administration does not act arbitrarily or 'beyond its powers', where powers means the authority delegated by Parliament. The ultra vires doctrine is a direct emanation of a constitutional positivism committed to a rigid doctrine of the separation of powers. Since the legislature has a monopoly on making law, the only

---

[27] *Roncarelli*, at 166–7.   [28] [1934] OR 421 at 428 (CA), cited at 167 of *Roncarelli*.

controls on public officials to whom it delegates authority are the controls set out in the statute.

Rand J's reasoning directly challenges that doctrine. While he did view Duplessis' intervention as sufficient to make the cancellation a wrongful act, he also found it important to stress that even if Archambault had acted on his own initiative, there would be an abuse of discretion. Fundamentally at stake, in Rand J's view, was the purpose which lay behind the cancellation, not the question of whether that cancellation had been dictated by someone who had no authority to do so. Indeed, he reasoned from the fact that Archambault was not entitled to cancel for this reason to the fact that Duplessis had no competence to issue an order on the basis of the same reason.

> To deny or revoke a permit because a citizen exercises an unchallengeable right totally irrelevant to the sale of liquor in a restaurant is equally beyond the scope of the discretion conferred. There was here not only revocation of the existing permit but a declaration of a future, definitive disqualification of the appellant to obtain one: it was to be 'forever'. This purports to divest his citizenship status of its incident of membership in the class of those of the public to whom such a privilege could be extended. Under the statutory language here, that is not competent to the Commission and *a fortiori* to the government or the respondent . . . There is here an administrative tribunal which, in certain respects, is to act in a judicial manner . . . [W]hat could be more malicious than to punish this licensee for having done what he had an absolute right to do in a matter utterly irrelevant to the *Liquor Act*? Malice in the proper sense is simply acting for a reason and purpose knowingly foreign to the administration, to which was added here the element of intentional punishment by what was virtually vocation outlawry.[29]

Notice how Rand J raises the stakes. The issue for him is not just that there is an abuse of discretion, but that the kind of abuse is one that undermines the appropriate relationship between citizens of a democracy and their state. Citizens have certain rights, for example, freedom of expression and freedom of religion, and it is beyond the scope of the government's authority in making a decision about the allocation of public resources to allow those decisions to be swayed by views about the actual exercise of these rights.

Rand J is not therefore distracted, as Cartwright J was, by the claim that discretions are by and large unreviewable if their subject matter is a privilege not a right and the decision about allocation was not subject

---

[29] *Roncarelli*, at 141.

to any statutorily prescribed controls. Put differently, he does not work within the formal categories of the day which divided the administrative world between quasi-judicial and administrative authority, a distinction which left vast tracts of the administrative state virtually uncontrolled by either the procedural controls of natural justice or by judicial scrutiny of the actual decision. Just how prescient his decision is may be revealed by the fact that it was not until *Nicholson* in 1979 that the Supreme Court began to subject such discretions to requirements of natural justice or fairness. And it was not until *Baker* in 1999 that the Court recognized that discretionary authority is not substantively different from authority to interpret the law, and so should be subject to the control of the tests developed by the Court to evaluate such interpretations.

One way of describing Rand J's approach is to say that it is functionalist, a term which, as we have seen, is supposed to contrast with the formalism of categories. A functionalist judge looks to the reality of the exercise of discretion rather than its form.[30] Certainly, Rand J was concerned with the actual impact of the administrative decision on Roncarelli. And so what makes the decision susceptible to judicial scrutiny, or 'judicial', is not some prior formal category but its effect. However, Rand J measures effect not just physically but also normatively, against the backdrop of a conception of the appropriate political relationship between citizen and state.

Once one sees this, it might also seem that what I described as the emptiness of Cartwright J's positivistic understanding of the rule of law is not a problem but a virtue. It is precisely that quality that reserves to the legislature the authority to fill the law with content and prevents judges from imposing their own views both on statutes and administrators. And trailing these problems is usually the spectre of judges whose hostility to the administrative state prompts them to try to hold it back under the guise of the rule of law.

However, this view of the rule of law departs dramatically from the rationale that has been offered down the centuries for its virtue – that the rule of law is worth having because it also allows us to escape the arbitrary rule of men. As we have seen, even when such a view is motivated by repugnance towards the administrative state, it is as likely to lead to the conclusion that that state is beyond the control of the rule of law as it is to lead to attempts to impose control. It is thus capable of throwing up its hands, as did Cartwright J, at what it regards as the arbitrary rule of men.

---

[30] See Andrée Lajoie, 'The Implied Bill of Rights, the Charter and the Role of the Judiciary' (1995) 44 *University of New Brunswick Law Journal* 337–54 at 340.

Rand J showed that he was not prepared to give up on this rationale in one of the two most famous passages from his judgment:

> The act of the respondent through the instrumentality of the Commission brought about a breach of an implied public statutory duty toward the appellant; it was a gross abuse of legal power expressly intended to punish him for an act wholly irrelevant to the statute, a punishment which inflicted on him, as it was intended to do, the destruction of his economic life as a restaurant keeper within the province . . . That, in the presence of expanding administrative regulation of economic activities, such a step and its consequences are to be suffered by the victim without recourse or remedy, that an administration according to law is to be superseded by action dictated by and according to the arbitrary likes, dislikes and irrelevant purposes of public officers acting beyond their duty, would signalize the beginning of disintegration of the rule of law as a fundamental postulate of our constitutional structure.[31]

Rand J's premise here is that the requirement that public officials act in accordance with the rule of law, or non-arbitrarily, is a constitutional requirement: 'a fundamental postulate of our constitutional order'. But he is also saying that if this requirement is interpreted as the rigid doctrine of the separation of powers requires, the result will be that the rule of law disintegrates. For on that understanding, officials may do as they like, they are a law unto themselves, as long as they do not bump against the explicit constraints of the statute.

But as Rand J makes clear, there is more to a statute than its explicit constraints. In the other famous passage from the judgment, he says:

> In public regulation of this sort there is no such thing as absolute and untrammelled 'discretion', that is that action can be taken on any ground or for any reason that can be suggested to the mind of the administrator; no legislative Act can, without express language, be taken to contemplate an unlimited arbitrary power exercisable for any purpose, however capricious or irrelevant, regardless of the nature or purpose of the statute. Fraud and corruption in the Commission may not be mentioned in such statutes but they are always implied as exceptions. 'Discretion' necessarily implies good faith in discharging public duty; there is always a perspective within which a statute is intended to operate; and any clear departure from its lines or objects is just as objectionable as fraud or corruption. Could an applicant be refused a permit because he had been born in another province, or because of the colour of his hair? the legislature cannot be so distorted.[32]

---

[31] *Roncarelli*, at 141–2.   [32] *Ibid.*, at 140.

The direction of argument here is very important. Logically, the constitutional positivist should not permit review even when there is fraud or corruption unless the legislature has explicitly provided for such review. However, once one allows in fraud or corruption, one has put a foot firmly onto a slope where in principle there are other values that have to be taken into account if the exercise of discretion is to be in good faith.

Here one should note that Rand J is particularly sensitive to the vulnerability of the person whose life and livelihood is subject to administrative decisions. But he is sensitive to this factor without evincing any hostility to the administrative state. His point is only that in an era when our lives have become increasingly subject to public regulation, such regulation should not be arbitrary.

> The field of licensed occupations and businesses of this nature is steadily becoming of greater concern to citizens generally. It is a matter of vital importance that a public administration that can refuse to allow a person to enter or continue a calling which, in the absence of regulation, would be free and legitimate, should be conducted with complete impartiality and integrity; and that the grounds for refusing or cancelling a permit should unquestionably be such and such only as are incompatible with the purposes envisaged by the statute: the duty of a Commission is to serve those purposes and those only. A decision to deny or cancel such a privilege lies within the 'discretion' of the Commission; but that means that decision is to be based upon a weighing of considerations pertinent to the object of the administration.[33]

Rand J's conception of the rule of law, then, is one that seeks to remove the elements of bad luck or arbitrariness that are endemic in the administrative state – the bad luck of having one's fate turn on the discretion of officials who are pursuing ends that undermine the citizen's status as equal before the law or who are failing to take into account considerations that have to be taken into account in order to sustain that status. It is an affront to the dignity and equality of the citizen if his or her fate turns on the luck of the draw of executive officials. But, as I will now show, if judges are to guard us against such arbitrariness, they have to depart quite dramatically from the formal account of the rule of law.

In one sense, Roncarelli was lucky, in that he had the public record of unabashed government. Rand J was very aware of this element of the case, and conceded that it was often 'difficult if not impossible in cases generally to demonstrate a breach of this public duty in the illegal purpose

[33] *Ibid.*

served' and that there might have been 'no means . . . of compelling the Commission to justify a refusal or revocation or to give reasons for its action'.[34] There is nothing in Rand J's judgment that indicates a readiness to find a duty to give reasons, a duty which was not announced until 1999 in *Baker*. But, in my view, speculation as to whether Rand J would have found such a duty in an appropriate case is not very fruitful. More interesting is that such a duty is necessary in order to fill out the conception of the rule of law to which he was committed.

In *Baker* the front line immigration officials had made the decision that Baker, an illegal 'overstayer' in Canada, should not be permitted to stay in Canada on 'Humanitarian and Compassionate Grounds'.[35] While the officials were under no statutory duty to give reasons, they had at the request of Baker's lawyers, divulged the notes which had been made by the official who had made the initial determination. The notes revealed that the fact that Baker had four Canadian-born children was regarded as an extra reason to get rid of her rather than as a humanitarian and compassionate ground which should weigh heavily in favour of permitting her to stay. Indeed, the notes reeked of prejudice and stereotype to the extent that the Supreme Court, as L'Heureux-Dubé J's majority judgment conceded, could have decided the case on the ground of bias.[36] But had the Supreme Court overturned the decision solely on the ground of bias, the message it would have sent to the executive was not to give its reasons in the future. Thus, if the Court wanted to face up to the arbitrariness that had been brought to its attention, it was necessary that it took the extra step and articulated a general duty to give reasons when an official decision affects an important interest of the individual. One way, then, of understanding L'Heureux-Dubé J's judgment is that she wished to remove the element of luck or arbitrariness which made it improbable that most applicants for review of discretion would be successful, even when the facts cried out for review, just because the facts would hardly ever be disclosed.

However, there is a deeper issue about luck. The language which L'Heureux-Dubé J used to describe the basis of the duty to give reasons makes it clear that one of the values – perhaps the main value – which the duty serves is the dignity of the individual. It would be an affront to the

---

[34] *Ibid.*, at 141.
[35] In this section I rely heavily on my chapter 'Baker: The Unity of Public Law?' in my edited collection, David Dyzenhaus (ed.), *The Unity of Public Law* (Oxford: Hart Publishing, 2004) as well as on Dyzenhaus, 'The Unwritten Constitution and the Rule of Law'.
[36] *Baker*, at 851.

dignity of the individual if her fate (literally meant) depends on the luck of the draw of executive officials.[37] Consequently, it is not enough that the officials who make decisions impacting important or fate-affecting interests of the individual disclose their reasons, in case they are acting in bad faith, in a biased fashion etc. For a duty to give reasons is rather ineffective if the message heard by the executive is that officials should in the future be very careful not to disclose reasons which provide evidence of bias etc., when these are the real reasons. And it would not be very difficult to recraft the notes in *Baker* so as to reach the same result without creating the suspicion of prejudice and stereotype. So a general duty to give reasons does not remove sufficiently the element of luck, which is why yet another step is necessary.

This step is the link L'Heureux-Dubé J established between the reasons for the decision and the review of those reasons and she held that these reasons should be reviewed on a reasonableness standard – they had to display a reasonable justification for the decision. This step might not look like a big deal in most common law jurisdictions, but it is. And I think it is important to see that that step had already been taken by Rand J in *Roncarelli*, for, as I have indicated, Rand J was not distracted by the distinction between quasi-judicial and administrative acts. For him discretions are controlled by the rule of law in a legal order which is committed to constitutionalism, whether or not there is a written constitution in place. He therefore had no trouble arguing, as we have seen, that there was a range of considerations which an official had to take into account which have to be weighed.

My claim is that in a constitutional state, one that is committed to government under the rule of law, judges have to put in place three elements or constitutional fundamentals. First, they have to be committed to the view that the rule of law has content – law is not a mere instrument of the powerful. Rather it is constituted by values that make government under the rule of law something worth having. Second, judges are entitled to review both legislative and governmental decisions in order to see whether these comply with the values. Third, the onus is on both the legislature and the executive to justify their decisions by reference to these values.

All these three elements are present in Rand's judgment in *Roncarelli*. Only a component of the third is missing – the duty to give reasons which

---

[37] *Ibid.*, at 848.

is the way in which the executive will justify its decisions so that the individual subject to the decision can know that among other things his dignity as an individual, his equal status before the law, has been respected, not only because the official has made the decision free from bias and bad faith, but also because the decision has been based on considerations appropriate to the particular statutory regime. The 'perspective within which a statute is intended to operate' is constituted not only by the statute. As L'Heureux-Dubé J put it in *Baker*, discretion must be 'exercised in accordance with the boundaries imposed in the statute, the principles of the rule of law, the principles of administrative law, the fundamental values of Canadian society, and the principles of the *Charter*'.[38]

I want to focus on the way in which these last two elements relate to each other. When it comes to intensity of review, recall that Rand J said that a 'decision to deny or cancel such a privilege lies within the "discretion" of the Commission; but that means that decision is to be based upon a weighing of considerations pertinent to the object of the administration'.

Rand J is not saying directly that the judge must reweigh the weighing, only that a process of weighing must take place. And it is important to be aware that the Supreme Court of Canada is now rather preoccupied with the idea that, whatever judges do, they should not 'reweigh' the factors officials have to take into account in order to demonstrate that their decisions are reasonable. Weight is, however, just a metaphor for a proper inquiry into the balance of reasons. It became part of the Canadian discussion because in *Baker* the majority was clearly influenced by the fact that Canada had ratified, though had not incorporated by legislation, the Convention on the Rights of the Child,[39] which in Article 3 required that in administrative decisions affecting children, the 'best interests' of the children had to be 'a primary consideration'.[40]

---

[38] *Ibid.*, at 855.

[39] Convention on the Rights of the Child, New York, 20 November 1989, in force 2 September 1990, 1577 UNTS 44.

[40] Iacobucci and Cory JJ issued a partial dissent, which claimed to object only to this aspect of the majority's reasoning and put the objection on classic dualist or positivist grounds – if the Charter is not directly involved, Parliament is the sole source of legal value. Thus the dissent claimed not to object to the majority's holding that the statute itself, as well as ministerial regulations, required that the children's interests be given 'substantial weight', nor that judges should check to ensure that officials had been 'alert, alive and sensitive to' the issue of whether appropriate weight had been given: *Baker*, at 864. As I have argued elsewhere, these grounds should also have led the dissenters to object to the finding of a general duty to give reasons as well as to the merging of categories of substantive review. See David Dyzenhaus and Evan Fox-Decent, 'Rethinking the Process/Substance Distinction: *Baker v. Canada*' (2001) 51 *University of Toronto Law Journal* 193–242.

But in the Court below – the Federal Court of Appeal – which upheld the decision to deport, Justice Strayer was clear that the most that a judge can do is check whether a relevant factor like the children's interests has been taken into account. For a court to evaluate how that factor was taken into account is to reweigh, which is illegitimate.[41] Since *Baker*, the Supreme Court has retreated from its position expressed there and has adopted the view, more like that of the Federal Court of Appeal, that judges must never evaluate the way that relevant factors figure in the official's reasoning. They can check that the right reasons were taken into account, but may not go into the balance of reasons, which is to say, reweigh the reasons. And it is no accident that this retreat from *Baker* took place in the first major decision in the national security area given by the Supreme Court after 9/11, *Suresh v. Canada (Minister of Citizenship and Immigration).*[42]

Similarly, in both the Federal Court Trial Division and the Federal Court of Appeal in *Baker*,[43] the judges found that the immigration officials had weighed the children's interests because they had taken into account that Baker had children. They thus seemed to understand the officials' view that the existence of Baker's Canadian-born children was a kind of aggravating circumstance or reason to get rid of her as one which could not be adopted without on the way considering the children's interests.

In the context of this case, it might seem that a court could comfortably invalidate the decision because the officials, far from giving appropriate weight to the children's interests, considered the existence of the children as a kind of aggravating factor in the light of their express concerns about the drain on Canada's resources that illegal overstayers like Baker, in their view, represented. But it could not be said that the officials had failed altogether to take children into account. So, if all a court is entitled to do is to check whether a factor has been taken into account that had to be taken into account, it is not at all clear that in this respect there was anything wrong with the officials' decision. In other words, if all the officials had to do was tick the box – 'considered children's interests' – this should satisfy a court if the court is not permitted to reweigh. The fact that the officials drew adverse inferences from the fact that Baker had

---

[41] See (1997) 142 DLR (4th) 554 at 557.

[42] [2002] 1 SCR 3. The Supreme Court adopted the view of Lord Hoffmann, expressed in *Rehman*, which is discussed below.

[43] The judges did not, however, concede that there was a duty to take the children's interests into account, just that in the circumstances the interests had been properly considered. Nor, however, did they see fit to quote the case notes, a striking omission to say the least. See [1997] 2 FC 127 at 136 and (1997) 142 DLR (4th) 554 at 557.

children might not be to the court's liking, but should not provide a basis for intervention.

There is something odd, even perverse, about this kind of reasoning. After all, noting the existence of children, whether or not one draws adverse inferences, is hardly equivalent to taking their interests into account. It is surely right that the very idea of taking children's interests into account when at stake is the deportation of their mother requires serious attention by the decision-maker to the question of what is in the interests of the children.

My contention is that while Rand J's conception of the rule of law, as well as L'Heureux-Dubé J's in *Baker* require such reweighing, a court can reweigh and at the same time defer, as long as deference is properly understood. And this basis is laid by the way in which Rand J articulated the idea that the rule of law is a constitutional concept that operates whether or not there is a written constitution in place.

Rand J shows that the controls of the rule of law are triggered just by the fact that a society desires to live by the rule of law and has in place the institutions necessary to sustain that rule. A society may choose to state its commitment in documents which entrench the values of the rule of law, and much else besides, in various ways. But while these documents do make a difference, sometimes a dramatic one, to the role of judges, they make a difference along a continuum which starts with ideas like the idea that judges are entitled to check whether the administration has acted in good faith. Moreover, Rand J not only accepts the necessity of the administrative state, but also its legitimacy. However, in his view, legitimacy comes with rule-of-law commitments. Public officials are under a duty to show that their decisions are non-arbitrary, or are made in accordance with the requirements of the rule of law. Once they have accepted and discharged that onus, judges have no reason to interfere with their decisions.

Here lies the solution to the paradox of the recognition of rationality. Recall that the paradox arises because for judges to recognize the rationality of administration is at the same time to claim a role in supervising the administrative process to ensure that it meets standards of rationality, even if a sincere attempt is made to conceive these differently. I mentioned earlier that in Canada's leading case on deference, *CUPE*, Dickson J warned that judges should be wary of characterizing an error as jurisdictional in order to make it reviewable on the correctness standard. But, as I also pointed out, in the wake of *CUPE*, some judges thought that when a tribunal or official offered reasons for a decision, judges should refrain from evaluating reasonableness by asking whether the reasons supported the decision. Rather, judges should focus solely on whether an error jumped out at them, a test akin to *Wednesbury* unreasonableness – the decision must be utterly irrational to make it reviewable. Their fear was that an exercise that focuses on the relationship between reasons and results inevitably draws judges closer to the point where the standard they apply is whether they themselves would have made that decision.

As other judges pointed out, however, it was very difficult to understand how one could establish that a decision was reasonable without scrutinizing the reasons given for it. They came to interpret Dickson J's judgment as staking the ground for a jurisprudence in which the privative clause is but one factor among those that a court must take into account in considering what standard of deference it owes to an agency. Put differently, it is now the case both that a privative clause is not necessary for deference and that the presence of such a clause is not always a sufficient basis on which to conclude that deference is due. At the same time, the Supreme Court developed the idea that the standard of deference could vary from patent unreasonableness through what was called 'reasonableness *simpliciter*' to correctness, depending on the combination of factors in the particular context. A reasonableness standard demands evaluation of the reasons – a 'somewhat probing examination' – as Iacobucci J put it in the decision in which this standard was first properly articulated.[44]

I cannot go into all the intricacies of the Canadian jurisprudence on deference. I do, however, need to note that its very sensitivity to issues such as the context in which the tribunal is operating, the kinds of interests that are affected by its decisions, as well as the variable standard of review, creates a structure so complex and elaborate that it might look like judges, whether they are minded to or not, will be constantly be tempted into correctness review.[45] Indeed, even judges of the Supreme Court are now

---

[44] *Pezim* v. *British Columbia (Superintendent of Brokers)* [1994] 2 SCR 557, following the implied rationale of *Bell Canada* v. *Canada (Canadian Radio-Television and Telecommunications Commission)* [1989] 1 SCR 1722.

[45] See Hunt, 'Sovereignty's Blight', pp. 353–4 for the following list of factors: the nature of the right in question; the nature of the particular context (for example, fair trial rights where judges feel more comfortable in contrast with balancing interests where they do and should feel more diffidence); special expertise; relative institutional competence to conduct the type of decision-making which preceded the primary decision-maker's decision; the degree of democratic accountability of the primary decision-maker as well as other mechanisms of accountability; the degree to which the primary decision-maker has engaged with the question of compatibility of the decision with relevant legal values. For the Canadian Supreme Court's list, see *Baker*, at 856–7. Compare the same kind of analysis when the question is the content of fairness: *Baker*, at 837–40. *Baker* is notable for several reasons: it is the first decision by the highest court in the common law jurisdictions discussed in this book to uphold a general duty to give reasons; it held that discretions should be reviewed

starting to worry openly in their judgments about the way that their Court has developed the jurisprudence of deference.[46]

I do not think that there is any option for judges but to grapple with these issues openly. The idea of deference inherent in *CUPE* is not deference in its primary Oxford English Dictionary meaning of submission to the commands of an authority. Rather, it is deference according to the secondary meaning, deference as respect – a judicial attitude of respectful attention to the reasons which are or could be offered in support of a legal authority's decision.[47] It is this idea which drives a wedge between a contemporary stance and the bad old days of judges who expressed their opposition to the administrative state either by cramming it into a bed of common law substantive rights or by deeming it beyond the control of the rule of law. The deferential stance accepts the legitimacy of the administrative state, but requires of its officials that they demonstrate their understanding of the distinction between power and legal authority.

CUPE, in other words, is not a mere concession to the fact that the administrative state is here to say. Rather, it involves a judicial cession of interpretative authority to the tribunal, within the scope of its expertise – the area of jurisdiction protected by the privative clause. This cession is a radical departure from the rigid doctrine of the separation of powers which underpins the evisceration approach. It thus at the same time challenges constitutional positivism.

This challenge is well illustrated by the approach of Justice Antonin Scalia, whom I used in the last chapter as an example of constiutitional positivism, to the American doctrine of deference to administrative officials, the '*Chevron* doctrine',[48] the doctrine of judicial deference which has been developed in US administrative law.

---

on the same criteria as executive interpretations of the substantive law; it suggested that courts should defer to an official's determination of what is procedurally appropriate; it endorsed the distinction between deference as submission and deference as respect; it relied on an unincorporated human rights treaty to inform the Court's understanding of reasonableness. Only this last aspect of the decision attracted a dissent by two judges. For a comprehensive treatment of *Baker*, see the essays in Dyzenhaus, *Unity of Public Law.*

[46] See LeBel J in *Toronto (City)* v. *CUPE, Local 79* [2003] 3 SCR 77.

[47] See *Baker*, at 858, referring to David Dyzenhaus, 'The Politics of Deference: Judicial Review and Democracy' in M Taggart (ed.), *The Province of Administrative Law* (Oxford: Hart Publishing, 1997), pp. 279–307.

[48] Antonin Scalia, 'Judicial Deference to Administrative Intepretations of Law' (1989) *Duke Law Journal* 511–21, analysing *Chevron USA, Inc.* v. *NRDC*, 467 US 837 (1984). For more extensive discussion, on which this particular one is based, see Dyzenhaus, 'The Unwritten Constitution and the Rule of Law'.

This doctrine consists of two steps. To begin with, the court must determine whether Congress had a 'clear' and 'unambiguously expressed' intent when enacting the statute in question. If the court finds that Congress did have such an intent that is 'the end of the matter' and the court has no authority to modify or interfere with the interpretation or implementation of the statute. However, if no such intent can be discovered, the court must determine whether the administrative agency came to its decision on the basis of a 'permissible construction of the statute'.[49]

Justice Scalia supports the *Chevron* doctrine – the introduction of an 'an across-the-board presumption that, in the case of ambiguity, agency discretion is meant'.[50] But he does not do so on grounds to do with agency expertise, nor with the separation of powers and the inappropriateness of judges deciding policy issues. In respect of expertise, he says that if it were true that officials were better situated to determine the purpose of legislation than judges this would constitute 'a good practical reason for accepting the agency's view, but hardly a valid theoretical justification for doing so'. In respect of separation of powers, he argues that the courts are constantly in the business of determining policy, especially when it comes to working out what is the intention or range of permissible intentions that can be attributed to a statute, so that this task cannot be reserved to the administration.[51]

Instead, his approval of *Chevron* is based on the rise of the modern administrative state. The kind of statute-by-statute assessment that was common prior to *Chevron* was becoming increasingly difficult to implement given the complexity of present-day administrative decision-making. In addition, he contends that in the majority of cases, Congress does not have a 'clear' intention and it does not mean to provide an agency with discretionary powers. Instead, it simply fails to consider the matter. Because of this, *Chevron* is 'unquestionably better' than that which preceded it. Not only does Congress now know that statutory ambiguities will be resolved by agencies rather than courts, but these agencies will be able to deal with them with sufficient flexibility to ensure that their decisions are not 'eternal' or 'immutable'. Indeed, he argues that one of the great benefits of *Chevron* is that it accords agencies the space to alter their interpretations and approaches in the light of changing conditions.[52]

Justice Scalia's view of the proper role of agencies is very much the Benthamite or political positivist picture of appropriate adjudication. Officials

---

[49] Here I rely on the quotations from Scalia, 'Judicial Deference', 511–12.
[50] *Ibid.*, 516.   [51] *Ibid.*, 514–16.   [52] *Ibid.*, 516–17.

who are charged with interpreting the law have wide discretion about how to apply the law and wide discretion when it comes to interpreting the law when the content of the law is indeterminate or ambiguous. But when it comes to the second activity of interpretation, the officials' decisions are not to have any precedential force, lest these come to be regarded as a constraint on the discretion of officials in the future.

However, Justice Scalia still has to make sense of his own role, qua judge. Here it is worth quoting at some length the link he draws between one's 'method' of interpreting statutory and constitutional documents and one's definition of 'clear' in the first step of *Chevron*:

> In my experience, there is a fairly close correlation between the degree to which a person is (for want of a better word) a 'strict constructionist' of statutes, and the degree to which a person favors *Chevron* and is willing to give it broad scope. The reason is obvious. One who finds more often (as I do) that the meaning of a statute is apparent from its text and from its relationship with other laws, thereby finds less often that the triggering requirement for *Chevron* deference exists. It is thus relatively rare that *Chevron* will require me to accept an interpretation which, though reasonable, I would not personally adopt. Contrariwise, one who abhors a 'plain meaning' rule, and is willing to permit the apparent meaning of a statute to be impeached by the legislative history, will more frequently find agency-liberating ambiguity, and will discern a much broader range of 'reasonable' interpretation that the agency may adopt and to which the courts must pay deference. The frequency with which *Chevron* will require *that* judge to accept an interpretation that he thinks is wrong is infinitely greater.[53]

Justice Scalia's positivism thus draws him to the view that his tests for statutory meaning are likely to come up with a plain meaning of the statute and that, once that meaning has been determined, there is no reason for the judge to defer. Since, as he argues elsewhere in the same article, it is rare that a judge, whatever his interpretative approach, will find that on his approach there is in fact 'equipoise' between conflicting interpretations, one can infer that generally Justice Scalia will find no reason for deference.[54]

The tension Justice Scalia encounters arises out of his view of the rule of law as the rule of a system of statute-based rules with determinate content. It arises because that view requires, on the one hand, that when the statute imposes constraints, these rigidly constrain officials in accordance with the judges' understanding of the correct interpretation of the law. On the other hand, it also requires that when that kind of constraint does not

---

[53] *Ibid.*, 521 (author's emphasis).   [54] *Ibid.*, 520.

exist, officials are accorded a more or less free-wheeling discretion – they are a law unto themselves.

The approach I advocate contests both aspects of this view and does so moreover in a way that is not best described as the product of the mind-set of one who 'abhors a 'plain meaning' rule, and is willing to permit the apparent meaning of a statute to be impeached by the legislative history' and who is thus prone 'more frequently [to] find agency-liberating ambiguity'. It starts with the regulative assumption that Parliament, the executive and judges are committed to a rule-of-law project which is about the realization of fundamental constitutional values, whether written or unwritten. Judges should thus try to find that legislation is legislation which seeks to achieve its particular objectives in the light of a wider legal project. Thus legislative meaning is not a top down communication – a 'one way projection of authority', as Lon L. Fuller described the positivist view. Rather, as Fuller preferred to put it, law is the product of a relation of reciprocity between ruler and ruled.[55] A corollary of the view of law as a product of a value-based, rule-of-law project is that no particular insti-tution in legal order has a monopoly on the best understanding of law and that is why judges have reason to defer to administrative interpretations of the law of the particular administrative mandate. But they should defer only if the officials do a reasonable job of justifying their interpretation of the law.

Justice Scalia is well aware of this kind of approach. He describes it in rather harsh terms as 'mealy mouthed' deference, which does 'not neces-sarily mean anything more than considering those views with attentive-ness and profound respect, before we reject them'. And he goes on to say that if one were to try to give more force to this idea of deference, if those views would be binding if they were judged reasonable, the result would be a 'striking abdication of judicial responsibility'.[56] But this claim begs the question of what judicial responsibility is. If judicial responsibility is to preserve a monopoly over interpretation of the law, then it follows that there is an abdication. If, in contrast, judges are to regard themselves as involved with the legislature and the government in a common, rule-of-law project, the result speaks rather to judicial recognition of the roles of each of the powers in maintaining that project. Judicial deference is trig-gered neither by alleged ambiguity nor by explicit legislative commands to defer, but by the assumption that the other powers are participating in this project.

---

[55] Fuller, *The Morality of Law*, p. 207. [56] Scalia, 'Judicial Deference', 513–14.

Moreover, it might be the case that the best interpretation of the Supreme Court of Canada's later jurisprudence is that the shift in focus from decision to reasons for decision, and the development of the third standard of review, reasonableness review, shears the correctness standard off the continuum of standards of review. In other words, even the most probing judicial evaluation is to some extent deferential, since judges operate with a presumption that the reasons offered by the tribunal for its decision could justify a decision, which is not necessarily the decision that the court would have reached had it operated in a 'vacuum'.[57] So, for example, generally judges should conclude not only that the content of fairness will vary according to context, but also that the legislature and the administrative decision-maker are better equipped than they are to work out what is most appropriate to context. In other words, generally speaking, judges should defer to legislative and administrative choice when it comes to institutional design, including the design of fair procedures. And in the case of deference to administrative choice, filling the vacuum is not desirable because of some natural abhorrence, but because what fills it is the expert understanding of the tribunal about how the law is to be interpreted in its specialized context. If that is right, then there is no correctness review, only more or less intense scrutiny of reasons, whether tribunals are engaged in interpreting the law of their constitutive statute, or of another statute, or the common law, or the provisions of a written constitution, including, if there is one, their bill of rights. As a result, the deference approach does not read privative clauses out of the particular statutes in which they occur. Rather, like Gordon, the approach renders them redundant by reading them into every statute that delegates authority to public officials. However, unlike Gordon, they are read in in a way which treats them as a legislative signal to judges to alert them to what is in any case their duty – to treat administrative interpretations of the law with respect, as long as these are serious attempts to carry on the common, rule-of-law project.

As the issue of the duty to give reasons shows, the discharge of that onus requires public officials to become truly public, to emerge from the shadows. Indeed, that duty has often been imposed by legislatures rather

---

[57] As La Forest J put it in the first decision in a trilogy of cases where the Supreme Court of Canada decided that a tribunal could entertain a *Charter*-based challenge to a provision in its statute – *Douglas/Kwantlen Faculty Association* v. *Douglas College* [1990] 3 SCR 570 at 605. For my detailed discussion of these issues, see David Dyzenhaus, 'Constituting the Rule of Law: Fundamental Values in Administrative Law' (2001–02) 27 *Queen's Law Journal* 445–509.

than by judges, which has led lawyers to remark that, in the case of the duty to give reasons, it was Parliament that supplied the omission of the judges. This remark contains an important insight – that Parliament's intervention is often crucial to maintaining the rule of law. And the same point can be made about the executive, since it will often be the executive that either has to put flesh on the bones of the legislature's skeletal design of an institution or which has more or less to build its own skeleton in the light of experience. And with emergence from the shadows comes judicial scrutiny, but also, as I have tried to argue, judicial deference. The dangers of not seeing this last point are, as I will now show, nowhere better illustrated than in the story of the reaction after 9/11 by judiciaries across the Commonwealth.[58]

Emerging from the shadows

In chapter 1, I discussed briefly the House of Lords' decision in the Second World War detention case, *Liversidge v. Anderson*.[59] As we have seen, Brian Simpson, a leading scholar of the common law, argues that Lord Atkin's dissent in *Liversidge* is itself an example of judicial lip service to the rule of law – an attempt by a judge to shore up his sense of role in the face of the reality of necessarily untrammelled executive discretion.[60] It is important to know that the circumstances of Liversidge's detention order were such as to make it, as Simpson describes it, as 'at the least, very close to being an example of an order made in bad faith'.[61] And this was reflected in the fact that the grounds in fact given to Liversidge before the executive

---

[58] Of course, as I indicated in chapter 1, the same story can be told of the courts in the United States. For an excellent account, see Masur, 'A Hard Look or a Blind Eye' 441–521. Masur argues, as I do, that in general there is every reason for judges to extend their methods of upholding the rule of law in 'ordinary' administrative law to executive decisions in emergency type situations.

[59] *Liversidge v. Anderson* [1942] AC 206.   [60] Simpson, *In the Highest Degree Odious*.

[61] *Ibid.*, p. 421. Liversidge was detained because he had lied about his background in order to join the RAF – his date and place of birth. He wanted to surmount the obstacle that a police file had been opened on him as a result of his business connection in 1928 with two brothers who were tried on a charge of conspiracy to defraud. See *ibid.*, pp. 333–7. Simpson demonstrates that Liversidge's patriotic motives were impeccable as was his service before detention. But as his account also shows, Liversidge's business activities just prior to the war involved contacts with foreigners 'and no doubt some were dubious people'; in addition, he seemed to have some connection with British intelligence, passing information to them which he had gleaned in the course of his dealings: *ibid.*, p. 335. It would thus have been open, I think, to the Home Secretary to give very bare particulars of the grounds for suspicion in regard to Liversidge's 'hostile associations'.

committee set up to oversee the detention regime were either so irrelevant or so bare as to be, as Simpson, says 'offensive'.[62] Thus it seems clear that if the government's case for detention could have been tested in open court, it would have been exposed as one either in bad faith or so close to bad faith that it was unreasonable. But, Simpson says, Lord Atkin was content to require such reasons as the government was willing to supply as long as these went beyond a reiteration that there was reasonable cause to detain. Lord Atkin was then willing to bestow the aura of the rule of law on the detention as long as he could find a way to carve out a role within the legal process to do so.

There is, as I have already accepted, a serious challenge here to my or any other aspirational account of the rule of law. But I still think that Simpson underestimates the power of Lord Atkin's dissent, and I think that one can demonstrate that power by seeing an unnoticed area of agreement between Lord Atkin and the speech of Viscount Maugham.

Regulation 18B was made by Order in Council under the authority of the Emergency Powers (Defence) Act 1939. The statute authorized the making by Cabinet of regulations as 'appear . . . to be necessary or expedient for securing the public safety . . .' and specifically authorized regulations to be made 'for the detention of persons whose detention appears to the Secretary of State to be expedient in the interests of the public safety or the defence of the realm'. Regulation 18B provided:

> If the Secretary of State has reasonable cause to believe any person to be of hostile origins or associations or to have been recently concerned in acts prejudicial to public safety or the defence of the realm or in the preparation or instigation of such acts and that by reason thereof it is necessary to exercise control over him, he may make an order against that person directing that he be detained.

The only protection detainees had was that they could make representations to a three-person advisory committee, within the administration, whose chairman had to inform them of the grounds of their detention, so that they could make a case to the committee for their release. The Secretary of State could decline to follow the advice of the committee but had to report monthly to Parliament about the orders he had made and about whether he had declined to follow advice.

The issue before the Court was whether it could require particulars about the grounds of a detention in order to test its validity. As we have

[62] *Ibid.*, p. 339.

seen, the majority held it could not despite the fact that in order to head off a revolt in Parliament the phrase 'reasonable cause' in Regulation 18B had been substituted by an executive committee for the more subjective sounding 'if satisfied that' of the original regulation.[63] In the majority's view, if the minister produced an authenticated detention order, the detainee had the onus of establishing that the order was invalid or defective, basically showing that the minister had not acted in good faith.

In the leading judgment for the majority, Viscount Maugham recognized fully the change in wording in Regulation 18B and that other parts of the regulations generally adopted an 'if satisfied that . . .' form of wording. He also acknowledged that the regulation impacted on liberty. But he rejected Liversidge's argument that legislation dealing with the liberty of the subject 'must be construed, if possible, in favour of the subject and against the Crown'. Rather, following the majority in *Halliday*,[64] the First World War House of Lords' decision on detention, he said that this interpretative rule has 'no relevance in dealing with an executive measure by way of preventing a public danger'. The Court should adopt the 'universal presumption' that if there were reasonable doubt about the meaning of the words, it must follow the 'construction which will carry into effect the plain intention of those responsible for the Order in Council rather than one which will defeat that intention'.[65]

He reasoned that while the prima facie meaning of 'reasonable cause to believe' is, in the 'absence of a context', 'if there is in fact reasonable cause',

---

[63] Simpson *ibid.*, especially ch. 3, points out that the government effectively pulled the wool over the judges' eyes. While the statutory scheme required the Secretary of State to have reasonable grounds and to communicate those grounds to the chairman of the advisory committee, not only were the grounds not communicated to the appealing detainee, but the Chair was also not given the reasons. To find out the true grounds, the public officials would have had to be subpoenaed and questioned in court. It was for such reasons that Liversidge's lawyer, D. N. Pritt, brought an action for false imprisonment in order to test the ministerial practice of responding to habeas corpus applications by swearing an affidavit which simply asserted that the minister had reasonable grounds for his belief. That is, the plaintiff alleged that the defendant has without justification imprisoned him and so the defendant bore the onus of justifying the detention. Pritt says that the point was to get the minister to see that he could not 'slide out' by an affidavit, and therefore he would have to 'face up to the case, give his reasons, and let the Court judge of their reasonability'. 'At worst', the Court would clarify the matter by deciding that the words 'reasonable cause' did not 'carry the meaning they had hitherto carried'. He confidently expected a decision in his favour; D. N. Pritt, *The Autobiography of D. N. Pritt: Part One; From Right to Left* (London: Lawrence & Wishart, 1965), pp. 304–7. See further Simpson, *In the Highest Degree Odious*, ch. 17.

[64] *R* v. *Halliday, ex Parte Zadig* [1917] AC 260.   [65] *Liversidge*, at 218–19.

the words need not have only that meaning.[66] He found several reasons to support his conclusion that, in this context, 'reasonable cause to believe' means the more subjective if the official 'thinks' he has such cause. First, there was the fact that, in his view, no judicial control could be exercised over the second limb of Regulation 18B – that the Secretary of State believes that it is 'necessary to exercise control' over the person. Moreover, if that matter was left to the 'sole discretion' of the official, it followed that the same was 'true as all the facts which he must have reasonable cause to believe'. Second, the Secretary of State was not acting 'judicially' when he made the detention order – he could act on hearsay, was not required to obtain legal evidence or to hear the person's objections. Third, the Crown could refuse on the ground of privilege to disclose any evidence it wanted to keep confidential. Finally, the discretion was entrusted to a high member of government, responsible to Parliament.[67]

In response, Lord Atkin excoriated his fellow judges for returning the Court to the days of the Star Chamber, where subjects could be detained on the say-so of the executive. They had, he seemed to suggest, abdicated their constitutional role of standing 'between the subject and any attempted encroachments on his liberty by the executive, alert to see that any coercive action is justified in law'.[68] But he also laid great stress on the fact that 'reasonable cause to believe' was the form of words used, citing over almost ten pages of a twenty-two page judgment from the common law and statute to show that these words meant that a court was entitled to test the basis for the belief.[69]

Simpson is decidedly unimpressed by Lord Atkin's dissent. It is, he says, 'quite unconvincing, for it fails to explain with any clarity at all how the supervisory role of the courts was to operate, granted the right, which [Atkin] conceded, to withhold information of a confidential character'. In Simpson's view, Atkin's real concern was not liberty but role – Lord Atkin's sense that the executive was riding roughshod over judges. 'All that he seems to have wanted was for the Home Office to exhibit deference to the judges by being a little more forthcoming about the basis for detention orders'.[70]

Simpson also argues that the majority decision reflects the reality better, since the courts were not intended then, nor since, to have 'any significant role in the business of state security'. He recognizes that outside the field of security, a 'massive body' of law has been developed in which the courts

---

[66] *Ibid.*, at 219.   [67] *Ibid.*, at 220–2.   [68] *Ibid.*, at 244.   [69] *Ibid.*, at 227–36.
[70] Simpson, *In the Highest Degree Odious*, p. 363.

have 'an important role to play' in 'controlling the exercise of power'. 'Subject', he says, 'to the fact that Parliament can overrule them, the courts decide what their role is, and the principles they then formulate to express their role are called the law.'[71] But this law, or the rule of law, he seems to think is not transplantable to the security field because of the veil of secrecy the executive draws there. There the law, or the rule of law, has 'nothing to contribute'. In the 'conflict between secrecy and the rule of law secrecy wins'.[72]

Simpson's realism is very reluctant. He is far from trusting the security services since, as he says, 'they are in the business of constructing threats to security, and the weaker the evidence the more sinister the threat is thought to be'.[73] He also notes that secret administration is incompatible not only with the rule of law, but also with parliamentary control and sovereignty.[74] And in the closing pages of his book, he even seems to relent a bit in his harsh evaluation of the judges who tried ostensibly to impose the rule of law on the administration of Regulation 18B. They could, he said, have 'prised more information out of the executive . . . and thereby empowered themselves to exercise a greater degree of supervision'.[75]

A closer inspection of the reasoning in Lord Atkin's judgment reveals that he was rather more sensitive to the issue of privilege and confidentiality than Simpson allows. Lord Atkin noted that the chairman of the administrative committee before which the detainee appeared if he wished to object had to inform the detainee of the grounds on which the order had been made against him, grounds which the Secretary of State would have to convey. And he expressed puzzlement at the thought that there could be such a duty to inform the objector of the grounds before the committee, but that it was 'impossible in the public interest to furnish the objector with them in court'.[76]

In contrast, the much fuller grounds furnished to Ben Greene, in a case decided simultaneously with Liversidge satisfied Lord Atkin, and he drew from this inference that it was possible in many cases to furnish satisfactory grounds without raising issues of confidentiality. Further, he pointed out that often the issue would be protection of the confidentiality of informants rather than of the information. In addition, the courts had, in terms of s. 6 of the Emergency Powers (Defence) Act 1939, power to order a trial to be held in camera and he could not see why challenges to detention orders presented more difficulties than the trial of a spy.[77]

---

[71] *Ibid.*, p. 420.   [72] *Ibid.*, p. 421.   [73] *Ibid.*, p. 410.
[74] *Ibid.*, p. 421.   [75] *Ibid.*, pp. 420–1.   [76] *Liversidge*, at 240.   [77] *Liversidge*, at 241–2.

Moreover, in contrast to Viscount Maugham, Lord Atkin reasoned that if a stricter standard was appropriate to judge whether the detainee met the test, the decision about the necessity to control had to be subject to judicial scrutiny as well. While if there were reasonable grounds for the belief that would usually dispose of the matter, he contemplated circumstances where, despite the fact that someone was clearly of 'hostile origin', that person had lived in the country for so long and had a record of utter loyalty to it, so that it could not be thought necessary to detain him.[78]

Even more important than the fact that Lord Atkin's understanding of appropriate judicial scrutiny seems rather more realistic than Simpson allows, is that there is some agreement between him and Viscount Maugham. Unlike his fellow majority judges, Lords MacMillan and Wright, Viscount Maugham did not waffle in a self-exculpatory way about how he loved liberty as much as the next man, nor about how the advisory committee was in any case an adequate rule of law safeguard for the detainees. Rather, he reasoned from the fact that often information and sources would have to be confidential that it would be futile to try to impose a general requirement that the Secretary of State justify detention orders to a court. He also said that if an appeal against the Secretary of State's decision 'had been thought proper, it would have been to a special tribunal with power to inquire privately into all the reasons for the Secretary's action, but without any obligation to communicate them to the person detained'.[79]

The area of agreement between Viscount Maugham and Lord Atkin pertains to the fact that both think it possible to have such detentions reviewed and both agree that context is all important in determining if and how it is to be reviewed. The difference between them resides in interpretative approach. For Lord Atkin, the interpretative context is structured by the common law principles that he takes to be at stake: the general principle that executive decisions are subject to the control of the rule of law and the particular principle that judges should strain to find that liberty is protected rather than undermined by any legislative scheme. So he is prepared to go as far as he possibly can to implement review, even if the review that is possible is not very effective. For him, the very fact that an internal panel has been set up is a legislative signal or intimation that detention decisions are susceptible to review, even if the committee did not have the teeth to perform that review.

---

[78] *Ibid.*, at 243.   [79] *Ibid.*, at 220–2.

In contrast, Viscount Maugham holds that, with one qualification, all that matters is the explicit terms of the statute as well as the regulations made under its authority. The qualification is that the minister's decision has to be in good faith, although as both he and Lord Atkin point out, the decision will be presumed to be in good faith unless the applicant can bring evidence that displaces the presumption. And in the absence of a duty to give reasons or particulars justifying the detention order, the duty to act in good faith has no content. In Viscount Maugham's view, effective review requires that the legislature should establish a quasi-judicial panel with authority to inquire into confidential material. Judges should not attempt to turn themselves into such a panel, and the difficulties in the way of any such attempt serve for him as secondary indications that no intention to have judges review these decisions should be imputed to the legislature or the Cabinet.

My argument is that once one takes seriously Viscount Maugham's idea of the appropriate kind of review panel, one that would have to be set up by the legislature, then one should be able to see that that idea actually proves the power of Lord Atkin's dissent. The very reasons that operate as secondary considerations for Viscount Maugham's construction of legislative intention and for Simpson's critique of Lord Atkin's dissent – the factors that made judicial review rather ineffective – can be seen as the point of that dissent. If rule-of-law controls are appropriate, but very difficult to impose given the structure put in place by legislation, judges should try in so far as they can to impose such controls. They should do so not only to deal with the bad faith or close to bad faith cases such as Liversidge's, but also to send a message to the legislature (and Cabinet) that it is high time for it to put its house in order. That judges are only able partially to enforce the rule of law is hardly a reason not to enforce it. Rather, they should go as far as they can towards enforcing it, both because that is their duty to the individuals who would otherwise be subject to executive whim and arbitrariness and because they should send a message to the legislature about the need for it to cooperate better in maintaining the rule of law. This message requires a rather different tone from Lord Atkin's judgment, as he tended to blame the executive and his fellow judges for Liversidge's plight, rather than the legislature and the Cabinet. Simpson is therefore right in so far as Lord Atkin suggests much too strongly that all is well with the rule of law as long as judges will not be satisfied by mere executive say-so.

On the view which I am developing, Lord Atkin would have been justified in reaching his conclusion even had Regulation 18B retained its original 'if satisfied that . . .' wording. In his judgment, he makes too much of 'reasonable cause to believe'. His citation of chapter and verse from legislation and the common law makes it look like he is grasping at a straw rather than making an argument from the position of strength of which 'reasonable cause to believe' was not the basis, but the evidence. This argument from strength would accept Viscount Maugham's claim that words receive their meaning in context. But it would also insist that the context is set by the rule of law, unless the legislation explicitly excludes the rule of law from operating.

'If satisfied that' does no more to exclude the rule of law from operating than does a privative clause, a statutory provision which seeks to exclude judicial review. Only a substantive privative clause, a provision which precludes judges from relying on particular principles of the rule of law as grounds of review, might exclude the constitutional rule of law approach which I think is the proper basis of Lord Atkin's judgment. Moreover, once that approach sets the context, 'reasonable cause to believe' is simply a confirmation from the legislative scheme of the constitutional basis for the scheme which the judge must assume to be in place until the legislature explicitly states otherwise. It is a legislative intimation of legality which a judge should take into account, but not as a decisive factor. It is important for the judge to signal, as we saw Rand J do in *Roncarelli*, that the basis for the judge's reasoning is the constitution so that legislative intimations of legality count only as evidence.

It was of course the case that it was the executive and not the legislature which made this intimation. Lord Atkin dealt with this fact by simply deeming the executive's intention to be the same as that of the legislature,[80] while Viscount Maugham chose to claim that the fact that the change in wording was made by the executive meant that less significance should be attributed to it than to a change in the drafting of legislation, which, he suggested would receive more attention.[81] However, it was well known that the change in wording happened because of parliamentary unease with an uncontrolled power to detain. While the executive might have thought it had achieved a compromise that successfully fudged the issue without in fact putting in place an explicit review mechanism, such fudges are not legally insignificant, if one adopts the constitutional approach to the rule of law.

The weaknesses in Lord Atkin's judgment do not so much inhere in its basis as in the fact that his excessive reliance on the wording of

---

[80] *Ibid.*, at 232.   [81] *Ibid.*, at 233.

Regulation18B derives, in my view, from embarrassment. As I have noted in chapter 1, and as he himself acknowledged,[82] the First World War decision of the majority of the House of Lords in *Halliday* affirmed the decision of a lower court of which he was a member. But Lord Atkin was unable to rely on Lord Shaw's dissent in *Halliday*, since he was committed to regarding it as irrelevant to his present concerns. He thus studiously avoided relying on Lord Shaw's sophisticated account of the common law approach to adjudication on matters of national security. Only this aspect of his position can explain the tension between the most famous lines of his dissent – 'In this country, amid the clash of arms the laws are not silent. They may be changed, but they speak the same language in war as in peace' and his suggestion that in wartime judges should 'perhaps' not lean towards protecting liberty.[83]

Recall that in *Halliday*, the question facing the House of Lords was not the interpretation of a regulation which authorized indefinite detention but whether the Defence of the Realm Consolidation Act 1914 authorized the government to make a detention regulation at all. The Act empowered the government to issue regulations which would secure 'the public safety and the defence of the realm'. It also provided that the government could authorize the trial and punishment of those found to have contravened such regulations. Among the regulations made by the government was Regulation 14B, which empowered the Secretary of State to order the internment of any person 'of hostile origin or associations' when 'it appears to [him]' that this is 'expedient for securing the public safety or the defence of the realm'. And, as in the scheme set up in the Second World War, the only recourse a detainee had was to an executive advisory committee.

In his dissent, Lord Shaw treated the matter as one of ordinary statutory interpretation, different only in so far as the power the regulation purported to confer had special dangers. 'Whether the Government has exceeded its statutory mandate is a question of ultra or intra vires such as that which is now being tried. In so far as the mandate has been exceeded, there lurk the elements of a transition to arbitrary government and therein of grave constitutional and public danger'.[84]

Lord Shaw was, however, was careful to explain that his judgment should not be taken as implying a hostility to regulation as such. Rather, much more than the judges in the majority, he went to great effort to understand the statutory scheme as a whole. On the basis of that scheme,

---

[82] *Ibid.*, at 238.   [83] *Ibid.*   [84] *Halliday*, at 287.

it seemed that the statute authorized the government to make regulations to secure public safety and defence and, in order to make such a scheme effective, it was also provided that violations of the regulations would be charged and punished, by summary trial, or by a court-martial, or by a jury:

> 'Regulation' means . . . the formulation of rules in the interests of public safety or defence . . . in obedience to which the citizens may co-operate for these ends, and for disobedience to which they may be punished. But the regulation now challenged is not of that character. It is not the formulation of a rule of action, behaviour or conduct to be obeyed by the citizen; but it is for the summary arrest and detention of his person, grounded, and grounded alone, on the subject's hostile origin and association.[85]

It followed from that fact that the regulation to detain people suspected of being of hostile origin or associations was not a regulation authorized by the Act. Parliament would not have gone to such great lengths to stipulate the impact violations would have on the interest in liberty if it had intended that the executive could set itself up as the arbiter of when and how deprivations of liberty should take place.

Only two arguments could, he thought, support the conclusion that the government had the authority to make such a regulation. The first was that that the government had the power in virtue of the prerogative. But, said Lord Shaw, the validity depended on a statute and if the prerogative were permitted to get 'into association with executive acts done apart from clear parliamentary authority' it would be 'an evil day; that way lies revolution'.[86]

The second argument was that the government had been delegated the authority to do as it liked, to act arbitrarily. Lord Shaw said that if this were so, then the power must logically extend to summary execution, and he reported that the Attorney-General had accepted this point.[87] The government would then be a modern equivalent of the Star Chamber and, quoting from Maitland's *Constitutional History of England*, it would, said Lord Shaw, be 'a court of politicians enforcing a policy, not a court of judges administering the law'.[88] This 'basic danger', Lord Shaw said, 'is found in especial degree whenever the law is not the same for all, but the selection of the victim is left to the plenary discretion whether of a tyrant,

---

[85] *Ibid.*, at 288–9.   [86] *Ibid.*, at 286–7.   [87] *Ibid.*, at 290–1.

[88] *Ibid.*, at 292. Lord Shaw has the quote wrong. It is: 'It was a court of politicians enforcing a policy, not a court of judges enforcing the law'; F. W. Maitland, *The Constitutional History of England* (Cambridge: Cambridge University Press, 1950), p. 263.

a committee, a bureaucracy or any other depositary of despotic power. Whoever administers it, this power of selection of a class, and power of selection within a class is the negation of public safety or defence. It is poison to the commonwealth'.[89]

Lord Shaw's reasoning supplies the premise which is not entirely artic-ulated in Lord Atkin's dissent. Legislation is legitimate only on condition that it does not grossly offend fundamental common law principles, and so judges should interpret legislation in light of such principles. Draw-ing on Blackstone, Lord Shaw reasons that the right to habeas corpus is of such fundamental importance to the constitution that judges will not allow it to be abridged except by express, unambiguous intention. As he put it, the judicial stance should be that 'if Parliament had intended to make this colossal delegation of power it would have done so plainly and courageously and not under cover of words about regulations for safety and defence'.[90] For judges to allow the right to be abridged is to revolutionize the constitution, perhaps, more accurately to undertake a counter-revolution. It amounts to what he called a 'constructive repeal of habeas corpus',[91] a repeal by the executive which is then ratified by judges. He would, he said, have come to his conclusion even though the language of the state 'had been much more plain and definite than it is'.[92]

However, even if one grants Lord Shaw's assumption, the question remains of how to follow through on that assumption. This ques-tion was perceptively raised in 1957 in a monograph which appears largely forgotten: John Eaves, Jr, *Emergency Powers and the Parliamentary Watchdog: Parliament and the Executive in Great Britain, 1939–1951*.[93] In his discussion of Regulation 18B, Eaves mentions the view of Sidney Sil-verman, a Member of Parliament, that when the words 'reasonable cause to believe' were substituted 'we all thought that was giving the courts a power to control what happens. That is why we altered it'.[94] But he also quotes the view of Lord Chorley to the effect that 'too much was given away' in the change. Lord Chorley says that had Lord Atkin's view pre-vailed, 'the result would have been an amendment of the regulation so as to bring it into accord with the needs of the situation'.[95]

Eaves seems at times to agrees with Chorley that judges are incapable of exercising a review authority over this category of executive decisions, and

---

[89] *Halliday*, at 292.   [90] *Ibid.*, at 291–2.   [91] *Ibid.*, at 294.   [92] *Ibid.*, at 293.
[93] (London: The Hansard Society for Parliamentary Government, 1957.)
[94] *Ibid.*, p. 51, note 3.
[95] *Ibid.*, p. 51, note 4, quoting from Lord Chorley, 'Law-Making in White Hall' (1946) 58 *Modern Law Review* 26–41 at 40.

so he thinks that trust has to be placed in Parliament to rein in the executive in exceptional times. Like Keith Ewing and Conor Gearty writing some forty years later,[96] his argument is that generally speaking Parliament did a reasonable job. But he stresses that one should not rely too heavily on members of the opposition being able to force the government to account for its actions, especially since in moments of great stress, the tendency will be for members of Parliament to rally round the flag, often in a government of national unity.

Thus he concludes his study with an inquiry into the way in which standing parliamentary committees can make the process of bringing officials to account internal to the workings of Parliament. In his view, such committees are essential to the 'future effectiveness of the House of Commons'.[97] It is their work which indicates that those 'who mourn the passing of Parliament have perhaps donned their black suits prematurely'. He takes from Sir Cecil Carr the observation that writers on the British Constitution must 'always be wary' since 'it does not stand still long enough to be photographed. Furnishings are constantly being shifted about on the stage; the decline of one safeguard may find another unobtrusively taking its place; but the stage is cluttered, and it is easy for the observer to be misled'.[98]

In the next section, I will show that Eaves was right, except that he did not see that essential to a well furnished state is an institution which can do the task that he thought impossible – the task of effectively reviewing the executive in national security matters. But, as will be clear, I do not want to underestimate the obstacles in the way of that insight, obstacles which persist to this day.

In the black hole

As Simpson has argued, political reality seems to triumph again and again over any effort to impose the rule of law in exceptional situations. He quotes as a reflection of this reality, Lord Denning's dictum in 1977 in *R* v. *Secretary of State, ex parte Hosenball*:[99] 'There is a conflict between the interests of national security on the one hand and the freedom of the individual on the other. The balance between these two is not for a court of law. It is for the Home Secretary. He is the person entrusted by Parliament with the task.'[100]

---

[96] See Ewing and Gearty, *The Struggle for Civil Liberties.*
[97] Eaves, *Emergency Powers*, p. 195.   [98] *Ibid.*, pp. 195–6.   [99] [1977] 1 WLR 766.
[100] Simpson, *In the Highest Degree Odious*, p. 419.

This case concerned the deportation of an American journalist on alleged national security grounds. Those subject to deportation on national security grounds had been statutorily deprived of the right of appeal that individuals subject to deportation on other grounds enjoyed and their only recourse was to an advisory procedure modelled on that set up to administer Regulation 18B. Hosenball argued that the common law required that he have a hearing from the minister prior to deportation.

Lord Denning recognized that if the case were an 'ordinary one' it might be thought appropriate that judicial review was in order on the basis of the common law principle that one is entitled to a hearing before the decision-maker who is to make the decision which affects one's fundamental interests. But because the context was national security, things were different: 'our history shows that, when the state itself is endangered, our cherished freedoms may have to take second place. Even natural justice itself may suffer a set-back. Time after time Parliament has so enacted and the courts have loyally followed'. And in support of these claims, he not only quoted with evident approval from the majority judgments in *Liversidge* and *Halliday*, but said that while these were wartime cases, 'times of peace hold their dangers too. Spies, subverters and saboteurs may be mingling among us, putting on a most innocent exterior'.[101] He did recognize that this meant that the liberty-interests of the individuals affected were at the mercy of the Home Secretary. But he then indulged, as Simpson puts it, in some 'rhetorical rubbish',[102] by saying that England was not like other parts of the world where national security has been used as 'an excuse for all sorts of infringements of individual liberty', since in England 'successive ministers have discharged their duties to the complete satisfaction of the people at large'.[103]

While Lord Denning was egregious in his willingness openly to renege on his duty to uphold the rule of law, an inspection of other decisions in the area of national security reveals a consistent pattern of executive-minded decisions in the national security area. In addition, when developments in 'normal' administrative law – when the issue was not national security – made it inevitable that judges asserted a comprehensive authority to control public power in general, including the prerogative, they also said eventually that the prerogative to deal with national security is subject to the rule of law and thus to judicial review. But in the same breath they said that the executive say-so as to what was required in the interests of

---

[101] *Hosenball*, at 778.
[102] Simpson, *In the Highest Degree Odious*, p. 421.   [103] *Hosenball*, at 783.

national security must prevail. In other words, they reinvented the prerogative under the guise of a doctrine of judicial deference.[104]

In the result, there appeared a bifurcated approach. In normal or ordinary administrative law, Lord Atkin's dissent was often cited, and if the prerogative were discussed, then Blackstone's definition of the prerogative which assumes that it is controlled by law was preferred to Locke's, which asserts that the prerogative is beyond law's control.[105] If national security was in issue, then, either explicitly or implicitly, Locke was preferred to Blackstone and the majority in *Liversidge* to the dissent.[106]

Nor have things changed in what one could think of as the United Kingdom's human rights era, the period in which the United Kingdom joined those countries which have constitutionalized human rights by enacting the Human Rights Act 1998. Prior to its enactment, in *Chahal* v. *UK*,[107] the European Court of Human Rights had rejected the United Kingdom's argument that national security grounds are inherently incapable of being tested in a court of law and held that the advisory panel

---

[104] *Council of Civil Service Unions* v. *Minister for the Civil Service* [1985] AC 374. For discussion, see David Dyzenhaus, *Hard Cases in Wicked Legal Systems: South African Law in the Perspective of Legal Philosophy* (Oxford: Oxford University Press, 1991), ch. 8.

[105] Blackstone in fact rather mischievously redefines Locke. Locke's definition was: 'This power to act according to discretion for the publick good, without the prescription of the Law and sometimes even against it, *is* that which is called *Prerogative*.' Locke, *Two Treatises*, p. 375. Blackstone said that the prerogative consists '(as Mr Locke has well defined it) in the discretionary power of acting for the public good, where the positive laws are silent, if that discretionary power be abused to the public detriment, such prerogative is issued in an unconstitutional manner'; Sir William Blackstone, *Commentaries on the Laws of England* (Chicago: University of Chicago Press, 1977), vol. I, p. 244.

[106] Lord Denning more than any other judge exemplified this bifurcation. In the same year in which his decision in *Hosenball* is reported, in a case of review of executive discretion affecting commercial interests, he quoted Blackstone with approval and said the following:

> It is a serious matter for the courts to declare that a minister of the Crown has exceeded his powers. So serious that we think hard about doing it. But there comes a point when it has to be done. The courts have the authority – and I would add, the duty – in a proper case, when called upon to inquire into the exercise of a discretionary power by a minister or his department. If it found that the power has been exercised improperly or mistakenly so as to impinge unjustly on the legitimate rights or interests of the subject, then these courts must so declare. They stand as, between the executive and the subject, as Lord Atkin said in a famous passage – 'alert to see that any coercive action is justified in law' . . . To which, I would add, alert to see that a discretionary power is not exceeded or misused. See *Laker Airways Ltd.* v. *Department of Trade* [1977] QB 643 at 705, 707–8.

[107] (1996) 23 EHRR 413.

for those subject to deportation on national security grounds did not give the 'effective remedy' required by Article 13 of the European Convention on Human Rights and Fundamental Freedoms.[108]

The UK government responded through Parliament with a statute in 1997 which established the Special Immigration Appeals Commission (SIAC), a three-person panel of which one member had to have held high judicial office, the second had to have been the chief adjudicator or a legally qualified member of the Immigration Appeals Tribunal, while the third would ordinarily be someone with experience of national security matters. The 1997 statute gave the individual who would have had the right to appeal against a deportation order but for the fact that national security was involved a right to appeal to SIAC and SIAC itself the authority to review the Secretary of State's decision on the law and the facts as well as the question whether the discretion should have been exercised differently. There was a further appeal to the Court of Appeal on 'any question of law material to' SIAC's determination. In addition, the statute provided for the appointment of a special advocate who could represent the appellant if parts of the proceedings before SIAC took place in closed session because it was considered necessary to keep information confidential. SIAC's decision is based on both the closed and the open session though its reasons do not disclose information from the closed sessions.

SIAC thus seems to be an answer to Lord Atkin's, Viscount Maugham's and Simpson's concerns: it is seized of jurisdiction through a statutory right of appeal; it has the explicit authority and the necessary expertise to review security decisions; it has before it the information on which the executive and the security services act, which is partly tested even if it is highly confidential. At least, it is the answer unless Simpson is right that judges are less motivated by a concern for the rule of law than about their place in the hierarchy of legal order, in which case the creation of such a body might be seen as an occasion for judicial perplexity, perhaps even jealousy.

Either perplexity or jealousy seem at least a small part of the explanation of the House of Lords' decision in *Secretary of State for the Home Department* v. *Rehman*,[109] though most of the explanation, in my view, has to reside in judicial loss of nerve. Here SIAC had rejected the government's

---

[108] The Convention for the Protection on Human Rights and Fundamental Freedoms also known as the European Convention on Human Rights, Rome, 4 November 1950, in force 3 September 1953, 213 UNTS 221.

[109] [2002] 1 All ER 123.

argument that the question of what could constitute a threat to national security was a matter for the exclusive decision of the Secretary of State. It said that the definition of national security was a question of law which it had jurisdiction to decide. It then found that the Secretary of State had interpreted the phrase 'national security' too widely since, properly understood, Rehman's alleged activities did not affect the United Kingdom's national security. National security, according to the Commission, included only activity which 'targeted the United Kingdom' or UK citizens 'wherever they may be', or activities against a foreign government which 'might take reprisals' against the United Kingdom. In addition, it found that the specific allegations against Rehman did not meet the test it deemed appropriate in such cases, which it termed a test of a 'high civil balance of probabilities', and it suggested that this failure occurred whether one adopted the Secretary of State's wide or its own narrow definition of national security.

The House of Lords held, on separation of powers grounds, that it was for the executive to decide what is in the interests of national security and on the issue of the particular allegations against an individual that these must stand unless they can be shown to be absurd. Most remarkably, Lord Hoffmann closed his speech with this passage:

> *Postscript*– I wrote this speech some three months before the recent events in New York and Washington. They are a reminder that in matters of national security, the cost of failure can be high. This seems to me to underline the need for the judicial arm of government to respect the decisions of ministers of the Crown on the question of whether support for terrorist activities in a foreign country constitutes a threat to national security. It is not only that the executive has access to special information and expertise in these matters. It is also that such decisions, with serious potential results for the community, require a legitimacy which can be conferred only by entrusting them to persons responsible to the community through the democratic process. If the people are to accept the consequences of such decisions, they must be made by persons whom the people have elected and whom they can remove.[110]

In taking this stance, the Court refuses to concede to SIAC the capacity to be a more effective enforcer of the rule of law than a generalist court which has at its disposal only the resources of the common law.[111] To bolster its sense of place in the legal order, the Court first interprets the legislation as giving courts some review authority, though one which clearly undersells the resources of the common law: courts can review only

---

[110] *Rehman*, at 142.   [111] See Lord Hoffmann *ibid.*, especially at 138–9.

if decisions are manifestly absurd. But in the same cause, the Court then cuts down SIAC's authority to fit the Court's parsimonious understanding of its own role. Given the generous delegation of authority to SIAC, the result is little different from that of the majority's claim in *Liversidge* that detention orders were not arbitrary since the courts could still check that they were made in good faith.

The question why this Court did not give full effect to the legislative message becomes even more pressing when one notes that two of the judges on this bench – Lords Steyn and Hoffmann – are responsible for articulating a principle of legality in ordinary administrative law which requires that all executive acts be demonstrated to be justifiable in law, where law is assumed to include fundamental values.[112] The puzzle, then, is why these two judges find that in some cases that they are driven to constitutional bedrock, which they find to be full of values and principles, while in others they find that the constitution amounts only to a very rigid doctrine of the separation of powers.

One response to this puzzle would be to point out that in the cases where this principle of legality was articulated, the people affected by the decisions were citizens of the United Kingdom whose fundamental rights – liberty, freedom of expression, and access to the courts – were affected by the executive decisions. This response is reinforced by Lord Woolf's judgment in *Belmarsh*, or *A v. Secretary of State for the Home Department*,[113] a decision which denies the rule-of-law value of equality before the law in accepting that non-citizens may be legitimately treated as not being full bearers of human rights.[114] It is also reinforced by the decision of Canada's Supreme Court in *Suresh*, the decision which I have

---

[112] Thus in *R v. Secretary of State for the Home Department, ex parte Pierson*, Lord Steyn said that 'Parliament does not legislate in a vacuum' but 'for a European liberal democracy founded on the principles and traditions of the common law' [1998] AC 539 at 587. And in *R v. Secretary of State, ex parte Simms*, [2000] 2 AC 115 at 131, Lord Hoffmann said that while Parliament can override fundamental rights, the principle of legality means that 'Parliament must squarely confront what it is doing and accept the political cost. Fundamental rights cannot be overridden by general or ambiguous words. This is because there is too great a risk that the full implications of their unqualified meaning may have passed unnoticed in the democratic process. In the absence of express language or necessary implication to the contrary, the courts therefore presume that even the most general words were intended to be subject to the basic rights of the individual. In this way the courts of the United Kingdom, though acknowledging the sovereignty of Parliament, apply principles of constitutionality little different from those which exist in countries where the power of the legislature is expressly limited by a constitutional document.'

[113] [2002] EWCA Civ 1502.

[114] For a similar stance, see the Australian decision *Al-Kateb v. Godwin* (2004) 208 ALR 124 discussed in ch. 2.

pointed out earlier signals the Canadian Supreme Court's post-9/11 loss of nerve, and in which Lord Hoffmann's postscript to *Rehman* was quoted with approval.[115]

There are at the moment two rays of light, the first of which is the decision of the House of Lords which overturned Lord Woolf's judgment in *Belmarsh*, which I will discuss at the beginning of chapter 4. The other is the English Court of Appeal's decision in *Abbasi*.[116] Here the Court had to deal with the detention of Mr Abbasi in what it described as a 'legal back hole'.[117] Abbasi was one of a number of British citizens captured by American forces in Afghanistan and transferred to Guantanamo Bay, an area controlled by the United States and so beyond the jurisdiction of English courts. Challenges in the courts in the United States had led nowhere, as, on the Court of Appeal's description, these courts had held that the 'legality' of the detention of foreign nationals rested 'solely on the dictate of the United States government, and, unlike that of United States' citizens, is said to be immune from review in any court or independent forum'.[118]

Abbasi's lawyers sought a finding from the Court that the Foreign Secretary owed Abbasi a duty to respond positively to his and his mother's request for diplomatic assistance. Two obstacles seemed to stand in Abbasi's way. First, the principle of comity requires that an English court will not examine the legitimacy of action taken by a foreign sovereign state. Second, an English court will not adjudicate upon actions taken by the executive in the exercise of its prerogative to conduct foreign relations.

In response to the first obstacle, the Court relied on previous authority in accepting Abbasi's contention that 'where fundamental human rights are in play, the courts of this country will not abstain from reviewing the legitimacy of the actions of a foreign sovereign state'.[119] Lord Phillips then went on to accept the argument that Abbasi's detention contravened 'fundamental principles recognised by both jurisdictions and by international law'. He referred here to both common law and US constitutional

---

[115] *Suresh*, at 25.   [116] *R (Abbasi)* v. *Secretary of State* [2003] 3 LRC 297.

[117] *Ibid.*, at 322.   [118] *Ibid.*, at 323.

[119] *Ibid.*, at 319. One of the authorities relied upon was the famous decision of the House of Lords in *Oppenheim* v. *Cattermole* [1976] AC 249, a decision in which the Court had to decide whether a decree passed in Germany in 1941 which deprived Jews who had emigrated from Germany of their citizenship should be recognized by the English court. Lord Phillips quoted at length the passage from Lord Cross' judgment at 277 which ends with this line: 'To my mind a law of this sort constitutes so grave an infringement of human rights that the courts of this country ought to refuse to recognise it as law at all.'

law[120] and to the International Covenant on Civil and Political Rights[121] which, in Article 4, provides the right of a detainee to have access to a court to decide on the lawfulness of his detention and, in Article 2, requires that the parties (which include the United States and the United Kingdom), ensure that the rights protected by the Covenant are accorded to all individuals 'without distinction of any kind, such as . . . national origin . . .'[122]

In responding to the argument about the non-justiciability of the foreign affairs prerogative, the Court rejected arguments that either the European Convention on Human Rights or the Human Rights Act 1998 supported the contention that the Foreign Secretary owed Abbasi a duty to exercise diplomacy on his behalf. But the Court did not conclude that therefore the government was right that decisions by the executive are non-justiciable when these pertain to its dealings with foreign states regarding the protection of British nationals abroad. Rather, the Court drew on *Council of Civil Service Unions* v. *Minister for the Civil Service*[123] for the following two propositions. First, the doctrine of legitimate expectation 'provides a well-established and flexible means for giving legal effect to a settled policy or practice for the exercise of an administrative discretion'. The expectation, which may arise from an express promise or the existence of a regular practice, is not necessarily that the promise will be fulfilled or the practice continue, but that the subject is entitled to have the promise or practice properly considered before any change is made.[124] Second, the mere fact that a power derives from the royal prerogative does not 'necessarily exclude it from the scope of judicial review'; rather, the issue of justiciability 'depends, not on general principle, but on subject matter and suitability in the particular case'.[125] Here the Court referred to one of its prior decisions where it was accepted, following the Australian High Court's decision in *Teoh*,[126] that ratification by the United Kingdom of an international convention could in principle create a legitimate expectation.[127]

---

[120] To Lord Atkin's dissent in *Liversidge* and to a dictum of Justice Brennan for the US Supreme Court in 1963, where Brennan adopted the claim of an English judge that habeas corpus was 'a writ antecedent to statute, and throwing its root deep into the genius of our common law', *Fay* v. *Noia*, 372 US 391 (1963) at 400, adopting Lord Birkenhead LC, in *Secretary of State* v. *O' Brien* [1923] AC 603 at 609.

[121] International Covenant on Civil and Political Rights, New York, 16 December 1966, in force 23 March 1976, 999 UNTS 171.

[122] *Abbasi*, at 322.   [123] See note 104 above.   [124] *Abbasi*, at 327.   [125] *Ibid.*, at 327–8.

[126] *Minister for Immigration and Ethnic Affairs* v. *Teoh* (1994-95) 183 CLR 273.

[127] *Abbasi*, at 311, citing *R* v. *Home Secretary, ex parte Ahmed and Patel* [1998] INLR 570 at 584.

The Court then noted that the Foreign and Commonwealth Office had a policy of assisting British citizens abroad when there is evidence of miscarriage or denial of justice. Since in Abassi's case, the denial was of a fundamental right, it followed that he had a legitimate expectation that the government would 'consider' making representations.[128] A British citizen had a legitimate expectation that if he is 'subjected abroad to a violation of a fundamental right, the British government will not simply wash their hands of the matter and abandon him to his fate'.[129] The Court stressed the limited nature of the expectation: the individual's request will be properly considered, that is, weighed against all the other non-justiciable and highly sensitive political factors.[130] The 'extreme case', the one where judges should make a mandatory order that the Foreign Office give due consideration to the applicant's case, would lie if the Office were, 'contrary to its stated practice, to refuse even to consider whether to make diplomatic representations on behalf of a subject whose fundamental rights were being violated'. Finally, the Court expressed its confidence that the appellate courts in the United States would prove to have the 'same respect for human rights as our own' and it noted that the Inter-American Commission on Human Rights had 'taken up the case of the detainees', though it was 'yet unclear what the result of the Commission's intervention would be'.[131]

The Court is thus engaged in a process of letting the executive know that it would be concerned if the executive departed from its practice and it is also sending a disapproving message to the government and courts of the United States, a message which it is worth noting has been strongly reinforced by Lord Steyn, who has made speeches in which he has suggested to both the US Supreme Court and his own that they put their rule-of-law house in order.[132] There is, however, more to the judgment than that.

As Charlotte Kilroy has pointed out,[133] the Court left open the possibility of more intrusive review in other circumstances, for example, if there were no outstanding court actions in regard to Abbasi, it might be thought appropriate for Abbasi to have a legitimate expectation that went beyond a mere 'consideration' of his case. But, as she also points out, the significance of the decision lies in its 'clear signal that where fundamental

---

[128] *Abbasi*, at 331.   [129] *Ibid.*, at 331.   [130] *Ibid.*, at 331.   [131] *Ibid.*, at 332.

[132] Johan Steyn, 'Guantanamo Bay: The Legal Black Hole' (2004) 53 *International and Comparative Law Quarterly* 1–15.

[133] Charlotte Kilroy, '*R. (on the application of Abbasi) v. Secretary of State for Foreign and Commonwealth Affairs*: Reviewing the Prerogative' (2003) 2 *European Human Rights Law Review* 222–9.

human rights are at stake, the courts will be reluctant to allow the government to hide too far behind its prerogative power',[134] and, I would add, reluctant to allow foreign governments to hide behind the doctrine of comity. And I think it is this issue that explains Lord Phillips' reference to the role of international human rights conventions in legitimately influencing a court's understanding of the legitimate expectations that individuals have. This reference is the only loose end in an otherwise very tight set of reasons, unless one takes it as a general placeholder for the Court's acceptance of the argument put forward by Nicholas Blake for Abbasi that the 'increased regard paid to human rights in both international and domestic law'[135] meant that international law could no longer be regarded as a matter of relations between states but as giving 'rise to individual rights'.[136] These rights might not manifest themselves in the domestic legal order as enforceable duties, but still can play a role in controlling public authorities.

The message of *Abbasi* is complex. On the one hand, the Court seems to be extending judicial control of the prerogative even further. The Court is engaged in a process of intimation different from a legislative or executive signal to the judiciary. The judges are letting the executive know that they would be concerned if it departed from its practice and they are also sending a disapproving message to the government and to the courts of the United States.

On the other hand, if one looks at the decision in the context of *Rehman* and the Court of Appeal's decision in *Belmarsh*, it might seem that the Court is willing to rely on the dissent in *Liversidge* and on the jurisprudence of normal or ordinary administrative law in security matters only when this makes no difference, when it can affirm the value of a practice in which the executive is already engaged. The Court also left rather unclear what its stance would be if the executive announced that it would no longer make it a practice to intervene in such cases.

Just this tactic was unsuccessfully adopted by the Australian government in the wake of the Australian decision on which the Court of Appeal relied, *Teoh*. In *Teoh*, the High Court of Australia held that executive ratification of a human rights treaty created a legitimate expectation that the rights would be taken into account by administrative decision-makers despite the fact that the treaty had not been incorporated by domestic legislation. Two of the judges suggested that it would be hypocritical for the government to do otherwise, in my terms, to intimate its respect for human rights to the international legal order but to refuse to live up to

---

[134] *Ibid.*, 229.   [135] *Abbasi*, at 310.   [136] *Ibid.*, at 314.

its commitments when it came to decisions within the domestic legal order.[137] The Australian government made a formal statement disavowing any domestic effect to ratification of treaties prior to their statutory incorporation. But, perhaps realizing that this statement merely heightened the hypocrisy, thus leaving judges the opportunity to choose the better face of government – the face turned to the international community – the government also announced that it would introduce legislation to enforce its stance. However, it has failed on more than one occasion to follow through on its threat.

Consider for a moment just how odd the situation would be if the government were to follow through. Once a government ratifies a treaty, there is a firm expectation that eventually there will be explicit incorporation of the treaty into domestic law. Indeed, it is customary before ratification for the government to undertake an internal audit to check that its domestic law is not in conflict with the international obligations it wished formally to recognize. Thus for a government to initiate legislation that disavows that recognition would be so odd that the term hypocrisy does not quite describe the situation.

The failure of the Australian government to renege on its self-incurred obligations is significant. It seems to show that once the executive steps onto the rule-of-law path, judges can, if they have the nerve, keep it on that path until the point when the legislature at considerable cost in terms of its domestic and international reputation orders the executive to step off.

Thus one can concede that the control in *Abbasi* is procedural and so very easily satisfied. But if that control is seen as purely procedural only because it is at the outer reaches of legal order since Abbasi was under the control of a foreign government, and if judges demonstrate their willingness to exercise more substantive controls as one moves within the sphere of national sovereignty, then even pure proceduralism does not look like window dressing or lip service. Moreover, Lord Phillips' judgment suggests that even beyond the outer reach there is no black hole, as international institutions might play a role and the courts of the foreign jurisdiction might come to their rule-of-law senses. It is the creation of the black hole within the sphere of national sovereignty that is the real problem and that issue boils down, as I just suggested, to failure of judicial nerve.

The invocation of the rigid doctrine of the separation of powers and a stance of submissive deference which we saw in *Rehman*, which has

---

[137] *Teoh*, at 291, judgment of Mason CJ and Deane J.

been echoed by the Canadian Supreme Court in its own retreat from the rule of law in national security cases, is merely the cover for this loss of nerve. It results in an inappropriately pure proceduralism, proceduralism where something more substantive is required, and it contradicts the development in both jurisdictions of a robust understanding of principles of the rule of law which are the basis of governmental accountability. Here it is important to recall the point I made earlier about the Canadian retreat from the understanding of the rule of law articulated in *Baker*. Review which applies a standard akin to *Wednesbury* unreasonableness, one which requires that officials merely go through the motions of justification, is no less purely procedural than a hearing requirement which requires that officials merely go through the motions of a hearing. Moreover, the legitimacy of judges holding government to account has been signalled not only by after the fact acquiescence by both legislatures and executives, but also by positive steps by these branches of government at the domestic and the international level to increase the reach and intensity of control by the rule of law.

It is not only institutions such as SIAC that I have in mind. Even more significant, as Eaves predicted, is the phenomenon of parliamentary committees which seek to make scrutiny of legislation and executive action for its compliance with the rule of law and human rights norms into a matter internal to the workings of the legislature. Most notable here is the Joint Committee on Human Rights, which came into being in 2001 after the passage of the Human Rights Act 1998. That committee has twelve members, six from the House of Lords and six from the Commons, and its task is to scrutinize every Bill for compliance with the European Convention on Human Rights and six international human rights instruments whose obligations have been accepted by the United Kingdom. The committee works under the direction of a Legal Adviser and it is important to know that the first adviser, David Feldman, and the second and present adviser, Murray Hunt, are among the leading human rights lawyers in the United Kingdom. At their prompting, the committee has become very active in requiring public officials at the highest level to respond to human rights concerns before a bill becomes law. It thus brings human rights concerns into the legislative process properly so called.[138] It requires that process attempt to be a fully deliberative one where appropriate attention is paid

---

[138] See David Feldman, 'The Impact of Human Rights on the UK Legislative Process' (2004) 25 *Statute Law Review* 91–115 and Robert Hazell, 'Who is the Guardian of Legal Values in the Legislative Process: Parliament or the Executive?' [2004] *Public Law* 495–500.

to the impact of public power on human rights before a decision is taken to exert or delegate authority.

There is also the Select Committee on the Constitution, established by the House of Lords in 2001, and whose mandate is to examine the constitutional implications of 'all public Bills coming before the House; and to keep under review the operation of the constitution'. While Robert Hazell has noted that this committee has not yet 'earned a place as a pillar of the constitution', he still emphasizes that it does offer the 'potential to do so'.[139]

As Feldman said in his reflection on his work at the Joint Committee: 'If human rights are to be properly taken into account at all stages of the legislative process, Parliament and the executive must work together and respect each other's responsibilities and functions. Each must act as guarantor of the other's commitment to fundamental values.'[140] He went on to say that 'friction' between the different institutions is not only to be expected but to be welcomed, since institutions which 'tolerate, and even celebrate, that friction demonstrate a commitment to human rights . . . [H]uman rights offer not harmony, but a practical framework in which a society, if it is sufficiently durable and flexible, can maintain an equilibrium between conflicting interests'.[141]

In establishing this practical framework, it is, I believe, impossible to draw any advance distinction between small 'p' politics or large 'P' politics which could demarcate the area of prerogative or the exceptional situation where the controls of the rule of law are inappropriate. Indeed, here I agree with Carl Schmitt though I want to reject the implication he wished to draw that law cannot control an exceptional situation. This implication would follow only if it were also impossible to have political accountability to the rule of law in some situations; for example, if it were impossible to conceive of an institution such as SIAC. It might take, that is, institutional imagination, a readiness on the part of legislature, executive and judiciary to experiment unbound by a rigid doctrine of the separation of powers, to give full expression to the rule of law. But whether or not one should do this is not determined by the brute nature of the political, by the alleged fact that in some category of highly intense political decisions the rule of law has no grip. Rather, the situation involves a political choice. Moreover, as I will now suggest, while this choice in a democracy is one

---

[139] *Ibid.*, 499. He also draws attention to the Delegated Powers and Regulatory Reform Committee, established in 1992; 495–7.

[140] Feldman, 'The Impact of Human Rights on the UK Legislative Process' 115.

[141] *Ibid.*

for the people through their representative body to make, it is not a choice open to judges, at least it is not open to judges who understand their duty to uphold the rule of law. Such judges will understand that their duty is to uphold the values of the rule of law, the constitution of law itself. So I will now return to the more abstract themes canvassed in the first chapter in order to answer the questions and challenges posed there, thus bringing the themes of the whole into one coherent picture of the rule of law.

4

The unity of public law

Introduction

In chapters 1 and 3, I briefly discussed the decision of the House of Lords in December 2004 which seems to show that judges in the United Kingdom have put a rule-of-law spine into the adjudication of national security – *A v. Secretary of State for the Home Department*.[1] As before, I will refer to it as *Belmarsh*, as it concerned the challenge by men held in indefinite detention in Belmarsh prison to the statutory provision which authorized their detention. *Belmarsh* might seem to put a stop to the trend, exemplified in the House of Lords' decision in *Secretary of State for the Home Department* v. *Rehman*,[2] discussed in chapter 3.

As we saw, *Rehman* adopts a stance on deference in matters of national security which proceduralizes judicial review of national security. In so doing, it substitutes for the claim that review is unavailable because of the political nature of the decision – that the decision is not justiciable – the claim that a kind of deference is appropriate which allows the executive to do pretty well what it likes. This approach to deference empties review of almost all substance, thus giving to the executive the ability to claim that it is operating under the rule of law while it is in fact largely free of legal constraints. And the stance from which it follows requires the rigid view of the separation of powers, according to which the legislature has a monopoly on law-making, the judiciary on interpretation of the law, and the executive on application of the law. In short, the trend indicates the resurgence of constitutional positivism.

Belmarsh is rightly regarded as a significant victory for the rule of law. But only the one dissenting judge confronted squarely the jurisprudence of *Rehman*, and that jurisprudence drove his reasoning. There is of course an understandable reticence on the part of judges explicitly to overrule a recent decision of their own Court and at times judges, including the judges of the House of Lords, have not even regarded themselves as having

[1] [2005] 2 WLR 87.   [2] [2002] 1 All ER 123.

the authority to do so. But, as I will now argue, the failure to confront *Rehman* squarely is not merely a matter of judicial tact or embarrassment; it is evidence of the grip which *Rehman*, and thus constitutional positivism, continued in different ways to exert even on the judges who declared the statutory provision incompatible with the human rights commitments of the United Kingdom.

The *Belmarsh* decision

After 9/11, the UK government had Parliament enact in s. 23 of the Anti-Terrorism, Crime and Security Act 2001 (the 'Anti-Terrorism Act') the power to detain indefinitely non-nationals in the circumstances where they had been determined to be a security risk but could not be deported because of some practical consideration or because deportation would subject them to a risk of torture. The power thus did not extend to nationals and the government conceded throughout that this meant that nationals who were security risks escaped the indefinite detention visited on non-nationals.

Before the bill was laid before Parliament, the Home Secretary notified the Secretary General of the Council of Europe that the government intended to take measures derogating from Article 5 of the European Convention on Human Rights,[3] which precluded such indefinite detention. Here the government relied on Article 15(1) of the Convention: 'In time of war or public emergency threatening the life of the nation any High Contracting Party may take measures derogating from its obligations under this Convention, to the extent strictly required by the exigencies of the situation, provided that such measures are not inconsistent with its other obligations under international law.' As a result the government made the Human Rights Act 1998 (Designated Derogation) Order 2001 which designated the detention powers under s. 14(1) of the Human Rights Act 1998.

The Anti-Terrorism Act did provide various safeguards: s. 24 provided for the grant of bail by SIAC, the Special Immigration Appeals Commission (the tribunal we encountered in the last chapter); s. 25 permitted a detainee to appeal to SIAC against his certification as a suspected international terrorist; s. 26 provided for SIAC to conduct periodic reviews of

---

[3] The Convention for the Protection of Human Rights and Fundamental Freedoms also known as the European Convention on Human Rights, Rome, 4 November 1950, in force 3 September 1953, 213 UNTS 221.

certification; s. 28 provided for periodic reviews of the operation of the detention scheme as a whole; s. 29 provided for the expiry of the scheme subject to periodic renewal and the final expiry on 10 November 2006 unless renewed. Section 30 gave SIAC exclusive jurisdiction in derogation matters.

The detainees claimed both that there was no public emergency threatening the life of the nation and that indefinite detention was not strictly required by the exigencies of the situation. It followed, they argued, that there was no valid derogation under Article 15. They also argued that the detention provisions were discriminatory in contravention of Article 14 of the Convention, which had not been notified for derogation. That Article precludes discrimination on various grounds, including 'national . . . origin'. SIAC rejected the argument that there was no public emergency. But it upheld the challenge on the basis that the provisions were discriminatory and, in addition, not a proportional response to the emergency. The Court of Appeal overruled SIAC on the last two grounds.[4] It held that, following *Rehman*, it had to defer to the government and the legislature in national security matters. It reasoned further that it was recognized in both international and domestic law that when it came to immigration law aliens did not enjoy the same rights as nationals. Finally, it held that if one's concern is the protection of liberty, it would be illogical to require the government to inflict indefinite detention on nationals as well as aliens in order to avoid discriminating against aliens.

In the House of Lords, Lord Bingham's speech attracted the agreement of six of the nine Law Lords who were, exceptionally, convened to hear the appeal. Like SIAC, he insisted that the matter be characterized as one about the right of the legal subject to liberty and equality and thus resisted the recharacterization of the matter by the government, which had been accepted by the Court of Appeal as an immigration matter in which the assumption is that non-nationals or aliens do not have the same rights as nationals. He thus upheld the challenge on the basis that it was disproportionate and discriminatory. However, he conceded that the Court should defer to the government's claim that there was an emergency. Lord Hoffmann also upheld the challenge but on the sole ground that there

---

[4] *A v. Secretary of State for the Home Department* [2004] QB 335. As Rayner Thwaites has pointed out to me, the more accurate description is that the Court of Appeal did not overrule SIAC expressly on proportionality; rather it held that findings on proportionality are a matter of fact not law and so not subject to appeal. In *Belmarsh* the House of Lords, Lords Hope at 141 and Rodger at 157–8 are properly attentive to this issue, while Lord Bingham at 114 is not.

was no emergency. Lord Walker dissented as he preferred the approach of the Court of Appeal.

The government argued, and Lord Walker agreed, that the kind of deference *Rehman* required in national security matters covered both the issue of whether there was an emergency and the issue of the appropriate response to an emergency. In Lord Bingham's summary, the Attorney-General submitted 'that as it was for Parliament and the executive to assess the threat facing the nation, so it was for those bodies and not the courts to judge the response necessary to protect the security of the public. These were matters of a political character calling for an exercise of political and not judicial judgment'.[5] In other words, the government argued along the lines we saw in chapter 1 that Carl Schmitt thought that states of emergency reveal as necessary: the political sovereign must decide both when there is a state of emergency or exception and how best to respond it.

While the majority agreed in effect about the issue of assessment, it disagreed about the issue of appropriate response. Lord Hoffmann, despite the fact that he had been responsible in *Rehman* for setting out the view adopted by the government of appropriate deference, disagreed with the government about the first issue, but did not, as he saw things, have to decide the second. Indeed, Lord Hoffmann did not even mention *Rehman*. As a result, the main puzzle raised by *Belmarsh* in the context of my argument about the role of judges in sustaining the rule-of-law project is the relationship between that decision and *Rehman*.

Lord Bingham's response to the Attorney-General's argument was that while Parliament, the executive and the judges have 'different functions', 'the function of independent judges charged to interpret and apply the law is universally recognised as a cardinal feature of the modern democratic state, a cornerstone of the rule of law itself'. It was thus wrong to 'stigmatise judicial decision-making as in some way undemocratic'. It was 'particularly inappropriate' when judges could declare only that a statute was incompatible with human rights, a declaration which did not affect its validity.[6] And Lord Rodger elaborated this point:

> If the provisions of section 30 of the 2001 Act are to have any real meaning, deference to the views of the Government and Parliament on the derogation cannot be taken too far. Due deference does not mean abasement before those views, even in matters relating to national security... Indeed, the considerable deference which the European Court of Human Rights shows to

---

[5] See *ibid.*, Lord Bingham at 110 , Lord Scott at 151.   [6] *Ibid.*, at 113–14.

the views of the national authorities in such matters really presupposes that the national courts will police those limits. Moreover, by enacting section 30, Parliament, including the democratically elected House of Commons, gave SIAC and the appellate courts a specific mandate to perform that func tion – a function which the executive and the legislature cannot perform for themselves – in relation to the derogation. The legitimacy of the courts' scrutiny role cannot be in doubt.[7]

But if judges have that function, it is not that easy to determine why Lord Bingham and the judges who agreed with his speech let the government off so lightly on the first issue. As the judges acknowledged, no other party to the Convention had found it necessary to derogate from it in the wake of 9/11, not even the Spaniards in the wake of the Al-Qaeda attack on Madrid in March 2004; and the government admitted that they could not claim that an attack was imminent. Moreover, Lord Hoffmann's speech, which poured scorn on the claim that the situation was one in which there was a war or other public emergency threatening the life of the nation, was a source of disquiet for the other judges. Three of the majority judges thus intimated or expressed their doubts about whether the government had a serious case.[8] However, they found shelter behind two claims.

First, SIAC in coming to the decision that it should defer to the government's claim that there was an emergency had seen confidential material from the government in closed session. The Attorney-General, however, had declined to ask the House of Lords to read the same material. Still the majority seemed to think that because SIAC had seen confidential material in closed session and come to a conclusion on its basis that the claim that there was an emergency must have been strengthened by that material.[9] And they thought this despite the fact that SIAC had expressly not relied on the confidential material in coming to its conclusion. But even on my argument in chapter 3 that the courts should be ready to defer to SIAC, should SIAC adequately justify its decision, and, correspondingly, that both SIAC and the courts should be ready to defer to the government when it provides such a justification, such deference cannot be blind, the kind of deference which I referred to in the last chapter as deference as submission. As we have seen Lord Rodger put it: 'Due deference does not mean abasement.' Even if a less strict standard of scrutiny is required for the question whether there is an emergency than for the question about how best to respond to it, the scrutiny has to be of the reasons if the

---

[7] *Ibid.*, at 158.
[8] *Ibid.*, Lord Bingham at 104, Lord Scott at 151, Lord Rodger at 155.   [9] *Ibid.*, at 104–5.

reasons are to be given the stamp of approval of adequacy. To give, as one judge put it, the government the 'benefit of the doubt' at the same time as he expresses 'very grave doubt'[10] about the government's case seems peculiar, especially when the government chose not to allow the Court to see evidence that might remove some of that doubt.

Second, the majority relied on decisions of the European Court of Human Rights which held that the Court should generally defer to a national government's determination that there is such an emergency.[11] But such reliance fails to give proper effect to the gap some of the judges acknowledged[12] between the situation in which the European Court defers to a decision by a government that has withstood challenges before that government's national courts and the situation in which the highest national court has to evaluate the government's challenge. That is, a stricter standard is arguably appropriate in the latter situation and the application of such a standard there would make more sense of the application of the more relaxed standard in the first situation.[13]

My point here is not that the majority were wrong to defer, but that they failed to require that a proper case for deference be made. In failing so to require, they in effect conceded to Schmitt the first limb of his claim about states of emergency – that it is for the executive to decide when there is a state of exception. Moreover, they concede that limb in the way which, as I have argued throughout this book, makes things worse from the perspective of the rule of law. They still adopt the regulative assumption that all exercises of public power are legally constrained. But their understanding of constraint is so thin that it becomes merely formal, with the result that they claim that the declaration of the state of emergency has met the test of legality, even as they empty the test of rule-of-law substance.

The majority did face a rather large problem though in confronting this issue. There was no doubt that the United Kingdom faced a serious threat of terrorist attacks and the events of July 2005 confirmed the government's claims. But the issue of whether that threat, or indeed actual attacks, amounted to an emergency in accordance with the Article 15 definition was not so much debated but asserted, as one can gather from both the

---

[10] *Ibid.*, Lord Scott at 151.   [11] *Ibid.*, at 105.

[12] *Ibid.*, Lord Bingham at 112–13 and Lord Hope at 139.

[13] See Tom R. Hickman, 'Between Human Rights and the Rule of Law: Indefinite Detention and the Derogation Model of Constitutionalism' (2005) 68 *Modern Law Review* 655–8. I am much indebted in my analysis of *Belmarsh* to this piece and to further discussion with Tom about it.

account in the judges' speeches of the government's arguments and by Lord Hoffmann's cursory dismissal of those arguments. One can sum up the majority view by saying that if there is some reason to suppose that there is an emergency, that is, it is not irrational to claim that there is, even if the judges doubt that there is, they still have to give the benefit of the doubt to the executive. And not only is that just the test that was suggested by Lord Hoffmann in *Rehman* for review of decisions concerning national security, but Lord Bingham seemed to accept that the jurisprudence of *Rehman* should determine this issue.[14]

In order for the judges to do more, they would need a better justificatory basis to scrutinize. For there to be such a basis, the government would have to be prepared to treat Parliament as more than a rubber stamp for legislation when the government thinks it needs more powers to confront an alleged crisis. Not only would the government have to forego its standard (and nearly always unjustified) line that there is no time to debate properly both the extent of the emergency and the appropriate responses to it. It would have to devise some system of parliamentary committees which could hear that part of the government's case which could not be publicly debated. To use the term introduced at the end of the last chapter, more constitutional furniture would have to be put in place in order to ensure that the government could meet its justificatory responsibilities before the judges could carry out their duty properly to evaluate the government's case. And for the judges to carry out that duty, they would of course have to be given some means of testing the arguments made in the closed committee sessions.[15]

The upshot for my critique of the majority on this first issue is not that I think the judges were obviously wrong to defer to the government's claim that there was a state of emergency. Rather, my critique is that they should have made clear both that they did not have an adequate basis for testing that claim and that the government should take suitable steps to make an adequate justification possible. They needed to do that because the two limbs of Schmitt's challenge cannot be separated. As we know, the majority denied the second limb of Schmitt's claim. They held, contrary to him and to the government, that judges can effectively, and are entitled to, second-guess the way that the executive chooses to respond to the emergency, and the logic of that holding extends to the question

---

[14] *Belmarsh*, at 111.

[15] Of course, the main reason for the government to put in place this furniture is not to enable judicial review but to fulfil a political responsibility to Parliament and thus to the democracy it serves.

whether there is an emergency. For the propriety of the response can only be assessed against a view of what the response is to, a view of whether there is an emergency and, if there is, of what kind.

As we have seen, Lord Hoffmann was the only judge willing to decide on the ground that the government lacked the basis for its claim that there was a state of emergency sufficient to derogate from constitutional commitments. He also seemed to reject what he (wrongly) took to be an implication of the reasoning of the other judges who allowed the appeal that the problem with the legislation could be cured by extending indefinite detention to include citizens.[16] In Lord Hoffmann's view, 'such a power in any form is not compatible with our constitution'.[17] It might thus seem that his speech is a complete about-face from the position he articulated in *Rehman*. But in fact, Lord Hoffmann accepted the second limb of Schmitt's challenge – that the executive is entitled to decide how to respond to an emergency, if in fact there is an emergency.

Moreover, for him the position that the judges may second-guess the executive when there is an emergency was entirely dependent on the only difference he took the Human Rights Act to make to the legal landscape of the United Kingdom. Before the Human Rights Act came into effect, Lord Hoffmann said, a court could not have questioned an Act of Parliament, so it could not have decided whether the threat to the nation was sufficient to justify suspension of habeas corpus. While the Act does not permit courts to say that a statute is invalid, a declaration of incompatibility enables Parliament to choose to maintain the statute or not 'with full knowledge that the law does not accord with our constitutional traditions'.[18] The difference is that since it came into effect, Parliament's power to derogate from human rights, which he takes to be both part of the constitutional tradition and necessary to it,[19] is subject to the risk of a judicial declaration of incompatibility. Parliament could not then cure that incompatibility by extending indefinite detention to citizens, since there did not exist a state of emergency sufficient to justify a derogation from the rights of anyone, aliens or citizens or both. But if there were a real state of emergency, it also follows that there would be no incompatibility with the United Kingdom's human rights commitments, because the circumstances would exist in which the 'exceptional power to derogate'[20] had been validly exercised and, it seems, the government would have thereby been released from those commitments.

---

[16] *Belmarsh*, at 135. It was not of course an implication. Extending detention would deal with the discrimination argument, but not with the proportionality argument.

[17] *Ibid.*, at 135.   [18] *Ibid.*, at 134.   [19] *Ibid.*, at 133.   [20] *Ibid.*

My objection is not to the claim that there can be a valid derogation from human rights, but to three related aspects of Lord Hoffmann's speech. The first is that, like Dicey, he sets up an account of the separation of powers as the battle between the competing supremacies of Parliament and its delegates, on the one hand, and judges on the other. He thus swings between a stance of utter deference, as in *Rehman*, and no deference at all, as in *Belmarsh*. Not only does this swing from one extreme to the other lead to a radical incoherence. It also squeezes out the space for a public justification by the executive of its claim, one that could supply reasons with which the judges might not wholly agree, but which would be strong enough to earn their respect.

The second aspect has to do with the all-or-nothing approach to which such swings lead. Either the rule of law rules with all its force, it is business as usual,[21] or we have mere rule by law, with none of the substance of the rule of law. This aspect is demonstrated in Lord Hoffmann's equation of human rights with the values of the common law constitution. The result of this equation, especially in light of Lord Hoffmann's position in *Rehman*, is that if there is a valid derogation, the common law constitution has no role to play in controlling exercises of executive power.[22] The rule of law is suspended by the derogation despite the fact that all it mentions explicitly is the United Kingdom's commitments to human rights.

Lord Hoffmann's position then is the same as that articulated by the majority of the Law Lords in the English wartime cases of *Liversidge*[23] and *Halliday*[24] discussed in the last chapter. Amidst the clash of arms the laws are silent. His speech is no more supportive of the rule of law than Justice Scalia's judgment in *Hamdi*, the US Supreme Court's decision on the due process rights of 'enemy combatants'.[25] As we saw in chapter 1, the rhetoric of Justice Scalia's dissent might lead one to believe that he had, contrary to reputation, become a defender of the rule of law in the face of an executive that wanted a free hand when it came to dealing with its perceived enemies. But all he required was proper creation of the legal black hole in which the Bush administration wanted to put the 'enemy combatants'. Like Justice Scalia and the majorities in *Liversidge* and *Halliday*, Lord Hoffmann is unperturbed by the existence of legal black holes, as long as they are properly created. Moreover, while he claims that judges are able to test whether there is a real basis for their creation, he (like the plurality in

---

[21] As we saw Oren Gross put it in ch. 1 – Oren Gross, 'Chaos and Rules, 1011–134.
[22] See Hickman, 'Between Human Rights and the Rule of Law', 664–5.
[23] *Liversidge* v. *Anderson* [1942] AC 206.   [24] *R* v. *Halliday, ex Parte Zadig* [1917] AC 260.
[25] *Hamdi* v. *Rumsfeld*, 124 S. Ct. 2633 (2004).

Hamdi) is willing to accept that once such a basis exists, black holes can be created by statutes that do not make clear statements about the suspension of habeas corpus. For he held that during both world wars habeas corpus had been suspended and 'powers to detain on suspicion conferred on the Government'.[26] But, as we have seen from *Halliday*, the issue in that case was whether there had been a suspension – whether an open-ended delegation of authority to the executive necessarily included a power to create indefinite detention. However, in *Liversidge* the issue was whether an explicit authority to detain meant that the minister's decision was in effect unreviewable. In other words, habeas corpus was not suspended by Parliament but by the effect of the decisions of the majority of the House of Lords. Following them, Lord Hoffmann excludes any real role for the courts in circumstances where there is a genuine public emergency threatening the life of the nation. In such circumstances all bets are off and the executive should have a free hand.

Lord Hoffmann's speech in *Belmarsh* shows that he is willing to read a privative clause ousting judicial review into a statute that validly derogates from human rights, even though the statute says nothing about the common law. He thus does not think that the political virtue in requiring Parliament to be subject to a process of judicially enforced public reflection about its human rights commitments applies to the rule of law. Here we should recall from chapter 1 that it was an intense public debate that led to the government's retreat in 2004 from the privative clause it had proposed introducing into the United Kingdom's immigration legislation. And that debate, one which placed in very sharp relief the question of the government's lack of commitment to the rule of law and the judges' willingness to maintain the common law constitution in the face of that lack, formed the context in which *Belmarsh* was decided.

Finally, and as we will see contrary to Dicey, Lord Hoffmann held that the power to create a legal black hole is a constitutional one,[27] thus locating the executive's authority to create a lawless void in the constitution. This is the third objectionable aspect of Lord Hoffmann's speech – that he wished to dignify legal black holes with the mantle of the rule of law.

Recall that in *Rehman* Lord Hoffmann was rightly understood to say that in a democracy the executive and the legislature are given almost total deference by the courts when it comes to the determination of what constitutes a risk to national security and who falls into that category. As we have seen, the government, perfectly logically, relied on that judgment

---

[26] *Belmarsh*, at 133.   [27] *Ibid.*

and in particular Lord Hoffmann's speech, to argue in *Belmarsh* that that position on deference entailed that the courts should be similarly deferential when it came to an executive determination that there is a state of emergency.[28] Here the Attorney-General took the same approach as the one we saw in chapter 1 advocated by Justice Thomas in *Hamdi*, which is also the approach advocated by Schmitt – that the executive has a free hand to determine both that a state of emergency exists as well as how to manage it.[29]

But, as we have seen throughout this book, such an approach is incompatible with a regulative assumption of the judicial role: judges must ensure that government is in accordance with the law. That assumption can be maintained at a formal, rhetorical level by positivist judges who are prepared to equate the rule of law with rule by law. They are willing to hold that government is in accordance with the rule of law, even when the principles of the common law constitution are suspended, as long as the suspension comes about through a valid statute. As I have argued, such judges do more damage to the rule of law than do judges like Thomas who abdicate altogether their duty to uphold the rule of law. They uphold the form of the rule of law but not its substance, and that tactic allows the government to continue to claim that it governs in accordance with the rule of law.[30] Of course, as I have acknowledged throughout, Parliament can override the common law constitution simply by enacting an explicit statute. But, as I have also argued, that a determined and powerful government can procure such an override does not show that the values of the constitution are less constitutional for that reason. All that it shows is that the powerful might decide that they prefer to rule outside the reach of the rule of law.

The Human Rights Act makes the choice to move outside of the rule of law much more complex than it would be when the only constitution is a common law one and it is important to appreciate that the complexity is at the legal–constitutional level. Lord Scott's concurring speech is instructive, albeit negatively, in this regard.

Lord Scott said that the effect of a declaration of incompatibility on 'the lawfulness under domestic law of the incarceration of the appellants

---

[28] See *Rehman*, at 137 and Lord Bingham's speech in *Belmarsh*, at 105–6.

[29] See Schmitt, *Political Theology*.

[30] This formal and substantively empty approach to the rule of law is not the sole preserve of conservative or right-wing judges; it is also supported by some left-wing academic lawyers. See for example Gearty, *Principles of Human Rights Adjudication*, pp. 67–8.

is nil'.[31] But he still expressed discomfort with the fact that, as he saw it, a declaration of incompatibility required the courts to go beyond their 'normal and proper function' of adjudicating on executive action that affects the rights of 'citizens' 'under domestic law'.[32] It was not, that is, 'normal' for courts to be required to rule on 'whether an Act of Parliament is compatible with an international treaty obligation entered into by the executive'. In being asked to perform that function, the courts had to do something that is 'essentially political in character rather than legal':

> A ruling that an Act of Parliament is incompatible with the [European Convention on Human Rights] does not detract from the validity of the Act. It does not relieve citizens from the burdens of the Act. It provides, of course, ammunition to those who disapprove of the Act and desire to agitate for its amendment or repeal. This is not a function that the courts have sought for themselves. It is a function that has been thrust on the courts by the 1998 Act.[33]

In addition, Lord Scott alone among the judges was perturbed by the fact that s. 14 of the Human Rights Act which permits derogations does not prescribe any limitation on the government's power to make a designated derogation order and that the Act does not directly incorporate Article 15 of the Convention and its test of strict necessity.[34] It was thus, he said, a 'puzzle' why s. 14 was included at all, since the Act did not restrict Parliament's power to legislate inconsistently with the Convention. Perhaps, he concluded, it was there 'simply to enable it to be made clear that the inconsistency was deliberate and not inadvertent, and thereby to constitute an aid to the courts in construing the statutory provision'.[35] So concerned was he about this issue, that he came back to it in the concluding paragraph of his judgment, and emphasized his view that the Court could rely on Article 15 only because the Attorney-General accepted that the government response to the emergency had to be consistent with that Article.[36]

Lord Scott's discomfort is created by the logic of dualism, itself the product of constitutional positivism. As we have seen, constitutional positivists

---

[31] *Belmarsh*, at 148.   [32] *Ibid.*, at 149–50.   [33] *Ibid.*

[34] *Ibid.*, at 150. Lord Rodger based the application of Article 15 on the fact that s. 30(2) and (5) of the 2001 Act provide that any derogation from Article 5(1) in terms of s. 14(1) of the 1998 Act can be questioned in legal proceedings before SIAC and in an appeal from their decision. And he observed: 'If the right is to be meaningful, the judges must be intended to do more than simply rubber-stamp the decisions taken by ministers and Parliament' (at 154). See Lady Hale to the same effect at 175.

[35] *Ibid.*, at 149–50.   [36] *Ibid.*, at 153.

regard statutes as the sole legitimate source of legal norms and thus pay no heed to executive commitments to international human rights instruments except in cases of ambiguity. It happens, though, that there is no ambiguity here, a fact that is underlined by the derogation order. However, on Lord Scott's view, the section which requires the order is not necessary because all it can do is to underline what is the case: the legislature has unambiguously legislated in a way that excludes certain human rights from figuring in the judicial understanding of legislative intention.

Lord Scott could not have been unaware that if the Court had found that the derogation order was valid, it would have been unable to make a declaration of incompatibility with respect to Article 5, the Article specifically derogated from in that order. So his point must be that in the absence of explicit authority for judges to strike down statutes that violate international human rights commitments, a determined government can get its way by being sufficiently explicit in legislation about its intentions. On his view, the Human Rights Act merely adds political hoops through which such a government has to pass, but no real legal constraints. All it does is thrust judges into a political role which is regrettable from the perspective of constitutional positivism because it requires them to raise a question mark about the wisdom of the Anti-Terrorism Act.

But there is another, better explanation of the presence of s. 14, the government's choice to treat its response as bound by Article 15 and the judicial role. Section 14 makes sense in part because, as Lord Scott says, it requires an explicit and deliberate recognition by government when it proposes legislation that derogates from one or more of the Convention rights which are contained in Sch. 1 of the Act. But its purpose is not to constitute, as he also claimed, an 'aid to the courts in construing the statutory provision', so that they will have an easier time understanding the statute by comparison with a statute that simply overrode human rights commitments without any government recognition of that fact. Rather, in choosing to derogate, a government is not simply stating as a matter of fact that it no longer is bound by its human rights commitments. It is making a public claim that it is legally justified in departing from particular commitments. Moreover, the claim that there is a legal justification presumes not only that there is a legally testable basis for the departure, but also that the mode of departure – the way in which it is structured – is legally justified.

In other words, derogation presupposes a commitment to the rule of law that responds to both limbs of Schmitt's challenge. The only difference between Article 15 of the Convention and s. 14 of the Human Rights

Act is that the former specifies just what sort of a test is appropriate for the mode of departure, while the latter does not. The government in accepting that the mode of departure was governed by both strict necessity and consistency with other international law obligations mandated by Article 15 indicated that it remained committed to the regime of legality presupposed in any claim that derogation is justified.[37]

Of course, the government sought at the same time to empty its regime of legality of most of its substance by relying on *Rehman*. That decision, it thought, permitted it to demand that in applying the substantive legal conditions for valid derogation the courts and SIAC defer utterly to its claims about its compliance with those conditions. In effect, the government argued that s. 14 of the Human Rights Act should be read as follows:

> In time of war or public emergency threatening the life of the nation, the United Kingdom government may take measures derogating from any or all of its human rights obligations. The decision that there is such a war or public emergency lies within the unfettered discretion of the government, so that neither that decision nor any of the measures it takes, are subject to review in a court of law on any basis whatsoever, whether fact or law.

Such a position makes human rights commitments optional – they apply when the government thinks it is convenient for them to apply. And, as we have seen before, when a government sends such a mixed message to judges, they are not only entitled but under a duty to pick that part of the message that is evidence of the government's commitment both to the rule of law and to the general regime of legality that comes out of the legal order's particular history. In the United Kingdom, that duty exists because the common law constitution requires judges to understand all

---

[37] As Hickman points out, 'Between Human Rights and the Rule of Law', 665–6, Lord Bingham used the language of proportionality rather than strict necessity in testing the mode of departure, in contrast to Lord Scott, Lord Rodger and Lady Hale. Hickman acknowledges that the two tests led in this case to the same result, but he emphasizes that it is important to be aware that this may not always be so. 'The strictly required test invites the Government to show, without any initial evidence from which the contrary is to be inferred, that it has considered all the alternatives and that no less intrusive possibility exists. It demands the most anxious scrutiny by the courts and insists upon convincing evidence that even carefully tailored measures are indispensable. Where measures are more widely framed than they need to be it will be extremely difficult – if not impossible – to show that they are strictly required.' It is of course highly significant that the detention regime was made subject to much more extensive due process controls through SIAC than the equivalents in the United States. As Lady Hale put it, 'Belmarsh is not the British Guantanamo Bay', *Belmarsh*, at 174.

the powers of the legal order as committed to the rule-of-law project. But the duty has another source in the Human Rights Act which explicitly tells judges their duty is to ensure that the executive and the legislature fulfil their commitments.

Only a constitutional positivist would suppose both that judges perform some inappropriately political function when they test legislation for its compliance with fundamental legal values and that, if the judges are unable to invalidate legislation that does not comply, the message they send to the legislature and to government is merely political. Lord Bingham's articulation of the judicial role in response to the Attorney-General's argument rejects Lord Scott's positivism in both respects. As we have seen, he said that judicial guardianship of legality is a cornerstone of a democracy, a political order by definition committed to the rule of law. And as Lady Hale put it, while the offending provision is not invalidated, 'Government and Parliament then have to decide what action to take to remedy the matter'.[38]

Her point is surely not that government and Parliament are entitled to do nothing. Either the government is convinced that the House of Lords got things wrong, in which case the government must appeal to Strasbourg, which entails a readiness on its part to accept the European Court of Human Rights' verdict. Alternatively, the government must accept the House of Lords' decision, which entails that it must remedy the incompatibility. If it fails to take the latter course, it is in the same position as it would be if it failed to respond positively to a decision of the European Court. The government would reveal itself as taking the optional view of the legal order's human rights commitments – they apply when convenient. Thus the majority's view entails that a government that fails to bring legislation which violates the legal order's commitments into line operates under a deficit of legality, under a cloud of legal doubt.

In other words, while the Human Rights Act does not give judges the authority to invalidate statutes, it legislates a view of the unity of public law, a unity of the common law and of international law, which is inconsistent with constitutional positivism. Indeed, the Act might be even more disturbing for constitutional positivism and its understanding of sovereignty than the entrenchment of rights in a bill of rights, with a corresponding authority for judges to review statutes on the basis of these rights. As we saw in chapter 2, a positivist judge can try to maintain his view of sovereignty and the monopoly of the legislature on making

[38] *Ibid.*, at 173.

law by understanding the rights as frozen in time at the moment of their entrenchment. Parliament is constrained, but the constraints are both domestic in origin and have in some sense the blessing of 'the people'. But if the legal norms which have constitutional status have their source in international law, and moreover in human rights regimes which are continually evolving, these damage control measures cannot work because constitutional positivism entails dualism. And this is the reason why Lord Scott had to go to such lengths to deny the constitutional status of the Human Rights Act.

It is also, I suspect, the reason why Lord Hoffmann hardly mentioned the Human Rights Act or the European Convention and said nothing about international human rights. In his view, the common law sufficed to uphold the appeal, since it was the source of liberty, a value which had to be exported to the lawless Europeans and then enshrined in a Convention for them after the Second World War. The only reason for the United Kingdom to have subscribed to the Convention was that it set out the 'rights which British subjects enjoyed under the common law'.[39] The United Kingdom could subscribe because subscribing made no difference, except, as we have seen, to the Court's ability to question a statute by making a declaration of incompatibility. His speech thus contrasts strongly with Lord Bingham's care in showing that the United Kingdom, despite the efforts of the Blair government, remains part of a family of nations that respects both the rule of law and international human rights.[40]

Of course, the government could amend or abolish the Act by determined use of its majority in the House of Commons. And in the wake of the attacks on London in July of 2005, the government has indicated that it might amend the Human Rights Act if a proposed statute which will dictate to judges how they are to balance human rights and security does not have the desired effect. This stance reveals that the government wishes to operate under the cloak of the rule of law by requiring of judges that they give it and Parliament the stamp of legality. This would result in a statutory endorsement of *Rehman*, which would mock the legal order's commitment to human rights. But it is still significant that the government

---

[39] *Ibid.*, at 133.
[40] It is instructive here that Lord Bingham relied not only on the jurisprudence of international human rights, but also on the reports of the Joint Committee on Human Rights as well as the Newton Committee, which is not a standing committee but one set up by the Anti-Terrorism, Crime and Security Act 2001 to review its operation.

prefers to risk being accused of mockery than to make explicit in the law its desire to be free of its commitments.

However, were the government to procure an amendment of the Human Rights Act that made it clear that the Act did not protect rights but merely stated an option for the government of the day, it would still have to contend with the common law constitution. Moreover, that constitution is, as I have indicated in several places, an evolving or living constitution and by this point in its development, the judicial understanding of its content has been irrevocably changed by the international human rights regimes and other constitutional experiments of the last fifty or so years. If the government really wanted to govern free of a substantive conception of the rule of law, one whose content includes respect for human rights, it would have to resort to introducing into legislation substantive privative clauses, provisions which, as we have seen in chapter 2, say that judges may not review executive action on the grounds of reasonableness, fairness, bias, and so on. In short, one would be back in the contest about how best to understand the rule of law and the role of the different powers of legal order in upholding it. And I will now bring my arguments about what I have called the constitution of law to a close, beginning with the theme of dualism.

Refuting dualism

> [T]he law of nations (whenever any question arises which is properly the object of its jurisdiction) is here adopted in its full extent by the common law, and is held to be a part of the law of the land. And those acts of parliament, which have from time to time been made to enforce this universal law, or to facilitate the execution of it's decisions, are not to be considered as introductive of any new rule, but merely declaratory of the old fundamental constitutions of the kingdom; without which it must cease to be a part of the civilized world.[41]
>
> Sir William Blackstone

We have seen at various times in this book that the conversation between Commonwealth judges about the rule of law and human rights can take a depressing turn, one which involves a retreat to constitutional positivism with its insistence on the rigid separation of powers and consequent dualism.

---

[41] Blackstone, *Commentaries*, 5th chapter of the Fourth Book, quoted by Hersch Lauterpacht in 'Is International Law a Part of the Law of England?' [1939] 25 *Transactions of the Grotius Society* 51–88 at 52.

In my view, this turn is best analysed through a discussion of the relationship between international law and domestic law. Constitutional positivism's rigid doctrine of the separation of powers seems unassailable in its dualism, its insistence that international human rights norms should have no domestic legal effect until these have been incorporated into law by the legislature. As we have seen, dualism about the relationship between international law and domestic law relies on spatial metaphors to understand that relationship. There is the space of domestic law, the space controlled by the sovereign, understood as the uncommanded commander of a political order, and there is the space in which such commanders have agreed to certain rules that will govern their relationships with each other. But those rules will be permitted entry to the domestic space only under certain conditions; they are aliens, unless, with certain exceptions, the sovereign explicitly says that they are entitled to permanent residence. Dualism thus sets up a contest between competing claims to supremacy by international law and domestic law.

But, as I will now show, it is at this point that dualism is at its weakest. Further, in seeing why we should do away with dualism about the relationship between international and domestic law, we are better equipped to do away with its exact equivalent within the domestic legal order – the dualism between statute law and the principles of the rule of law, principles which are manifested in the common law.[42] And once dualism of this kind is scotched, together with its image of the competing supremacies of Parliament and the judiciary, we are also equipped to deal with the last kind of dualism we have encountered – the dualism which is claimed to be required to deal with emergencies – a dualism between the rule-of-law state, which deals with ordinary matters, and the prerogative state, which responds to the emergency.

Sir Hersch Lauterpacht relied on the epigraph to this section in an address to the Grotius Society on 25 May 1939 on the relationship between international law and domestic law – 'Is International Law a Part of the Law of England?' It is, I think, not untypical that at a time of heightened international tensions, when not only international legal order but also liberal democracy was at stake, that Lauterpacht would choose to give an optimistic account of the relationship, with narry a mention of the tensions.

---

[42] The best elaboration of this view in the English context remains Murray Hunt, *Using Human Rights Law in English Courts* (Oxford: Hart Publishing, 1997), especially ch. 1.

Lauterpacht gives a resoundingly positive answer to the question he posed in his title, one which he finds, going back to Lord Mansfield and Blackstone, to be the answer of the common law tradition. Lauterpacht is not fazed in giving this answer by the doctrine of parliamentary supremacy. He points out that there is a commonly accepted rule of statutory construction that statutes are to be interpreted 'so as not to be in conflict with International Law'.[43] Any affirmation of the absolute supremacy of Parliament is, given this rule of construction, a 'theoretical affirmation', one which has 'the probably not unintended effect of stressing the duty of Judges to do their utmost to interpret statutes so as not to impute to the Legislature the intention of disregarding International Law'. He continues that it is 'easier to interpret away a provision of an Act of Parliament on the face of it inconsistent with International Law if previously due obeisance has been made to the supremacy of the Legislature'. And he admits that the 'presumption that Parliament did not intend to commit a breach of the law of nations has been a powerful weapon wielded with a determination which on occasions has come near to a denial of the supremacy of Parliament'.[44]

Lauterpacht's argument here is quite similar to the one we saw in chapter 2 that Sir William Wade was to make later about privative or ouster clauses. But I hope to show that Lauterpacht's insights are in the end more helpful in resolving the difficult issues posed by such clauses, despite one obvious difference between the problem of the relationship between international and domestic law and the problem of privative clauses. The former problem arises because of the absence of the statute which is thought to be required before international legal norms have domestic effect, while the latter problem has to do with the fact that a statute exists, one of whose provisions says that judicial enforcement of domestic legal norms is ousted.

Lauterpacht argues that the insistence on an incorporating statute was not a reaction to a common law claim that international law is part of domestic law. Rather, it was a reaction to the uncertainty of international law in particular areas. That is, where the requirements of international law are uncertain, and given that international law is part of the common law, the way to resolve uncertainty is for Parliament to clear up the uncertainty.[45] In making this point, Lauterpacht shatters the dualist understanding of the requirement of statutory incorporation of international law.

---

[43] See Lauterpacht, 'Is International Law a Part of the Law of England?'
[44] *Ibid.*, 58–9.   [45] *Ibid.*, 61.

Recall that dualism holds that statutory incorporation is required to give any effect to international law. Dualist judges will, however, mention at the same time as they refuse to apply international law, that if a statute is ambiguous judges should interpret it in favour of international law. They also purport to recognize that customary international law is part of domestic law, unless its operation is ousted explicitly by a statute. But they find that the statutes in which the first kind of issue arises are unambiguous. In addition, because in any hard case whether international law has achieved customary status is by definition arguable, dualists can attempt to preserve their rigid doctrine of the separation of powers at the same time as they proclaim their respect for international law. Put differently, they can claim to be part of the civilized world while refusing to apply its standards.

Lauterpacht's point shows precisely why that claim fails. The doctrine of incorporation or adoption is not, as dualists have it, about the incorporation of particular norms of international law by statute, but about the incorporation of the whole of international law by a domestic legal order. This is not, he is anxious to stress, an assertion of the supremacy of international law, for there is an act of will of the individual state on which such incorporation depends. But that act is a general submission to international law – a voluntary act of submission which as long as it lasts 'has the effect of elevating to the authority of a legal rule the unity of international and municipal law'.[46] From the 'point of view of municipal law' that submission may, Lauterpacht says, be 'validly refused or withdrawn, but the sanction of such action must be, in Blackstone's words, that the state would "cease to be part of the civilized world"'.[47]

In other words, voluntary submission is needed to maintain what Lauterpacht calls 'a fundamental jurisprudential identity'[48] between domestic and international law. That identity, which I prefer to term a unity, is manifested in various ways, including the dualist recognition of the importance of international law in interpretation of statutes as well as the force of customary international law in the absence of an explicit statutory override. The only way for dualist judges to achieve consistency is to deny any force to international law whatsoever, in the absence of explicit statutory incorporation. But that denial would fly in the face of the practice of countries as well as in the face of their proclamations of good citizen status in the international legal order. It would also have the odd result for judges preoccupied by a rigid doctrine of the separation of powers, and who like to inveigh against 'backdoor

[46] *Ibid.*, 64–5.   [47] *Ibid.*, 65.   [48] *Ibid.*

incorporation of treaties', of amounting to a judicially-driven act of secession.

The root of dualism is then not tradition or history but, Lauterpacht says, the rise of positivistic doctrines of absolute state sovereignty.[49] And he makes the point that just as it is not asserted that the common law fails to be part of the law of the land because statutes may override the common law, so one should reject the claim that international law is not part of the law of the land because statutes may override it.[50] In short, the problem of the identity of international law and domestic law is no different from the problem of the identity or unity of statute and common law, unless one adopts what Lauterpacht describes as a 'barren type of legal positivism'.[51]

In this observation, we can see the intolerable contradiction in which the two partial dissenters placed themselves in *Baker*,[52] Canada's Supreme Court's decision which we saw in the last chapter allowed the ratified but unincorporated Convention on the Rights of the Child[53] to inform its understanding of reasonableness. The two judges agreed with the majority in its finding that there is a duty to give reasons at common law when a public official makes a decision affecting important interests of the legal subject. And they agreed that the interests of Baker's children had to be taken into account when officials decided whether her deportation should be stayed on humanitarian and compassionate grounds and that the appropriate standard of review was reasonableness. In order to agree with these findings, the two judges had also to agree that the issue of how to interpret the statutory delegation of discretion did not turn on a claim about statutory ambiguity. Rather, it turned on a commitment to interpreting the statute if at all possible in the light of the fundamental values of the legal order. But, in that light, they could not without contradiction invoke the rigid doctrine of the separation of powers against the majority's reliance on international human rights norms in determining the content of reasonableness. Similarly, we have seen other dualist judges contradict themselves when they assert, on the one hand, that explicit statutory incorporation is required to give effect to international human rights norms and, on the other, that statutory ambiguity should be resolved in favour of international law and that customary international law applies until explicitly overruled by statute.

Once we see that these are contradictions, we are also better equipped to deal with the question of the proper rule-of-law response to both

---

[49] *Ibid.*, 72.   [50] *Ibid.*, 76.   [51] *Ibid.*, 87.

[52] *Baker* v. *Canada (Minister of Immigration)* [1999] 2 SCR 817.

[53] Convention on the Rights of the Child, New York, 20 November 1989, in force 2 September 1990, 1577 UNTS 44.

privative clauses and executive and legislative assertions of emergency powers. Lauterpacht's critique of dualism tells us that there is a possibility that a valid law might come into existence which is inconsistent with, or even contradicts, an aspirational conception of the rule of law. But he also tells us that at that moment, the 'fundamental jurisprudential identity' of law with its aspirations is in peril. That fact must at the least put the particular law 'under a cloud of legal doubt', to use (against him) Latham CJ's phrase in his dissent to the Australian High Court's decision in the *Communist Party* case.[54] Even if the offending law cannot be invalidated and is enforced against those who fall within its scope, its status as law – its very claim to have authority – is in doubt. And what will create the doubt is that the commitments to the aspirational conception remain intact, even if they are put under strain.

This insight not only puts paid to dualism, it also breaks the slender thread which seemed to prevent the ultra vires doctrine of judicial review from becoming an aspirational conception of the rule of law. As we have seen in chapter 3, that doctrine holds that the rule of law is maintained by judges seeing to it that the administration does not act arbitrarily or 'beyond its powers', where powers means the authority delegated by Parliament. The ultra vires doctrine is a direct emanation of a constitutional positivism committed to a rigid doctrine of the separation of powers. Since the legislature has a monopoly on making law, the only controls on public officials to whom it delegates authority are the controls set out in the statute.

In recent years, proponents of this doctrine have suggested that the common law basis of judicial review is legitimate in so far as the values of the common law can be said to apply by dint of tacit or implied legislative intent. So ultra vires theory, like dualism, now seeks to give some role to the aspirational conception of the rule of law, while making the role conditional on statutory silence. Indeed, in its most sophisticated version, the ultra vires doctrine has now departed from what we can think of as an internal dualism about statute and common law, in which it is asserted that the common law presumptions play a role only when a statute is ambiguous.[55] It has moved to the position that judges are entitled to interpret a statute in the light of such presumptions until the point that

---

[54] *Australian Communist Party* v. *Commonwealth* (1951) 83 CLR 1 at 164.

[55] Sir William Wade is the most eminent public lawyer to have pinned the colours of judicial review to the ultra vires mast, now followed by Christopher Forsyth and Mark Elliott; see Wade and Forsyth, *Administrative Law*; the essays by Forsyth and Elliott in Forsyth, *Judicial Review* and Mark Elliott, *The Constitutional Foundations of Judicial Review* (Oxford: Hart Publishing, 2001).

the legislature explicitly says that they may not. This move is a clear echo of the interpretative obligation imposed by s. 3 of the Human Rights Act, which requires that '[s]o far as it is possible to do, primary legislation and subordinate legislation must be read and given effect in a way which is compatible with the Convention rights'.

In accepting that judges are under such an interpretative obligation, ultra vires theory gives up the red herring that statutory ambiguity is the only legitimate port of entry of common law norms into the regime of statute law.[56] At the same time, it accepts induction into the aspirational conception of the rule of law, save for its claim that an explicit statutory override of the rule of law has complete legal authority. From this claim ultra vires theorists conclude that Parliament is supreme in the absolute sense. But as I have indicated in this section, and as I will continue to explore in the rest of this chapter, what they fail to understand is that a particular law can be valid while lacking legal authority. And with that part of its claim undermined, ultra vires theory is defunct.

Black holes and the rule of law

> There are times of tumult or invasion when for the sake of legality itself the rules of law must be broken . . . The Ministry must break the law and trust for protection to an Act of Indemnity. A statute of this kind is . . . the last and supreme exercise of Parliamentary sovereignty. It legalises illegality . . . [It] . . . combine[s] the maintenance of law and the authority of the Houses of Parliament with the free exercise of that kind of discretionary power or prerogative which, under some shape or other, must at critical junctures be wielded by the executive government of every civilized country.[57]
>
> A. V. Dicey

In a recent article, John Ferejohn and Pasquale Pasquino claim that the constitutional authority to use law to suspend law, thus creating an exceptional regime alongside the regime of ordinary law, is a universal feature of the 'nonabsolutist western legal tradition'.[58] As evidence, they argue that Dicey recognized the necessity of martial law in a Note within the Appendix to his *An Introduction to the Study of the Law of the*

---

[56] Hunt, *Using Human Rights Law in English Courts*, pp. 18–21.
[57] Dicey, *Law of the Constitution*, pp. 412–13.
[58] John Ferejohn and Pasquale Pasquino, 'The Law of the Exception', 210–39 at 239.

Constitution.[59] They do not deal with Dicey's claim in the body of his book that English constitutional law excludes martial law in the sense of the French state of siege, that is, an exceptional regime alongside the regime of ordinary law.[60] But it is undeniable that Dicey can be interpreted as delivering a mixed message about the ability of the state to use the law to suspend the law. Consider, for example, the following passage:

> [W]e must constantly bear in mind the broad and fundamental principle of English law that a British subject must be presumed to possess at all times in England his ordinary common-law rights, and especially his right to personal freedom, unless it can be shown, as it often may be, that he is under given circumstances deprived of them, either by Act of Parliament or by some well-established principle of law. This presumption in favour of legality is an essential part of that rule of law which is the leading feature of English institutions. Hence, if any one contends that the existence of a war in England deprives Englishmen of any of their common-law rights . . ., the burden of proof falls distinctly upon the person putting forward this contention.[61]

Dicey seems to be saying both that the rule of law is a constitutional requirement of the English legal order and that a statute can suspend it, so long as those who claim that it is suspended can prove that that is what has in fact happened. Indeed, he even seems to suggest that something short of a statute can suspend the law – 'some well-established principle of law'. And Ferejohn and Pasquino think that just such a principle is to be found in Dicey's claim that 'martial law comes into existence in times of invasion when, where, and in so far as the King's peace cannot be maintained by *ordinary means* . . . [because of] urgent and paramount necessity'[62] and that: 'This power to maintain the peace by the exertion of any amount of force strictly necessary for the purpose [principle of proportionality] is sometimes described as the *prerogative of the Crown*.'[63]

Now Ferejohn and Pasquino fail to mention that Dicey is sceptical about the description of this power as a prerogative one. It is, he says,

---

[59] Note X in the Appendix to the eight edition of A. V. Dicey, *An Introduction to the Study of the Law of the Constitution* (8th edn, London, MacMillan & Co., 1915), pp. 396–415. This note disappeared from subsequent editions. I will refer to it as Dicey, 'Note X'. All other references to *Introduction to the Study of the Law of the Constitution* are to the tenth edition.

[60] Dicey, *Law of the Constitution*, pp. 287–8.   [61] Dicey, 'Note X', pp. 538–9.

[62] *Ibid.*, p. 539, quoted by Ferejohn and Pasquino, 'The Law of the Exception', 238, their emphasis and insertion.

[63] Dicey, 'Note X', again their emphasis and insertion. (They misquote Dicey here, substituting 'defined' for his 'described'.)

'more correctly' described as the power that every citizen has to use force to preserve or restore the King's peace and since every citizen has it, so too does the Crown. Dicey adamantly rejects the thought that there is a legal or constitutional principle which he calls the 'doctrine of political necessity or expediency'.[64] At most, there exists what he calls 'the doctrine of immediate necessity',[65] which entitles all individuals to use force to counter immediate dangers. Moreover, he is clear that the exercise of this power will, once the emergency has been passed, have to be shown to meet the test of necessity if the person who wielded it is to escape punishment for having committed an illegal act. The existence of a good faith attempt to respond to a genuine state of emergency is not enough for any individual to escape punishment. That person has in addition to show that whatever action taken was strictly necessary to respond to the danger. In so far as acts go beyond strict necessity, they will then be punished unless an Act of Indemnity is passed, which, as Dicey says, amounts to Parliament legalizing illegality.[66]

In my view, there is more riding on these points than the fact that two distinguished scholars had to offer a very partial account of Dicey in order to sustain the claim that the greatest book on the English constitution cannot help but recognize what they claim to be a universal feature of a legal tradition. While they could retort that, whatever Dicey says, he has to recognize this feature, it is still the case that most of what he says is inconsistent with such recognition. Moreover, my argument is that it is only through making sense of the text that seems inconsistent with such recognition that one has the basis for responding to Schmitt's challenge. As I will show, Dicey does respond directly to both limbs of that challenge. Not only is it the case that it is for the court to decide whether the government had a justified claim that there was an emergency – the first limb – but the courts must assess whether the actual responses to the emergency were legal – the second limb.

I will also argue that Dicey's response is more powerful because it is made within the context of a common law legal order, one in which he acknowledges that an explicit statute can legalize both immorality and illegality. Schmitt's challenge is to the liberal ideal of the rule of law, however that ideal is institutionalized. It applies not only to common law legal orders, but also to legal orders where entrenched constitutions protect both the separation of powers and rights, whether or not these constitutions make provision for emergency powers and whether or not,

---

[64] Dicey, 'Note X', pp. 551–5.   [65] *Ibid.*, p. 552.   [66] *Ibid.*, p. 554.

if there is such provision, the limits on emergency powers are detailed and clear. But if that challenge can be met in a legal order where there are no explicit constitutional constraints, it can all the more easily be met by a legal order in which constraints of the right sort are explicitly constitutionalized.

Indeed, it is important to rescue Dicey from Ferejohn and Pasquino precisely to fulfill the ambition if not the structure of their own argument. While they wish to claim that responses to emergencies require a dualist legal order, one divided between ordinary law that responds to the normal situation, and emergency law which responds to the exceptional situation, they also seem to favour the idea that the emergency legal system should be a legal order – a rule of law order, to the extent possible.[67] And they imply that any derogation from the rule of law requires a justification.[68]

So while they concede both limbs of Schmitt's challenge, they try to blunt its force. In particular, they want to resist his suggestion that a sovereign who is determined to do so can change a dictatorship by commission, one limited in scope and time in order to attempt to ensure a return to normality, into a constitutional dictatorship, one which is able to use emergency powers to construct a new kind of order.[69] My argument is that in order for that ambition to be realized, one has to resist that kind of dualism. One needs to maintain the idea they associate with absolutism that legal order is unitary.

Put differently, one needs to maintain Hans Kelsen's Identity Thesis: the thesis that the state is totally constituted by law.[70] According to that thesis, when a political entity acts outside of the law, its acts can no longer be attributed to the state and so they have no authority. Dicey, on my understanding, subscribes to the same thesis, and differs from Kelsen only in that he clearly takes the claim that the state is constituted by law to mean that the law that constitutes the state and its authority includes the principles of the rule of law, which has the result that a political entity acts as a state when and only when its acts comply with the rule of law. There will of course be thicker and thinner versions of the Identity Thesis, and Dicey's is much thicker or more substantive than Kelsen's.[71]

[67] Ferejohn and Pasquino, 'The Law of the Exception', 228.
[68] *Ibid.*, 222.   [69] See Schmitt, *Die Diktatur.*
[70] Hans Kelsen, *Introduction to the Problems of Legal Theory. A Translation of the First Edition of the Reine Rechtslehre or Pure Theory of Law*, translated by Stanley L. Paulson and Bonnie Litschewski-Paulson (Oxford: Oxford University Press, 1992), pp. 97–106.
[71] But see Lars Vinx, 'Legality and Legitimacy in Hans Kelsen's Pure Theory of Law', PhD thesis, University of Toronto (2005) for the argument that Kelsen's understanding of the rule of law is far richer than commonly supposed.

Not only was Dicey concerned about the implications of describing any extraordinary powers in emergency situations as prerogative powers, he was in general deeply opposed to the claims of the royal prerogative, just because those claims purport to stand above or beyond the law.[72] In other words, his conception of constitutional order rejects the idea that the state can operate qua state in a legal black hole and so does not tolerate either an extra-legal power or a constitutional or statutory power to create such a black hole. But as we also saw in chapter 1, he accepts that in a common law legal order, a statute, rule by law, can achieve whatever ends legislators desire. It seems to follow that a statute can create a legal black hole – rule by law can do away with the rule of law.

From this perspective, there is no prerogative attaching to any institution of state to act outside of the law. Put differently, one can concede that there is an outside to law without being a dualist so long as one also denies that that there is authority, within or without the law, to authorize the state to act outside of the law. The Identity Thesis denies the existence of the prerogative or its analogues and requires resistance to attempts to use political power to install the analogues within the law. Thus, if the executive is given the equivalent of such a prerogative either by the constitution or by statute, it is the duty of judges to try to understand that delegation of power as constrained by the rule of law. To the extent that the delegation cannot be so understood, judges must treat it as, to use terminology developed by Ronald Dworkin, an embedded mistake. This is a legal fact that judges have to recognize, but which they must try to limit to the extent possible by refusing to concede to it 'gravitational force' or the ability to have any legal effect beyond what is absolutely necessary.[73] They are entitled to do this because they should adopt as a regulative assumption of their role that all the institutions of government are cooperating in what we can think of as the rule-of-law project, the project which tries to ensure that political power is always exercised within the limits of the rule of law.

As we have seen throughout this book, it is important to depart in some significant respects from Dicey in order to provide a workable version of the Identity Thesis. The regulative assumption just sketched does not require that judges are always the principal guardians of the rule of law. Certain situations, and emergencies are one, might require that

[72] Recall from ch. 3 Lord Shaw's similar remarks in his dissent in *Halliday*.
[73] Ronald Dworkin, 'Hard Cases' in Ronald Dworkin, *Taking Rights Seriously* (London: Duckworth, 1977), pp. 81–130, at p. 121.

Parliament or the executive, play the lead role. The rule-of-law project does not require allegiance to a rigid doctrine of the separation of powers in which judges are the exclusive guardians of the rule of law. Nevertheless, judges always have some role in ensuring that the rule of law is maintained even when the legislature and the executive are in fact cooperating in the project, and they have an important role when such cooperation wanes or ceases in calling public attention to that fact.

It is in seeing that judges are but part of the rule-of-law project that one can begin to appreciate the paradox which arises when rule by law, rule through a statute, is used to do away with the rule of law, to create a legal black hole. There is a contradiction in the idea of legal black hole created by the fact that one cannot have rule by law without the rule of law. But, as I have shown, precisely because judges are but part of the rule-of-law project, one cannot conclude that judges are always entitled to resist statutes that create legal black holes. Whether they are so entitled will depend on the constitutional structure of their legal order. But whatever that structure, they are under a duty to uphold the rule of law. Even if they are not entitled to invalidate a statute that creates a legal black hole, it is their duty to state that the legislature has made a decision to govern arbitrarily rather than through the rule of law. In doing this, they take up the weatherman role I sketched in the Introduction – the role of alerting the Commonwealth to storm clouds on the horizon when the rule of law which secures the fabric of civil society is put under strain.

In chapter 1, I mentioned the ambiguity in the idea of the rule of law between, on the one hand, the rule of law, understood as the rule of substantive principles, and, on the other, rule by law, where as long as there is a legal warrant for what government does, government will be considered to be in compliance with the rule of law. Only if one holds to a fairly substantive or thick conception of the rule of law will one think that there is a point on a continuum of legality where rule by law ceases to be in accordance with the rule of law. But the point I want to extract from Dicey goes beyond this thought. It is that a thick conception of the rule of law is committed to the conclusion that it is possible to use rule by law to take one right off the continuum of legality. One does not have rule by law let alone the rule of law. Here it is important to see that the difference between a statutory creation of a legal black hole in anticipation of officials acting in violation of the law and an Act of Indemnity which, to use Dicey's phrase in the epigraph to this section, 'legalises illegality' retrospectively, is not just a question of timing.

The closest Dicey comes to acknowledging the existence of prospectively created legal black holes is in his discussion of Habeas Corpus Suspension Acts – statutes which suspended habeas corpus for those charged with treason during periods of 'political excitement'.[74] But he says that, while they are popularly thought of as Habeas Corpus Suspension Acts, this name is inaccurate. All such a statute can do is to make it impossible for a detainee 'to insist upon being discharged or put on trial'. But it 'falls very far short of anything like a general suspension of the right to the writ of habeas corpus' and does not 'legalise any arrest, imprisonment, or punishment which was not lawful before the Suspension Act passed'.[75] It thus falls far short, Dicey claims, of a constitutional suspension of guarantees and this is illustrated by the fact that before the Act runs out its effect is 'almost invariably, supplemented by legislation of a totally different character, an Act of Indemnity'.[76]

Dicey's point is that without such an Act of Indemnity, the officials who imprisoned detainees would likely be guilty of a number of unlawful acts. Indeed, the 'unavowed object of a Habeas Corpus Suspension Act is to enable government to do acts which, though politically expedient, may not be strictly legal'.[77] It follows that the combination of a Suspension Act with the prospect of an Indemnity Act does 'in truth arm the executive with arbitrary powers'.[78] However, the relief the Indemnity Act will in fact grant is 'prospective and uncertain', dependent on its terms, and it is unlikely that it will cover acts of 'reckless cruelty'.[79] Moreover, despite the fact that an Act of Indemnity is an 'exercise of arbitrary sovereign power' it is, Dicey insists, still legislation and so 'very different from the proclamation of martial law, the establishment of a state of siege, or any other proceeding by which the executive government at its own will suspends the law of the land'.[80] It thus 'maintains in no small degree the real no less than the apparent supremacy of law'.[81]

But a legal black hole is very different from a suspension of habeas corpus followed by an Act of Indemnity, no matter how confidently the latter can be predicted. For a legal black hole comes about through an immediate statutory combination of the two. It creates a zone in which officials can act unconstrained by the rule of law and in advances declares what they do to be legal. It declares, that is, that official decisions are by definition either necessitous or made in good faith.

---

[74] Dicey, *Law of the Constitution*, p. 229.   [75] *Ibid.*, p. 230.   [76] *Ibid.*, p. 232.
[77] *Ibid.*, p. 234.   [78] *Ibid.*, p. 236.   [79] *Ibid.*   [80] *Ibid.*, p. 237.   [81] *Ibid.*

In contrast, a Suspension Act does not suspend the law but only the remedies to which the person would otherwise be entitled. It is not, that is, a total derogation from law, but a temporary denial of access to certain parts of the law. Moreover, when the Act of Indemnity is enacted it does not remove from the illegal acts that were done the substantive quality of illegality. It merely immunizes the officials from criminal and civil liability for what they did. The substantive law to which the officials were accountable is, in other words, unaffected and moreover the law that gives them immunity does not come about by executive fiat but through legislation. While the two occasions of rule by statute law, suspension followed by indemnity, do introduce arbitrariness into the legal order, the arbitrariness is contained, and so the statutes do not wholly do away with the rule of law.

It is for this reason that Dicey says that it would be erroneous to suppose that the Acts of Indemnity which follow Suspension Acts merely substitute the 'despotism of Parliament for the prerogative of the Crown'. '[T]he fact that the most arbitrary powers of the English executive must always be exercised under Act of Parliament places the government, even when armed with the widest authority, under the supervision, so to speak, of the courts.' In his view, the judges would exercise a control on executive action informed by their understanding of the 'general spirit of the common law'. And he claimed that in England 'Parliamentary sovereignty has favoured the rule of law . . . [T]he supremacy of the law of the land both calls forth the exertion of Parliamentary sovereignty, and leads to its being exercised in a spirit of legality.'[82] In other words, the rule of law is preserved to the extent that the officials who acted illegally are still accountable to a statute and because judges will interpret that statute to ensure that the officials acted in good faith and in a fashion that did not amount to reckless cruelty.

However, the extent to which the rule of law can be preserved is obviously dependent on the terms of the Act of Indemnity. An Act of Indemnity could make it clear that any acts, including acts done in bad faith and acts that are recklessly cruel, were covered, and that judges were not entitled to review official action during the emergency to see whether it fell within the terms of the Act. And Dicey might conclude that just as in the case of a statute that ordered that blue-eyed babies be put to death, judges would be powerless in the face of such a statute. This Act of Indemnity would establish a legal black hole – a zone of illegality – retrospectively and Dicey would surely have no hesitation in labelling it despotic.

[82] *Ibid.*, pp. 412–13.

But even if judges are powerless before such a statute, Dicey's legal theory is not. Rule by law and the rule of law are for Dicey two sides of the same coin, which is why he claimed that the two features of the English constitution are the sovereignty of Parliament and the rule or supremacy of law.[83] So when the rule of law is under stress, a question is raised about whether we even have rule by law. We might have, that is, the true legalization of illegality, a state of affairs brought about by law but one in which there is neither the rule of law nor rule by law. If suspension and indemnity are combined in the same statute, whether prospectively or retrospectively, not only is the rule of law done away with but also rule by law. For law – even on a very thin conception of law – no longer guides the officials who are given power by the statute. My claim is not that law's function should be taken to be exclusively about providing guidelines. Rather, it is that even for those who hold this to be law's main or exclusive function there comes a point where rule by law subverts itself.

Dicey did not, as far as I know, contemplate how a statute might prospectively provide for an executive response to a state of emergency in a fashion that preserved the rule of law.[84] And that had a lot to do with the fact that, as we have seen, he was averse to any legislative delegation to the executive of an authority that would amount to a discretion that could be exercised free of judicial control. He thought that the administrative state is an affront to the rule of law precisely because he thought that a state in which officials were given vast discretionary powers to implement legislative programmes necessarily placed such officials beyond the reach of the rule of law. Put more generally, Dicey was deeply opposed to the administrative state.[85]

But Dicey's reflections on Acts of Indemnity open up the conceptual space for prospective legislative responses to states of emergency which give officials authority to act, for example, to detain individuals, but which require that at the time as they act they justify to an independent tribunal their decisions as both necessary and made in good faith. In order for such a tribunal effectively to review such decisions, it must be the case not only that it is independent but that it has access to all the information which the

---

[83] *Ibid.*, pp. 183–4.

[84] I misinterpreted Dicey on this issue at p. 66 of 'The State of Emergency in Legal Theory', pp. 66–89 in that I claimed that Dicey clearly expresses a preference (in *Law of the Constitution*, pp. 412–13) that Parliament gives to officials in advance resources to deal with emergencies in accordance with the rule of law. The correct interpretation follows this note in the text.

[85] See for instance, *ibid.*, pp. 227–8.

officials claim support the judgment that the individual detained is, say, a threat to national security. In addition, it must be the case that, contrary to the suggestion of the plurality of the US Supreme Court in *Hamdi* explored in chapter 1, the state bears the onus of demonstrating that the individual is a threat. Such responses do exactly what Dicey hoped a Suspension Act and an Act of Indemnity could achieve in tandem; they provide a statutory basis for official decisions and at the same time seek to ensure that the decisions are made in a spirit of legality. And they have the additional advantage of rendering each decision, as it is made, testable to see whether it complies with the regime of legality established by the statute.

Now it is important to see that this idea is no mere thought experiment. As we have seen, SIAC is such a tribunal. It does have defects, most notably, that when confidential information is tested in closed session before it, the detainee and his lawyer do not have access to the information, but have to rely on a special advocate to contest the government's case. But more important is that it goes much further than the United Kingdom had gone before in trying to ensure that a rule-by-law response to a perceived emergency is coupled with the rule of law.

Almost as important is that in previous detention regimes created by statute or under the authority of statute, the government was anxious to avoid appearing to create black holes, to do away with all legal protections. Instead, it created grey holes, that is, protections which did not give detainees anything substantive. But even the impulse to create grey holes shows some recognition that rule by law has to be accompanied by the rule of law. And to the extent that holes created by statute are grey rather than black, judges, as long as they are not minimalists, can use the legal protections provided as a basis for trying to reduce official arbitrariness to the greatest extent possible. In doing so, they challenge the government either to make clearer its intention that detainees should be placed outside the protection of the law or to come up with some better way of fulfilling its claim to be committed to the rule of law.

As I suggested in chapter 1, one must keep a grip on the fact that at one level the debate about the rule of law is a theoretical and normative one and as much about what is appropriate during ordinary or normal times as it is about the kind of test that emergency situations pose for different conceptions of the rule of law. For if we can keep that grip, we keep alive the possibility that a substantive conception of the rule of law has a role to play in legal responses to emergencies. And with that possibility vivid, we maintain a critical resource for evaluating the legal responses to emergencies as well as the judicial decisions about the legality of those responses.

The solution, in my view, lies in appreciating the paradox that a concession that a statute is a valid one is not necessarily a concession that it has legal authority. Dicey is helpful here because he can help us, despite some of his own contrary views, to avoid what I called in chapter 1 the validity trap – the trap we fall into if we think that a sufficient condition for the authority of particular laws is that they meet the formal criteria of validity specified by a legal order. It follows from the trap that if the legal order provides no institutional channel to invalidate a law, then no matter how repugnant we might think its content, it has complete legal authority. The better position, as I have suggested, is to see that a law might be both valid and yet have only a doubtful claim to legal authority because it overrides explicit fundamental principles of the rule of law.

Instructive here is Robert Alexy's example of a constitution which declares in its first provision that the political entity it creates is unjust.[86] Alexy rightly thinks that whatever our theoretical position about law, such a provision looks crazy. It confronts judges and others with what looks like a contradiction installed by law within the legal order. Judges, I suspect, would have to deal with such a provision by ignoring it. More pertinent in the present discussion are constitutional or statutory provisions which seem to give the executive the authority to act outside the rule of law – a provision which does not exclude justice at large but the justice of the rule of law. Such provisions create, in my view, even more severe tensions for judges, if they adopt the regulative assumption that all the institutions of legal order are by definition committed to the rule-of-law project.

Such issues arise in a situation in which the executive or the legislature or both have ceased to cooperate in the rule-of-law project. But an answer to Schmitt need not accept the terms of his challenge. Indeed, my critique of positions which seem to accept part or all of Schmitt's line on emergencies can be summed up in just this fashion. One succumbs to that challenge when one accepts that a substantive conception of the rule of law has no place in a state of emergency, whether this is because one thinks that it is appropriate only for ordinary times or because one thinks that a thin conception is appropriate across the board. To answer that challenge one needs to show that there is a substantive conception of the rule of law that is appropriate at all times. The issue is not how governments and officials should react to an emergency situation for which there is no

---

[86] Robert Alexy, 'A Defence of Radbruch's Formula' in David Dyzenhaus (ed.), *Recrafting the Rule of Law: The Limits of Legal Order* (Oxford: Hart Publishing, 1999), pp. 15–39 at pp. 27–8.

legislative provision. Rather it is whether, when there is the opportunity to contemplate how the law should be used to react to emergencies, it is possible to react in a way that maintains the rule-of-law project, an enterprise in which the legislature, the government and judges cooperate in ensuring that official responses to the emergency comply with the rule of law.

It is thus, as I suggested in chapter 1, a mistake to take regimes of constitutional dictatorship as a test for a substantive conception of the rule of law, for such regimes have already conceded defeat to Schmitt by embedding the potential to create a black hole in the constitution even as they try to confine it. Similarly, it is a mistake to take as the test legislative regimes which explicitly announce an intention that officials may do more or less as they please in responding to an emergency. Such regimes establish a dual state in the sense used in the first chapter, where one has alongside the rule-of-law state a state that governs by law, in effect by delegating analogues of prerogative power to officials.[87] But it does not follow from the fact that such dualism has existed that it is necessary and hence that Schmitt's challenge is unanswerable. The real test for his challenge is whether legislative responses to emergencies necessarily create black holes or grey holes which are in substance black but, as we have seen, in effect worse because they give to official lawlessness the façade of legality.

As we saw in chapter 2 through the comparison of the majority judgments with Latham CJ's dissent in the *Communist Party* case, this kind of illegality retains its character only if one's conception of the rule of law is the aspirational one that holds that the rule of law is the rule of principles. But it is quite consistent with such an aspirational conception to hold that there can be a zone of illegality, a space where arbitrary power and not law rules. Thus I wish to add a refinement to Murray Hunt's recent argument that English law took a 'false doctrinal step' when it introduced 'spatial metaphors into the language of judicial review' by presupposing that there are certain areas within which public officials are 'simply beyond the reach of judicial interference'.[88]

Hunt's argument is correct but the refinement I think it needs is that spatial metaphors become apt when the law is used to put officials beyond the law, into, that is, a legal black hole. If law is a matter of rule-of-law principle, there are no holes within legal order, since a hole is by definition outside the reach of law.

---

[87] Fraenkel, *The Dual State.*   [88] Murray Hunt, 'Sovereignty's Blight, p. 338.

Spatial metaphors, Hunt says, express a vision of constitutionalism which embraces 'competing' but irreconcilable 'supremacies', the sovereign Parliament and the sovereign individual, whose guardian is the courts. So one gets in the same package two 'radically opposed narratives', political positivism[89] and liberal constitutionalism. To make things worse, as Hunt points out, one finds that adherents of this view tend to flip arbitrarily from one narrative to another.[90] And, as I have shown in this book, issues such as emergency or security legislation, or immigration, tend to push judges away from a Dworkinian or liberal constitutionalism towards the version of political positivism I have called constitutional positivism, the stance of positivist judges who work within a legal order in which their positivism is not at home.

Sovereignty thus casts, according to Hunt, a 'double blight' on the common law grasp of constitutionalism. It hides the fact that Parliament is subject to constitutional constraints as well as the fact that Parliament 'has an important role in both the definition and protection of fundamental rights and values'. In addition, it gets in the way of the 'proper articulation of what may be perfectly legitimate reasons for deferring' either to Parliament or to its delegates, 'obscuring them behind a vocabulary of spaces and boundaries which are asserted as if the underlying assumptions about the constitutional division of powers were not contentious'.[91]

The view that there are such legitimate reasons presupposes, as I have argued, that the rule-of-law project is a common one, so that, as long as the judgments of the legislature and the executive are either justifiable or justified as interpretations of the relevant rule-of-law values, judges should defer to these judgments. The kind of deference here is not deference in its primary meaning of submission to an order of a superior, deference understood as 'abasement', to repeat Lord Rodger in *Belmarsh*. Rather, as we have seen in chapter 3, it is deference as respect – respect for a successful attempt at justification.[92]

When a statute is challenged, it might contain a preamble that makes such an attempt, but often the justification will be offered only when a judge hears a challenge. With administrative decisions, often the very possibility of there being a challenge to a decision turns on whether reasons

---

[89] Hunt calls this kind of positivism 'democratic positivism', *ibid.*, p. 370, a label I also used to find apt. For reasons explained in chapter 2, and to which I will return at the end of this chapter, I think 'political' is more appropriate than 'democratic'.

[90] *Ibid.*, pp. 343–4.   [91] *Ibid.*, p. 339.

[92] For my most detailed attempt to elaborate this distinction, see Dyzenhaus, 'The Politics of Deference', pp. 279–307. For Hunt's account of what follows from the same distinction, see Hunt, 'Sovereignty's Blight', pp. 351–4.

were offered justifying the decision; hence, the growing recognition in common law countries of a duty on public officials to give reasons for their decisions. Imposing such a duty does of course have costs. But whatever the result of a cost-benefit analysis of a general imposition, it is important to see that its imposition may be understood as a kind of compliment to the administrative state, rather than as an intrusion performed in order to facilitate judicial colonization of the administration.

Consider, for example, the fact that until the 1960s and 1970s judges in the common law world held the view that delegations of authority to officials that gave them 'administrative' as opposed to 'quasi-judicial' authority neither attracted the requirements of natural justice nor were subject to review on the basis of the content of the discretionary judgment, except in quite exceptional situations. In Hunt's terms, it was one of the areas treated as if it were 'beyond the reach of legality, and within the realm of pure discretion in which remedies for wrongs are political only'.[93] One of the indicia of a delegation of administrative authority was that the official was given authority to act by a subjective, 'if satisfied that . . .' provision, instead of the more objective sounding 'if the minister has reasonable cause to believe . . .' That is, a subjective delegation of discretion was regarded as both a substantive and a general privative clause, as a clause which told judges not to review on the basis of rule-of-law principles and that their review authority was in any case excluded. When common law judges held that there is a general duty at common law for public officials to act fairly unless the constitutive statute expressly indicated otherwise, one reaction was that they were illegitimately usurping legislative authority.

But, as I have argued in chapter 3, the thought that the administrative state is not lawless but subject to the rule of law, including the legal value of fairness, is a thought that goes further than including the administrative state into the legal order in a way antithetical to the rigid doctrine of the separation of powers. It also supposes that the administrative state is legitimate in part because it is answerable to the fundamental values of legal order. And that thought goes beyond the claim that bodies that are not courts must make decisions in accordance with values that were previously thought to apply only to courts or court-like, quasi-judicial bodies.[94] As indicated above, it should include the further claim that,

---

[93] *Ibid.*, p. 339.

[94] It is important to signal here my awareness of the fact that judges have not yet found a general duty at common law for them to give reasons. Perhaps judicial resistance to a general duty at common law for officials to give reasons is partly influenced by judges' supposing that public officials can't be held to a higher standard of fairness than they

generally speaking, judges should defer to public officials' interpretations of the law, as well as to legislative and administrative choice when it comes to institutional design, including the design of fair procedures.

There is, however, a rather large difference between, on the one hand, a genuine statutory or administrative attempt to design fair procedures and, on the other, a legislative or administrative declaration that no fairness is appropriate. Where it is the administration that refuses, clearly judges are entitled to review. But where the legislature puts in place a substantive privative clause matters are more complicated. Recall that a substantive privative clause does not remove a judge's authority to review, but simply tells her that she may not rely on common law grounds for review, for example, the principle that officials are under a duty to act fairly. And I argued in chapter 2 that whether judges are entitled to react to a substantive privative clause by voiding it will depend largely on their understanding of their written constitution, if their legal order has one.

Even more complex is the situation where the legislature stipulates some degree of fairness and is explicit that no more is appropriate, where the kind of decision seems to cry out for much more. The challenge to the legality of the military tribunals put in place after 9/11 in the United States is a challenge in this kind of situation. These tribunals do not operate in a legal black hole, but in grey holes – space which is not adequately controlled by legality. And here it is important to recall that SIAC has been much criticized.[95] In part, this criticism comes about because SIAC's role has been expanded to review the decisions to detain indefinitely foreign nationals who are considered a security threat but who cannot be deported because of the risk of torture. Critics are particularly concerned that the subjects of these decisions play no role in contesting the evidence given in the closed sessions. They thus argue that while SIAC is advertised as an institution that implements the rule of law, in fact it provides a mere cloak for potential abuse of authority.

It might seem then that I have just made two fatal concessions. I have conceded that the question whether judges are entitled to uphold fundamental principles of legality depends on whether there is a written constitution which permits them to do so, a concession which then

themselves are subject to. And their continued reluctance to find that they are subject to such a duty night signal a sense that their independence is compromised through the logic of accountability that a duty to give reasons unfolds.

[95] See for example, Lucy Scott-Moncrieff, 'Detention Without Trial' (2004) 26 *London Review of Books* 22. See also the Seventh Report of Session 2004–05 of the House of Commons Constitutional Affairs Committee, 'The Operation of the Special Immigration Appeals Commission (SIAC) and the Use of Special Advocates'.

undermines the claim that there are such values inherent in legal order. And I have conceded that imaginative experiments which are designed to uphold the rule of law run the risk of undermining it. I do not however believe that I have made the first concession and the second is not so much a concession but a fact about risk which has constantly to be borne in mind.

In respect of the first issue, I have only conceded that there is such a question when the legislature very explicitly announces its intention to exclude such a value. That condition for excluding fairness is in itself a significant legal constraint since it requires a clear statement to override it. I have argued that this constraint is constitutional, even though it might be the case that in the absence of a written constitutional protection of the judges' review authority over such matters, the judges cannot enforce the constraint in the face of a clear legislative statement. In fact, the idea that the non-enforceability of a norm by judges in the face of a clear legislative statement means that it lacks constitutional status is a product of the mindset which includes the narratives of competing supremacies. The aspirational view of the rule of law, in contrast, recognizes that any of the branches of government may fail on occasion to live up to law's aspirations.

Consider again s. 33 of the Canadian Charter of Rights and Freedoms which permits the federal and provincial legislatures to override by statute judicial determinations that their statutes violate certain Charter-protected rights and freedoms for a period of five years, after which the override must be legislatively renewed if it is not to lapse. The override does not render any of the overridable values unconstitutional. It merely gives to the legislature a limited opportunity to operate unconstitutionally for a period, but on condition that it owns up to that fact. The override is meant to, and does, both incite and renew democratic debate about the government's decisions to govern outside of the constitutional order. Thus when judges uphold such an overriding statute, they do not uphold it merely because it is technically valid. Rather, they uphold the statute because, while it lacks authority from the perspective of Canada's explicit constitutional commitments, it has authority from the fact that it is the product of a properly conducted democratic procedure. In a country with these explicit constitutional commitments, the government's decision to govern outside of the constitutional order will put strain on its claim to be democratic. Moreover, that strain is increased by the fact that the terms of a valid override require the public to take note of the fact that the constitutional order is at risk. I have suggested that the Human Rights Act creates a very similar structure for the United Kingdom.

Put differently, while that law will lack complete legal authority because it overrides the rule of law, it will have some authority in a democracy because it has complied with the technical criteria of manner and form, but not merely because it has complied with such criteria. Indeed, a judge might be willing to concede some authority to the law merely because it is valid law on the Hobbesian basis that any order is better than chaos.[96] But the more the judge is driven to rely on her sense that her legislature is choosing to govern outside of the rule of law, the less she will think that there are democratic reasons to regard the law as authoritative, unless she adopts the very crude account of majoritarian democracy with which I began this section. Correspondingly, the more she will be driven to the Hobbesian basis as the only reason for according the law authority and at that point she should be close to giving it no authority at all.

A common law legal order in which the constitution is wholly unwritten does not then, as I have tried to argue, differ from Canada or the United Kingdom today in that it lacks genuine constitutional principles. The main respect in which there is a difference is that in such a common law legal order, there is no formal requirement that will force the public to take note of a violation of constitutional commitments. Rather, one will need judges determined to uphold the rule of law and ready to articulate fully (not minimally) their reasons for doing so, in order to help to ensure that the public is aware of the implications for the rule of law of legislative decisions.[97] Thus, I have not conceded that the question whether judges are entitled to uphold fundamental principles of legality depends on whether there is a written constitution which permits them to do so.

In all of these legal orders, judges are under a duty to uphold constitutional principles, including the principles of the unwritten constitution. That the principles can be overridden speaks to the existence of a political culture in which parliamentary judgment is given a great deal of respect, even when it puts a strain on fundamental principles. But this fact neither detracts from the constitutional status of these principles, nor undermines a claim that judges are always under a duty to uphold them. They uphold their duty by making explicit that the legislature's choice is to govern outside of the rule of law, or the written constitution, as the case may be.

---

[96] Though as I will point out below, it is doubtful that Hobbes was in this sense a Hobbesian.

[97] Of course, segments of the public might be more legally aware than judges and the media might in fact at times do a better job than judges can do, or even do the job when judges won't.

In regard to the issue of risk to the rule of law through institutional experiments, I must admit that a conception of law as a matter of principles is not immune to damage through the wrong kind of institutional experiment. Whether law is conceived as a matter of rules or principles, it is dangerous to permit governments the luxury of claiming that they govern in accordance with the rule of law when in fact law provides them with a formal façade that serves only to cover abuse of power. However, it is important to understand that in liberal democracies and beyond, it has become almost unthinkable for governments to govern outside of the framework of the rule of law. In addition, the allegedly permanent nature of the international terrorist threat that forms the backdrop for many of the cases discussed in this book makes, in my view, a legislative response inevitable. Finally, and most importantly, it is desirable, as Dicey argued, that the response be a legal one, which means that one should experiment only is so far as experimentation is justifiable by rule-of-law principles.

One must then hold in place the assumption that government is bound to govern in accordance with the rule of law, what we might think of as the assumption of constitutionality. And that assumption displaces the foundational status of Schmitt's distinction between the normal and the exceptional. It transforms it from its role in Schmitt as an assumption into a conclusion which has to be argued for. Moreover, where it seems appropriate to say that a situation is truly exceptional, that is it beyond the reach of the rule of law, this is not because, as Schmitt would have it, norms cannot apply to exceptions; rather, it is because power may triumph over law. If there were no models available for what we might think of as experiments controlled by legality or the rule of law, it would seem that the challenge posed by the exception left us in a highly uncomfortable position. But, as I have indicated, there is ample evidence of the right sort of experiment, presented by the development of the common law of judicial review in the last forty or so years. Since security issues will be dealt with by delegating authority to public officials, one should look to the common law of judicial review for a source of ideas about how such authority can remain subject to the rule of law.[98]

As should now be clear from my argument, I hold the view that governments which have the luxury of time to craft a response to emergency situations should do so in a way that complies with the rule of law. It does not follow, however, that all possible acts by public officials should

---

[98] For extensive argument on this theme in the context of the United States, see Masur, 'A Hard Look or a Blind Eye'.

be subject to the rule of law. Torture is absolutely prohibited by international law as well as by the domestic legal orders of many states for many good reasons, to do both with our understanding of ourselves as human beings and with the fact that even the prudential reasons for torture are so dubious. But the humanitarian reasons are so strong that no decent regime could permit torture. As a result, if officials consider that they have to torture to avoid a catastrophe, the ticking bomb situation, such an act must happen extra-legally, more or less the position the Israeli Supreme Court has taken. In this situation, all a court should say is that if officials are going to torture, they should expect to be criminally charged and at trial they may try a defence of necessity.[99] But in saying that, a court is simply recognizing, as we saw Dicey did, that in some situations where officials act outside of the law they merit after-the-fact recognition that they made an excusable decision because it was necessary that they act and the law did not provide them with the resources they needed.

The twist with torture is that a decent regime is precluded from providing prospective legal resources which attempt to legalize what would otherwise be illegal. Torture is, in other words, 'unlegalizable'. What precisely falls into this category of the unlegalizable will, of course, be controversial. Does preventive detention fall into this category, or trials which fall far short of the standards prescribed for criminal justice?

My point here is that in an era when the rule of law has a currency such that at least lip service to its ideals is required, governments will generally seek to use law prospectively to indemnify official illegality. Governments will prefer to use executive authorizations rather than explicit legislation ones, just because the use of an open-ended statutory delegation of authority can be read by judges minded to do so in the general spirit of the common law. And in requiring governments to opt for altogether explicit legislative authorization, judges can force governments to come clean in a way which increases political accountability and which might permit judges to find the authorization unconstitutional.

---

[99] See Judgment of the Supreme Court of Israel, sitting as the High Court of Justice, 6 September 1999, concerning the Legality of the General Security Services' Interrogation Methods. The Court did indicate the possibility that the Legislature might enact a statute that put in place prior authorization to torture, modelled on the defence of necessity. But my sense is that this indication was a dare which the Court thought the legislature could not afford to take up and that if it did there would be grounds for invalidation. For discussion, see David Dyzenhaus, '"With the Benefit of Hindsight": Dilemmas of Legality in the Face of Injustice' in Emilios Christodoulidis and Scott Veitch (eds.), *Lethe's Law: Justice, Law and Ethics in Reconciliation* (Oxford: Hart Publishing, 2001), pp. 65–90 at pp. 86–9.

Of course, the preferable result is that judges prompt governments and legislatures to undertake the imaginative experiments in institutional design that result in tribunals such as SIAC. With the caveat mentioned above about the category of the unlegalizable, I do think it is worthwhile running the risk of preserving legality through institutional experiments. However, judges must insist, as we saw in chapter 1 Justices Souter and Ginsburg did in *Hamdi*, that there is both an absolutely explicit legislative mandate for such experiments and that the experiments be conducted in accordance with the rule of law.

Further, when it comes to the category of the unlegalizable, the idea of the bill of attainder is helpful. Recall from chapter 1 Dicey's example of the statute that orders that all blue-eyed babies be put to death. Dicey used this example to illustrate two things. First, the utter immorality of a statute does not suffice to make it illegal. Second, it is highly unlikely both that legislators would be inclined to enact such a statute and that their electorate would permit them to do so.

I agree with Dicey but wish to point out that his example was a bad one, since a statute that in effect finds a person or a group guilty of a crime and orders their execution is a bill of attainder. So the opposition to such a bill, whether within or without Parliament, would not be only that it was immoral, but also that it was illegal, or, more accurately, that it flouted the fundamental moral values of legality; just the sort of opposition which we saw in chapter 1 was incited in the United Kingdom by the government's proposal to protect immigration decisions by a draconian privative clause.

As we have seen in chapter 2, one way of understanding the offence of such a bill is in terms of an idea of the separation of powers, where the judiciary has the role of determining in an open trial both guilt and appropriate punishment. T. R. S. Allan argues in the leading theoretical treatment of the rule of law that the substance of the intuition against bills of attainder pertains to the fact that the statute in issue offends the constitutional guarantee, written or unwritten, of an independent judiciary presiding in open court over determinations of guilt and punishment. A bill of attainder, he says, is just 'the paradigmatic example of legislation whose violation of the principles of equality and due process contravenes the rule of law'.[100] The repugnance of the common law tradition to such statutes is born of the idea that while the legislature can enact into law its understandings of subversion and other offences, the rule of law requires both that that offence be framed generally and that anyone accused of

[100] Allan, *Constitutional Justice*, p. 148.

such an offence be tried in a court of law. Once we see this, we can also see that it is not so much the separation of powers that is at stake as the reasons for the separation of powers. The constitutional role of the judges is to see to it that the fundamental values of legal order are preserved, by whatever means are most appropriate.

Those with legal power, including those at the very top of the hierarchy of legal order, must understand these values, so that they can take part in the common project of their realization. On this view, a doctrine of the separation of powers should be seen as instrumental to realizing the legal order's ideals. If in order to ensure the integrity of legal order, it is necessary to imagine institutions for the enforcement of legality that go against the grain of received views about the separation of powers, one should not let those views stand in the way of enforcing legality. Moreover, I want to suggest that this claim applies to all societies that assert they are governed by the rule of law. As long as there is a basis for the assertion, those subject to the law will be able to hold public officials to account, their accountability not being just to the positive law but also to the values of legality.

Thus while Parliament can place officials in a zone uncontrolled by law, a legal black hole, this does not show that what the officials are doing or did is legal, only that political power can be exercised in a brute fashion, permitting those who wield it to break free of the constraints of constitutionality and legality. Only in this situation, the situation where a space uncontrolled by law is deliberately created, do spatial metaphors become appropriate.

But what those who wield such power cannot do, or more accurately should not be allowed to do, is have their cake and eat it too in claiming that because they can use law to break free of law, what they are doing is therefore legal. In this point lies the answer to the question of why judges are always legally entitled to read down a general privative clause, but may not be entitled to do the same with a substantive privative clause.

The answer depends on seeing that the problems privative clauses create occur at different levels. A general privative clause – one that seeks to exclude authority to review – creates two different kinds of contradiction. It creates a contradiction within the statute between the positive injunction to courts not to review for jurisdictional error and the positive limits the statute sets out. It also creates a contradiction between the positive injunction and the limits set on the tribunal by the values of legality to be found in the common law constitution. In creating the internal contradiction, the legislature sends a mixed message to judges which it is their constitutional responsibility to resolve by applying a presumption that the legislature must be taken to intend its statutes to be governed by legality. That presumption entitles the courts to interpret the privative clause as if the legislature intended it to work other than by excluding either positive or constitutional limits. Putting in place criteria and then saying government need not abide by them is an even worse kind of hypocrisy than that involved in ratifying a human rights convention and saying that it should have no effect internally. To think along these lines would be for judges to suppose that the legislature has removed itself from the common project of aspiring to the rule of law.[101]

In contrast, a completely explicit substantive privative clause, one which precludes judges from relying on principles of the rule of law as grounds of review, creates only the second kind of contradiction – one between the positive law of the statute and the values of legality. If the judge has no explicit constitutional basis for invalidating the provision, she can still point out its illegality in her judgment, in effect doing what s. 4 of the Human Rights Act permits judges to do in issuing a declaration of incompatibility. Section 4 then formalizes the requirement that I think applies to all judges who understand their duty to uphold the rule of law. One should not here underestimate the political clout that attaches even to such an informal declaration. The judges cannot be accused of judicial activism but still they send a signal to the public and the legislature which should be taken very seriously, as proved to be the case in the United Kingdom in the wake of *Belmarsh* until the terror attacks of July 2005.

My argument has been not only that the rule of law can be imposed in national security matters, but also that judges are under an obligation to impose the rule of law until they are explicitly told by the legislature that it wants government to govern outside of the rule of law. The full realization of the rule of law will require the cooperation of all three branches of government, but judges must adopt as a regulative assumption of their practice that the other two are cooperating. Hence, judges should treat positive intimations of the desire to be governed by the rule of law, whether these come from the legislature or the executive, as evidence of the basis of constitutional principles which all three branches are committed to realizing. But intimations to the contrary should be ignored. It is not enough, for example, for a government to send a message to the judges by avoiding the declaration of a state of emergency and instead enacting

---

[101] On the issue of hypocrisy, see Mason CJ's and Dean J's judgment in *Minister for Immigration and Ethnic Affairs* v. *Teoh* (1995) 183 CLR 273 at 291.

a terrorism statute that introduces a series of partial exceptions into the ordinary law of the land. Just as judges should treat a state of emergency as governed by the rule of law, except in so far as there is an explicit legislative command to do otherwise, so they should treat these attempts to normalize or make permanent a state of emergency through a terrorism statute as subject to the rule of law.

Those who wield executive power might successfully act against the law, but for judges to validate such executive actions would be for them to confuse power with authority. If the law gives to officials in completely explicit terms the power to disregard rule-of-law principles, judges might find that, in the absence of a written constitution, they are powerless to do anything about this. They are still, however, under a duty to uphold the rule of law. Hence, they should certainly not give in to the temptation to assert that all is well in order to maintain that they still have their role. Judicial assurances of legality are to be shunned since they are usually attempts to disguise the fact that the judges have lost their nerve. Rather, it their duty to point out publicly in their judgments that a matter which is susceptible to the control of the rule of law, and which is very important for the rule of law to control, has been deliberately removed from such control.

In sum, the nature of politics, or of the political as Schmitt would put it, does not undermine the claim that there is a constitutional basis for the control of states of emergency or exception by the rule of law. A choice has to be made, which is itself political, and which Schmitt conceals. At its starkest, the choice is between government under the rule of law and government by arbitrary power. As we saw in chapter 1, one might argue that national security is different because judges will always lose their nerve when it comes to national security, or that the executive will do what it deems fit in an emergency, thus bringing the law into disrepute if one seeks to impose the rule of law too strenuously. Or one might argue that there are some situations which are so exceptional that it would be better to avoid an attempt to regulate them by the rule of law since that attempt will muddy the issue of the reach of the rule of law in less exceptional situations. But none of these arguments can support the claim that there is something exceptional about national security that makes executive decisions in the security area unsusceptible to the constitutional control of the rule of law.

There are, however, two better closely related arguments. First, there is the argument that judges cannot have any significant independent role in scrutinizing executive decisions about national security without access to independent sources of information. Since the judicial branch cannot establish its own intelligence service, effective review is not possible. But this is not an objection confined to judicial review of national security alone. Rather, it is an objection to review in all those situations where the information on which the executive acts is not by and large in the public domain, so that the applicant for judicial review has to rely on the ability of lawyers to test the executive's claim that the information it presents as the basis for its decision does provide a reasonable justification of the decision.[102] All that makes the area of national security special, and even then it is not uniquely special, is the issue of sensitivity and confidentiality of the information. And as we have seen, if a government is minded or required to think imaginatively about how to design institutions which implement the rule of law, it can create through legislation something like SIAC, a review panel which goes a long way to providing effective review while protecting confidentiality.

The second argument has to do with judicial ability to evaluate the information in the national security area. The concern here is not only with lack of expertise. It is also with the thought that as soon as judges get involved in the process of evaluating reasons for decision, whatever they claim about respecting a distinction between review and appeal, between an assessment of the legality of the decision and substituting their sense of the merits for the executive's sense, they do in fact turn review into appeal.

In my view, the answer to the concerns again lies in imagination in institutional design. Recall that my point in linking *Liversidge* through *Chahal*[103] to *Rehman* and *Belmarsh* was that Lord Atkin's dissent in *Liversidge* could not by itself provide a basis for effective review of detention decisions. Rather, the dissent should be regarded as a prompt to government and the legislature either to accept the political costs of doing away with a charade of the rule of law established by the phrase 'reasonable cause to believe' and by the ineffective advisory committee or to turn the charade into something real and effective. And real and effective requires that those engaged in the review do not accept the say-so of the executive, whether it comes in the form of 'we can't tell you the reasons but there are reasons', as in *Liversidge*, or, as in *Rehman*, 'we will give you the reasons because we have no choice, but as long as we have reasons which are not absurd, our decisions must withstand review'.

---

[102] See Masur, 'A Hard Look or a Blind Eye'.
[103] *Chahal* v. *United Kingdom* (1996) 23 EHRR 413.

Moreover, as before, the concerns are not confined to the national security area. They are concerns about judicial review more generally, given
that judges had moved away from a more positivistic conception of the
rule of law to a more substantive, common law model. Telling here is that
when the Supreme Court of Canada retreated from its earlier jurisprudence in the wake of 9/11, a retreat in which Lord Hoffmann's judgment
in *Rehman* was very influential, it did not describe its retreat as confined
to the situation of national security. Rather, on rigid separation of powers
grounds, the Court made a general claim that that earlier jurisprudence
was wrongly interpreted if one thought that it supported the proposition
that when judges review they are entitled to 'reweigh' the factors or reasons that the decision-maker has to take into account. All they are entitled
to do is to check that reasons are present.[104]

I will now conclude this study of the constitution of law and the role of
the rule of law within that constitution by sketching its implications for
philosophy of law.

The rule of good law

The most influential discussion of the rule of law of the last thirty years is
Joseph Raz's 'The Rule of Law and Its Virtue'.[105] Raz argues that the virtue
of the rule of law is like the virtue of a knife.[106] The virtue of a knife is
sharpness but it can of course be used in the service of very bad as well as
good purposes. Similarly, the virtue of law is its effectiveness in guiding
human planning, a virtue which it has because law communicates to legal
subjects through rules of determinate content. But the law can be used in
the service of very bad as well as good purposes. Therefore, one should not
confuse the rule of law with the rule of good law. Everything will depend
on the purposes which those who have authority to do so make law serve.

The great influence of this paper does not come from its standard
positivist line but from the way in which Raz elaborated it. He argued that
in order for law to exhibit this virtue, it must live up to certain internal
criteria, the principles of the rule of law. He thus seemed to respond to the
claim that there is a difference between the rule of law and the arbitrary
rule of men, the kind of claim which drives aspirational conceptions of the
rule of law, such as the common law one, developed most prominently by

---

[104] *Suresh v. Canada (Minister of Citizenship and Immigration)* [2002] 1 SCR 3 at 26–7.
[105] Joseph Raz, 'The Rule of Law and Its Virtue' in Joseph Raz, *The Authority of Law: Essays
on Law and Morality* (Oxford: Oxford University Press, 1979), pp. 210–29.
[106] *Ibid.*, p. 226.

Lon L. Fuller.[107] And it is imperative for positivists so to respond if they wish to show that a positivist account of law is more than the 'gunman situation writ large'.[108]

This memorable phrase was used by H. L. A. Hart to describe the command theory of law, the theory he took to be put forward by his positivist predecessors, Jeremy Bentham and John Austin. Hart and Raz after him wish to show that the rule of law does more than replace the arbitrary rule of men with the arbitrary rule of one man, with enough power to enforce his wishes. Hart thought that his most important contribution to legal theory, the key to solving the central problems of jurisprudence, is the idea of the rule of recognition, the rule which in any legal order those with sovereign power must follow if they are to succeed in making law.[109] Raz's essay on the rule of law then takes Hart's project further by showing that the rule of law places even more constraints on power because there are criteria internal to law's rule which those who claim to rule through law must respect if they are to live up to that claim.

However, the point of Raz's elaboration is to show that these internal criteria, the equivalents of Fuller's principles of an internal morality of law, do not make the rule of law the rule of good law, even though they might make it less arbitrary than the rule of men. The constraints on rule that come from these criteria are constraints that if followed make law more effective, a better instrument of the purposes of those with power. Raz thus seems to provide an account of the rule of law that attends to the fact that it does provide us with a distinctive mode of political ordering, but one which permits us to observe that a society which adopts that mode of ordering can be dedicated to using the law in the service of injustice.

Raz's attempt to respond to this fact about the rule of law fails. He is compelled by his positivism to argue that principles such as that judges should be independent, that public officials should act fairly, and that judges should have the authority to review officials to check that they have complied with rule-of-law principles, are principles that ensure that law is better able to provide effective guidance to it subjects.[110] In his view, these requirements serve to assist those with authority to interpret the law in the process of working out its determinate content so that that content can then be transmitted to legal subjects. But as we have seen, such requirements make sense only if they are understood as instrumental not

---

[107] Fuller, *Morality of Law*. For an illuminating discussion, see John Finnis, *Natural Law and Natural Rights* (Oxford: Clarendon Press, 1980), pp. 270–6.

[108] Hart, 'Positivism', p. 59.   [109] Hart, *The Concept of Law*, ch. 5.

[110] Raz, 'The Rule of Law and Its Virtue', pp. 214–18.

to guidance in this sense, but to ensuring that the law corresponds to the greatest extent possible to its aspirations, expressed in the fundamental or constitutional values of legal order. A society which followed Raz's criteria would not have the rule of law but very effective and faithful implementation by public officials of the commands of the sovereign.

The roots of this failure lie in the fact that Raz starts, with one exception, not from the basis of our intuitions about the rule of law, intuitions which derive from its practice, but with a conceptual argument about the very idea of authority.[111] The exception is that Raz notes that all authorities are committed to claiming to be legitimate. Raz argues that while authorities will make this claim, they are legitimate if and only if their directives serve the interests of their subjects better than would the subjects were they to follow their own sense of right and wrong. But, and here is the conceptual move, the directives can serve this purpose only if they effectively replace the subjects' sense of right and wrong. And that requires that the content of the directives be derived by tests about what the authority in fact intended, not from the reasons which led the subjects to regard the authority as authoritative. In other words, for Raz, the positivist claim that law is a matter of rules with determinate content is not an observation about legal practice but an entailment of a conceptual claim about the nature of authority.

Notice that this conception of authority is highly authoritarian. Legal subjects, those who are subject to the law, must accept that they are under a duty to obey the law whatever its content since, if they understand the nature of authority, they will also understand that the content of the law replaces their sense of right and wrong. However, it is also anarchistic, since Raz argues that an authority is in fact legitimate if and only if its directives serve the liberal ideal of individual autonomy. The legal subject is thus under no moral duty to obey the law, unless the law serves autonomy. In other words, legal subjects are saved from authoritarianism in appreciating that the criteria for the legitimacy of law come from a morality that is extrinsic to law.

Raz's picture of the authority of law undermines the moral reasons that Hart provided in 1957 for adopting legal positivism. Hart suggested that legal positivism can help us to avoid the problem of anarchism, the stance that says that law has authority only if it is moral, by which is meant if

---

[111] See Joseph Raz, 'Authority, Law, and Morality' in Joseph Raz, *Ethics in the Public Domain: Essays in the Morality of Law and Politics* (Oxford: Oxford University Press, 1994), pp. 194–221. See also Joseph Raz, 'The Obligation to Obey: Revision and Tradition' in Raz, *Ethics in the Public Domain*, pp. 325–38.

it complies with my sense of right and wrong. It also helps us to avoid the problem of conservatism or 'obsequious quietism', which says that it follows from the fact that X is the law that X is moral.[112] But, as I have tried to show, Raz's picture of authority creates precisely the dilemma that Hart thought positivism would help us to avoid. Either one adopts the stance of the legal subject, in which case positive law supplants one's conscience, or one adopts the stance of the liberal individual, in which case law has no authority unless its content is right by one's own moral lights. To use terms I introduced earlier, either one adopts a stance to authority of deference as submission or one adopts a stance of no deference at all.[113]

My point is not that Raz strayed from Hart's path. Rather, it is that Hart no less than Raz was incapable of doing justice to his moral reasons for adopting for legal positivism, and that is because Hart too argues for legal positivism on largely conceptual grounds, hence the title of his most famous book. In my view, the moral reasons are sound but they lead to a rejection of what I have called earlier conceptual legal positivism. And the best illustration of why this is the case comes from the person who is often credited both with founding legal positivism and with constructing a highly authoritarian or gunman-writ-large conception of authority – Thomas Hobbes.

In the Preface to *Leviathan* Hobbes set out exactly the same aspirations for his theory of politics and law that Hart set out in 1958. He said that he wished to show how we might 'pass unwounded between the opposing swords of those who contend on one side for too great liberty, and on the other side for too much authority'.[114] But Hobbes did not think that this path could be secured through driving a wedge between the conditions for an authority being legitimate and our understanding of the content of authoritative directives. While Hobbes did argue that authority and not truth makes law, his conception of authority sets internal conditions on authority, which go a long way to ensuring that the claim that authorities make to be legitimate is justified.

Hobbes did want law-making power located in one supreme body or person, the sovereign. But he regarded the articulation of the content of

---

[112] Hart, 'Positivism', pp. 53–4.

[113] See Ronald Dworkin, 'Thirty Years On' (2002) 115 *Harvard Law Review* 1655–87. Dworkin not only criticizes each step in Raz's argument but points out that Raz's account of authority leads to two different and contradictory stances to authority: either almost complete deference or no deference at all.

[114] Hobbes, *Leviathan*, edited by Richard Tuck (Cambridge: Cambridge University Press, 1991), p. 3.

any sovereign judgment as an exercise in which public officials, including judges, have a legitimate role. Moreover, in articulating the content of this judgment, the officials are under a duty to interpret the positive or civil law in the light of their understanding of the fundamental or constitutional values of legal order, the laws of nature, since the sovereign's positive laws are to be understood as attempts to give concrete expression to the very same values.[115] While Hobbes was opposed to the common law tradition and its claims about judicial guardianship of the artificial reason of the law, he therefore shared with it one crucial assumption – that the legislature, the executive and the judges are best understood as engaged in a common project that aspires to realize the fundamental values of legality.

Thus while Hobbes had, through John Austin, an immense influence on Dicey, and would ordinarily be considered one of the chief culprits for coining the vocabulary of sovereignty to which we have seen Hunt object, he did not in fact conceive of sovereignty in the absolutist way which we have seen drives constitutional positivism. His understanding of law is very similar to Hunt's, when Hunt sketches in the English context an idea of law as promoting a culture of justification, informed by a 'rich conception of legality and of the rule of law'.[116]

Hobbes, in my view, hardly differs at all from Hunt in advocating a conception of the rule of law that legitimates a role for courts 'in enforcing legal standards on public decision-makers' while creating 'space for a proper role for democratic considerations, including a role for the democratic branches in the definition and furtherance of fundamental values'.[117] The only difference is that Hobbes would put more emphasis on the sovereign law-giver and would speak of 'natural law considerations'.

This commonality between Hobbes and the common law tradition, their shared aspirational conception of the rule of law, does not prevent them from issuing different prescriptions about the institutional arrangements that will best implement the rule of law. Thus, Hobbes wished to confine the legal force of judges' judgments to the particular case, while the common law tradition often exalted such judgments over the judgment of the legislature. But whatever these different prescriptions, it is clear that those who have this view do not regard any particular arrangement of powers as fundamental; rather, they see such arrangements

---

[115] So much should be obvious from the Introduction to Hobbes' *Leviathan*, pp. 9–11, but chapter 26 'Of Civill Lawes' should settle any doubt. For more detailed discussion see David Dyzenhaus, 'Hobbes and the Legitimacy of Law' (2001) 20 *Law and Philosophy* 461–98.

[116] Hunt, 'Sovereignty's Blight', p. 350.   [117] *Ibid.*, p. 340.

as instrumental or functional to a larger purpose – the realization of principles.

While I cannot attempt to tell the complete story here, I think it is plausible to regard Austin's, Hart's and Raz's legal positivisms as attempts to find a conceptual or scientific basis for an absolutist account of parliamentary sovereignty whose origins lay in political developments in the nineteenth and early twentieth centuries. While all three see the need to understand law as something more than what Fuller called a 'one-way projection of authority',[118] they avoid at all costs finding that the constitutive conditions of authority provide internal moral limits on what can be done in the name of the law. But conceptual positivism is of no use to judges who find themselves in a legal order which is not constructed in accordance with that absolutist account. And it is of no use for two reasons.

The first reason harkens back to Dworkin's initial and devastating critique of Hart's positivism. A conception of law which understands law as a matter of rules with determinate content communicated from ruler to legal subject cannot account for the pervasive role of principles in adjudication, nor with the fact that that role is regarded by those with interpretative authority as determinative of their conclusions about what the law requires. Not can it account for the fact that in order to sustain the conclusions, judges provide detailed reasoned arguments in which all the reasons are legal.[119] Indeed, we should note that these two facts are all one needs to support Dworkin's right answer thesis, the thesis that there is in principle a right answer to all questions of law. At most one needs to supplement these two facts by saying that if judges reach different results using this method, the right answer is that given by the better or best argument.

Legal positivism responded to this critique in two ways, both of which have a basis in Hart's work. Exclusive legal positivists, most notably Raz, argue that to demonstrate that principles pervade adjudication is to demonstrate that judges have discretion – that judges' conclusions are not fully determined by law. But that argument is, as I have indicated, a conceptual one, falling out of a claim about the very nature of authority. Its only practical consequence for judges and other public officials is to ask them to accept that they have a strong discretion to decide the cases

---

[118] Fuller, *Morality of Law*, p. 207.
[119] Ronald Dworkin, 'Model of Rules I' in Dworkin, *Taking Rights Seriously*, pp. 14–45.

that come before them and that their practice of giving reasons for their conclusions is an elaborate charade. Judges must accept that they work entirely in the penumbra and so must accept that the rule of law is their rule – the rule of judges and officials and thus largely the rule of an elite, largely composed of men. The argument thus adds a second group of gunmen to the gunman at the apex of the pyramid of power, an addition which has the result of turning law into a series of exceptions, which those with authority deal with on an ad hoc basis by pretending that their preferences represent the requirements of law. While this theory is plausible as a sociological critique of the claims of the rule of law, it cannot make sense of a project whose aspiration is to replace the arbitrary rule of men with the rule of law.

In contrast, incorporationist or inclusive legal positivists, whose camp Hart belatedly joined, try to make sense of the fact that law is a matter of principles as well as rules and of the fact that these principles are regarded by judges and other officials as determining their conclusions about what the law requires.[120] As Dworkin has pointed out, this position looks like a wholesale capitulation to his critique of legal positivism, except for the fact that it holds out as a kind of face-saving device the logical possibility that a legal order could exist in which principles did not play this role. But logical possibilities are of no use to judges or other officials and moreover we would have good reason to think that the order imagined by these positivists as a logical possibility would not have any serious claim to be a legal order.

It is worth noting that exclusive legal positivism and unmodified ultra vires theorists are close cousins, as are their adaptations in inclusive legal positivism and modified ultra vires theory. Both exclusive legal positivists and unmodified ultra vires theorists regard morality as playing a role in law only when it is explicitly incorporated by the law. The main difference is that unmodified ultra vires theorists explicitly argue, on what they take to be democratic grounds, that the incorporating law must be a statute.

In contrast, both modified ultra vires theorists and inclusive legal positivists seem comfortable with the thought that morality is included unless the law explicitly excludes it. The difference is that while modified ultra vires theorists are preoccupied with the prospect of a particular law that strains or contradicts an aspirational conception of the rule of law, inclusive legal positivists are preoccupied with the prospect of a whole legal order that does the same. But both are examples of how some members

---

[120] Hart, *The Concept of Law*, pp. 250–4.

of the legal positivist family have tried to adapt themselves to a world in which the legal orders with which they are familiar have travelled along a path of realizing the aspirations of the rule of law in ways that make it difficult to sustain positivist claims about the contingent nature of connections between law and morality.

Indeed, even exclusive legal positivism is an example of such adaptation. When exclusive legal positivists write about the rule of law in particular legal orders, or about the process of judicial interpretation, what they have to say differs little from Fuller or Dworkin.[121] The main divide between them and their inclusive counterparts is the hair-splitting one that the latter concede more than that legal orders generally incorporate morality; they also concede that the incorporated morality is fully capable of determining answers to questions of law. And with that concession, as in the move by ultra vires theory to a view that common law presumptions about the rule of law create an interpretative obligation on judges, so both collapse into an aspirational conception of the rule of law, though the collapse is muddied by the urge to cling to a positivist vocabulary.

In sum, legal positivism as a theoretical endeavour has made itself into something which has become increasingly detached from legal practice. And it has become that because of its relentless conceptualism which has taken it away from the political roots of a noble tradition. Once we see this, it becomes unsurprising that judges who are positivists are not conceptual but constitutional positivists. They attempt to find some political anchor for their positivism, which is why they usually opt on democratic arguments to support a rigid doctrine of the separation of powers which reserves law-making authority to the legislature. Such political arguments harken back to Bentham's dream of a legal order as the mere instrument for the democratically determined judgment of the people. But the arguments are shaky to say the least. Because their legal orders have not been reformed on Benthamite lines, the judges have to try to come to terms with the fact that the legislature is not in fact the sole source of legal norms even if they consider it to be the sole legitimate source. They have, that is, to find ways of compromising with the fact that in a common law legal order their judgments potentially have authority beyond the particular case, that they are required to give reasoned arguments for their conclusions in which all the reasons are legal, and with the fact that international law, as well as written constitutional texts, claim authority over them.

---

[121] See Joseph Raz, 'The Inner Logic of the Law' in Raz, *Ethics in the Public Domain*, pp. 222–37 and 'The Politics of the Rule of Law', *ibid.*, pp. 354–62.

It is not, however, a mere accident that Bentham's dream was never put into practice.[122] Significant in this regard is that Bentham saw the need to have a staff of judges in place and that he gave them an even larger role than does the Human Rights Act, since he permitted them to suspend the application of a statute in a case where it wrought injustice; they would then inform a parliamentary committee of the need for statutory reform.

In making these institutional recommendations, Bentham saw the need to move from the normative foundation of his political and legal theory to the level of institutional design. It is true that, unlike Hobbes, he did not think that there were constitutive conditions internal to the exercise of authority. It is also true that he regarded rights talk with contempt so that he must have disapproved of Hobbes' attempt to show that there are laws of nature, derived from a right of nature, which together make up those conditions. Indeed, these two facts are deeply connected because Bentham sees law as the medium for transmission of utilitarian judgments about welfare, unmediated by any legal filter besides requirements of publicity and clarity.

But still it is a striking feature of Bentham's legal theory that Parliament cannot, to revert to John Eaves' image from the last chapter, do without some interesting bits of constitutional furniture that clutter the space between the command of the sovereign and the obedience of the subject. It is even more striking that in the work of the neo-Benthamites, Keith Ewing and Conor Gearty are distinguished examples,[123] who seek to revitalize Parliament, legal space becomes even more cluttered by constitutional furniture. And it becomes more cluttered because not only do these neo-Benthamites support the cause of human rights, but also because they see that cause as intimately connected to a principle of legality or the rule of law. They thus share an aspirational conception of the rule of law but do not trust judges to implement it. Rather, they put their faith in Parliament, suitably reformed.

Ewing and Gearty represent, in my opinion, the only plausible candidate for taking forward the tradition which I called in chapter 3 'left legalism'. The functionalist school, associated with the London School of Economics, venerated the executive as the driver of a social democratic programme and so had a view of law even more instrumental than that of legal positivism: law is the instrument of policies initiated by government

---

[122] See Gerald Postema, *Bentham and the Common Law Tradition* (Oxford: Clarendon Press, 1986), ch. 13.

[123] Ewing and Gearty, *The Struggle for Civil Liberties.*

and implemented by government, where Parliament is simply the body that gives legal form to policy mandates. Thus, democracy was no less instrumentally conceived. But, as I pointed out in chapter 3, functionalism loses its plausibility as soon as government departs from that political programme; indeed, when government with much popular support not only departs from that programme, but gets into the business of using law to dismantle itself, functionalism's veneration for the executive becomes worse than implausible – it becomes incredible.

The only hope for the legal left, for those who wish to construct a normative account of how law can make our societies better, is to argue for a renewed and reinvigorated legislature. And in order to support that argument, they have to rely on the role of the legislature in promoting social progress through law, that is, through institutions and mechanisms that respect legality, taking into account that our understanding of legality today is deeply influenced by our sense that the subject of the law is the individual bearer of human rights.

Indeed, I think one can make the case that this understanding is not so much new but a retrieval of Hobbes' natural law conception of the rule of law, in which the laws of nature do not come from outside of the law but are the constitutive conditions of legal authority. In Hobbes the idea of the legal subject is highly ambiguous between the passive object of authority, he who is subjected to law, and the active subject, on whose consent authority depends. In Hobbes' account, power legitimates itself if it is exercised through law but that is because the transformation of power into law requires respect for those constitutive conditions. What these conditions are is generated by asking what is required for peace and stability, given the one inalienable human right in Hobbes, the right to resist the sovereign when one's existence is threatened.[124] Thus, the transformation we have witnessed in public law of the idea of the individual from one who is subjected to the law, through the individual as citizen, to the individual as bearer of human rights is of great significance, but it might have deeper intellectual roots than one might at first suppose.

As Hobbes' own theory shows, one cannot in constructing such an argument do away with judges, nor marginalize them altogether. And one cannot do this even though, as I have shown in this book, distrust

---

[124] See Yves Charles Zarka, 'The Political Subject' in Tom Sorell and Luc Foisneau (eds.), *Leviathan After 350 Years* (Oxford: Oxford University Press, 2004), pp. 167–82 at pp. 180–1.

of judges is often supported by the judiciary's willingness to be sheep as long as they can do so in rule-of-law clothing. For it is still the case that it is on those occasions when judges rise to the challenge of the exception, drawing on resources that they have developed in less dramatic situations, that we start to get a grip on the content of legality and its connection to human rights. It is there that we encounter what I called in chapter 1 the moral resources of the rule of law.

I have also argued that even judges who do not lose their rule-of-law spine need allies. For the rule of law to approach its ideals, to get closer to realizing its aspirations, one needs furniture like SIAC and parliamentary committees like the Joint Committee on Human Rights. Such furniture is the concrete embodiment of the normative commitment of both Parliament and the executive to be part of the rule-of-law project. And without such furniture, the role of judges in upholding the rule of law in times of stress is confined to what I described in chapter 1 as the judge as weatherman. So while I think that the label neo-Benthamite is an apt one for the position of Ewing and Gearty, they are not, in any meaningful sense of that word, positivists. They have an argument about the best possible way to arrange the furniture. But that argument starts from the premise that what we are after is realizing commitments to the rule of law and human rights.

One way of understanding the point of this book is that those who value the rule of law and human rights should be greatly depressed. The advances since the Second World War seem at the moment to be on the point of being reversed. Politicians, judges and other elites seem determined to turn their backs on the lessons of their own history. However, I think I can end on an optimistic note.

We have seen that even the most parsimonious conception of the rule of law requires a few sticks of rule-of-law furniture. And without those sticks, without, say, independent judges, a legislature committed to enacting general, public, clear and prospective statutes, and a staff of public officials who are regarded as exercising delegated and hence limited authority, a political order will not look like a legal order, on any conception of law. Once those sticks are in place, judges and others have powerful resources to enforce the rule of law as long as they understand that the furniture is there for a purpose – to help them to ensure that law lives up to the ideals of legal order. And it is that furniture that is the concrete embodiment of the constitution of law.

My inquiry into what I called at the beginning the 'Commonwealth Constitution' was not designed to show the superiority of the

Commonwealth model to others, for example, to the US Bill of Rights model, in which it might appear that judges are in fact supreme when it comes to interpreting the Constitution. While I do as a matter of fact think that this model might promote better than others a cooperative rule-of-law project between legislature, judiciary and government, I have not engaged in advocating that model. Rather, I have tried to show how even in the common law legal orders out of which the Commonwealth model grew, legal orders in which parliamentary override of fundamental legal values is not only possible but actual, these values can claim constitutional status. In this sense, we can see how an understanding of the common law constitution tells us something significant about the constitution of law itself. That is, we cannot understand law itself unless we see law as a project which aspires to realize the values of the rule of law.

We can then place different legal orders on a continuum of legality, depending on how far along in that project they are. In this process it does not matter much from the perspective of the rule of law how the furniture is arranged: whether the legal orders are civil or common law, or have entrenched bills of rights, or statutory bills, or a division of powers constitution or no written constitution at all. What places them on the continuum is the level of their commitment to the constitutional project of realizing the values of the rule of law. The further along the continuum a legal order is, the better judges are able to fulfil their roles, both as guardians (though not exclusive guardians) of the rule of law and as rule-of-law weathermen. Not only will the judges have allies in their task, but, in addition, different sites where the values are articulated.

Legal positivism does not envisage this continuum of legality because a legal order designed along strictly positivist lines does not aspire to anything more than being as effective an instrument as possible. From its own perspective, there are no further points along the continuum of legality once the order is as close to perfection as it can be for transmitting the judgment of those with legal power to those subject to it. Indeed, to go further is to step off the continuum because any further step involves adopting principles which organize order in a way that potentially disrupts transmission.

In contrast, from the perspective of the aspirational conception of the rule of law for which I have argued in this book, a positivist legal order can be seen as a step along a continuum of legality because it insists on non-arbitrariness in the sense that no official may act unless there is a warrant in a valid law of that order. The importance of this step should not be underestimated. To the extent, for example, that the prerogative can still be invoked as the basis for an official act, a common law legal order has not yet fully taken that step.[125]

But, as we have seen, once this step has been taken, legislators can still attempt to enact the equivalent of the prerogative into the law by inserting privative clauses or subjectively framed delegations of discretion. Here, if judges adopt a doctrine of deference which amounts to deference as submission or abasement rather than deference as respect, the legal order will have taken that step in form, but not in substance. And when the idea still lingers in the legal culture that officials may claim special deference when their statutory powers are powers they could have claimed in the past as prerogative powers, one will find functional equivalents of the prerogative power in areas such as security and immigration control, despite the fact that these areas are subject to elaborate statutes and regulatory regimes.

It is only if law is answerable to the principles of the rule of law that judges will regard themselves as under an interpretative obligation to ensure that the law always complies with such principles and thus to resist the idea that public power can be exercised other than in accordance with the rule of law. But, as we have seen, in order for judges to make sense of their review authority, it is not enough that they regard the law that rules when one has the rule of law as simply valid law with a determinate content. Even on that positivist view of the law there is a puzzle when the law seems to exempt officials from legal controls. But that puzzle is not one which positivism of any sort has the resources to solve. For positivists start with the idea that law is valid law with a determinate content – a content that can be determined in accordance with factual tests, that is, not by tests that require that law up to some moral ideal. By definition, the rule of law exists when a law has been determined to be a valid law of the legal order and a determinate content for it has been ascertained. There is no further question about the law's authority qua law once it has been determined to be valid.

Thus a positivist legal order is only a step along the continuum of legality since a full realization of the rule of law requires the observance of principles of the rule of law beyond those that assist in determining the content of the law. Moreover, I doubt that that step can be taken without also putting in place significant elements of a rule-of-law regime. The logic of rule by law requires elements of the rule of law, for example, review by independent, judge-like officials of the decisions of public officials in

---

[125] See Tomkins, *Our Republican Constitution*, pp. 103–9.

order to ensure that the officials have stayed within the limits of their legal authority. Such compliance with the rule of law is not required as a kind of moral addition to legal order, so that positivists can retort that a legal order which fails to comply with the rule of law is nonetheless a legal order. The aspirational conception holds that what law is is answerable to the rule of law, so that when an actual law of a legal order fails to comply with the rule of law, there is a serious question about that law's authority.

I have argued that the question of how the institutions of a particular legal order attempt to bring to realization the ideal of the rule of law is less important than that they do. While one can go much further along the continuum of legality than a positivist legal order, it is not as clear that US style judicial review is necessarily even further along the continuum than say the United Kingdom, or Canada, or even a pure common law legal order, one where there is no written constitution. When judges in the United Kingdom today call for a constitutional authority to invalidate statutory provisions, it is because the government is signalling that it will react to decisions upholding the rule of law by finding ways for it to escape its constraints. But when a government is willing to do that, it is highly unlikely that any constitution, even if it is zealously guarded by judges, can stop it. Ultimately, as I pointed out at the end of chapter 1, and as Dicey so clearly saw, it is we the people's dedication to a culture of legality that is the guardian of the constitution. When push comes to shove, all that judges can do is take up the role of weatherman and make real to the people what kind of choice their government is making.

And in this thought lies some reason for optimism about the future of the rule of law. The more constitutional furniture there is in place, the more judges and politicians will look hypocritical if they try to derail the rule-of-law project. It is thus worth remembering that before Blair joined Bush in a momentous decision to secede partially from the rule of law, both internationally and domestically, he was at the forefront in putting more furniture in place to take forward that project. While judges of the Court of Appeal and the House of Lords might seem at times intent on either ignoring the furniture, or in trying to alter it to fit an agenda hostile to the rule of law, they and the politicians cannot wish it away. To remove it would I think exact a political cost which I hope no politician is yet willing to bear. And as long as the furniture is there, it stands not only in rebuke of the judges and politicians – legality's rebuke to those who wish to govern arbitrarily. It also stands in wait of a time when we will come back to our rule-of-law senses.

BIBLIOGRAPHY

Ackerman, Bruce, 'The Emergency Constitution' (2004) 113 *Yale Law Journal* 1029–91

Agamben, Girgio, *State of Exception*; translated by Kevin Attell (Chicago: Chicago University Press, 2005, first published in 2003)

Alexy, Robert, 'A Defence of Radbruch's Formula' in David Dyzenhaus (ed.), *Recrafting the Rule of Law: The Limits of Legal Order* (Oxford: Hart Publishing, 1999), 15–39

Allan, T. R. S., *Constitutional Justice: A Liberal Theory of the Rule of Law* (Oxford: Oxford University Press, 2001)

Aronson, Mark, Bruce Dyer and Matthew Groves, *Judicial Review of Administrative Action* (3rd edn, Sydney: Lawbook Co., 2004)

Arthurs, H. W., 'Rethinking Administrative Law: A Slightly Dicey Business' (1979) 17 *Osgoode Hall Law Journal* 1–45

Austin, John, *Lectures on Jurisprudence* (5th edn, London: John Murray, 1885), vol. II

Bickel, Alexander M., *The Least Dangerous Branch: The Supreme Court at the Bar of Politics* (2nd edn, New Haven: Yale University Press, 1986)

Blackstone, William, *Commentaries on the Laws of England* (Chicago: University of Chicago Press, 1977), vol. I

Chorley, Lord, 'Law-Making in White Hall' (1946) 58 *Modern Law Review* 26–41

Cole, D., 'Judging the Next Emergency: Judicial Review and Individual Rights in Times of Crisis' (2002–03) 101 *Michigan Law Review* 2565–95

Dicey, A. V., *An Introduction to the Study of the Law of the Constitution* (8th edn, London: MacMillan & Co., 1915)

Dicey, A. V., *Introduction to the Study of the Law of the Constitution* (10th edn, London: MacMillan, 1959)

Dicey, A. V., *Lectures on the Relationship Between Law and Public Opinion in England During the Nineteenth Century* (1st edn, London: MacMillan & Co., 1905)

Djwa, Sandra, *The Politics of the Imagination: A Life of F. R. Scott* (Vancouver: Douglas & MacIntyre, 1987/Toronto, McClelland and Stewart, 1987)

Dworkin, Ronald, *Freedom's Law: The Moral Reading of the American Constitution* (Cambridge, Mass.: Harvard University Press, 1996)

Dworkin, Ronald, 'Hard Cases' in Ronald Dworkin, *Taking Rights Seriously* (London: Duckworth, 1977), 81–130

Dworkin, Ronald, 'Hart's Postscript and the Character of Political Philosophy' (2004) 24 *Oxford Journal of Legal Studies* 1–37

Dworkin, Ronald, *Law's Empire* (Cambridge, Mass.: Belknap Press, 1986)

Dworkin, Ronald, 'Model of Rules I' in Ronald Dworkin, *Taking Rights Seriously* (London: Duckworth, 1977), 14–45

Dworkin, Ronald, 'A Reply to Critics' in Marshall Cohen (ed.), *Ronald Dworkin and Contemporary Jurisprudence* (London: Duckworth, 1984), 247–300

Dworkin, Ronald, 'Thirty Years On' (2002) 115 *Harvard Law Review* 1655–87

Dyzenhaus, David, 'Constituting the Enemy: A Response to Carl Schmitt' in Andras Sajo (ed.), *Militant Democracy* (Utrecht: Eleven International Publishing, 2004), 15–45

Dyzenhaus, David, 'Constituting the Rule of Law: Fundamental Values in Administrative Law' (2001–02) 27 *Queen's Law Journal* 445–509

Dyzenhaus, David, 'The Deep Structure of *Roncarelli v. Duplessis*' (2004) 53 *University of New Brunswick Law Journal* 111–54

Dyzenhaus, David, 'Disobeying Parliament: Privative Clauses and the Rule of Law' in Tsvi Kahana (ed.), *Legislatures and Constitutionalism: The Role of Legislatures in the Constitutional State* (Cambridge: Cambridge University Press, forthcoming)

Dyzenhaus, David, 'Form and Substance in the Rule of Law: A Democratic Justification for Judicial Review' in Christopher Forsyth (ed.), *Judicial Review and the Constitution* (Oxford: Hart Publishing, 2000), 141–67

Dyzenhaus, David, 'The Genealogy of Legal Positivism' (2004) 24 *Oxford Journal of Legal Studies* 39–67

Dyzenhaus, David, *Hard Cases in Wicked Legal Systems: South African Law in the Perspective of Legal Philosophy* (Oxford: Clarendon Press, 1991)

Dyzenhaus, David, 'Hobbes and the Legitimacy of Law' (2001) 20 *Law and Philosophy* 461–98

Dyzenhaus, David, 'Holmes and Carl Schmitt: An Unlikely Pair' (1997) 63 *Brooklyn Law Review* 165–88

Dyzenhaus, David, *Judging the Judges, Judging Ourselves: Truth, Reconciliation and the Apartheid Legal Order* (Oxford: Hart Publishing, 1999)

Dyzenhaus, David, *Legality and Legitimacy: Carl Schmitt, Hans Kelsen and Hermann Heller in Weimar* (Oxford: Clarendon Press, 1997)

Dyzenhaus, David, 'The Politics of Deference: Judicial Review and Democracy' in Michael Taggart (ed.), *The Province of Administrative Law* (Oxford: Hart Publishing, 1997), 279–307

Dyzenhaus, David, 'The State of Emergency in Legal Theory' in Victor Ramraj, Michael Hor and K. Roach (eds.), *Global Anti-terrorism Law* (Cambridge: Cambridge University Press, 2005), 66–89

Dyzenhaus, David, 'The Unwritten Constitution and the Rule of Law' in Grant Huscroft and Ian Brodie (eds.), *Constitutionalism in the Charter Era* (Markham, Ontario: LexisNexis Butterworths, 2004), 383–412

Dyzenhaus, David, 'With the Benefit of Hindsight': Dilemmas of Legality in the Face of Injustice' in Emilios Christodoulidis and Scott Veitch (eds.), *Lethe's Law: Justice, Law and Ethics in Reconciliation* (Oxford: Hart Publishing, 2001), 65–90

Dyzenhaus, David (ed.), *The Unity of Public Law* (Oxford: Hart Publishing, 2004)

Dyzenhaus, David and Fox-Decent, Evan, 'Rethinking the Process/Substance Distinction: *Baker v. Canada*' (2001) 51 *University of Toronto Law Journal* 193–242

Eaves, John Jr, *Emergency Powers and the Parliamentary Watchdog: Parliament and the Executive in Great Britain, 1939–1951* (London: The Hansard Society for Parliamentary Government, 1957)

Elliott, Mark, *The Constitutional Foundations of Judicial Review* (Oxford: Hart Publishing, 2001)

Ewing, K. D. and C. A. Gearty, *The Struggle for Civil Liberties: Political Freedom and the Rule of Law in Britain, 1914–45* (Oxford: Oxford University Press, 2000)

Feldman, David, 'The Impact of Human Rights on the UK Legislative Process' (2004) 25 *Statute Law Review* 91–115

Ferejohn, John and Pasquale Pasquino, 'The Law of the Exception: A Typology of Emergency Powers' (2004) 2 *International Journal of Constitutional Law* 210–39

Finnis, John, *Natural Law and Natural Rights* (Oxford: Clarendon Press, 1980)

Forsyth, C. F., *In Danger for Their Talents: A Study of the Appellate Division of the Supreme Court of South Africa from 1950–80* (Cape Town: Juta, 1985)

Forsyth, C. F. (ed.), *Judicial Review and the Constitution* (Oxford: Hart Publishing, 2000)

Foxton, David, '*R v. Halliday ex Parte Zadig* in Retrospect' (2003) 119 *Law Quarterly Review* 445–94

Fraenkel, Ernest, *The Dual State: A Contribution to the Theory of Dictatorship* (New York: Octagon Books, 1969)

Friedman, Bernard, *Smuts: A Reappraisal* (London: George Allen & Unwin Ltd, 1975)

Friedrich, Carl J., *Constitutional Reason of State: The Survival of the Constitutional Order* (Providence: Brown University Press, 1957)

Fuller, Lon L., *The Morality of Law* (rev. edn, New Haven: Yale University Press, 1969)

Gadamer, H. G., *Truth and Method* (London: Sheed & Ward, 1979)

Galligan, Brian, *Politics of the High Court* (Brisbane: Queensland University Press, 1967)

Gardbaum, Stephen, 'The New Commonwealth Model of Constitutionalism' (2001) 49 *American Journal of Comparative Law* 707–60

Gearty, Conor, *Principles of Human Rights Adjudication* (Oxford: Oxford University Press, 2004)

Gordon, D. M., 'The Relation of Facts to Jurisdiction' (1929) 45 *Law Quarterly Review* 459–93

Gordon, D. M., 'What Did the Anisminic Case Decide?' (1971) 34 *Modern Law Review* 1–11

Griffith, J. A. G., *The Politics of the Judiciary* (5th edn, London: Fontana, 1997)

Gross, Oren, 'Chaos and Rules: Should Responses to Violent Crises Always be Constitutional?' (2003) 112 *Yale Law Journal* 1011–34

Gross, Oren, 'Stability and Flexibility: A Dicey Business' in Victor Ramraj, Michael Hor and Kent Roach (eds.), *Global Anti-terrorism Law* (Cambridge: Cambridge University Press, 2005), 90–106

Gudridge, Patrick O., 'Remember Endo?' (2003) 116 *Harvard Law Review* 1933–70

Hart, H. L. A, *The Concept of Law* (2nd edn, Oxford: Clarendon Press, 1994)

Hart, H. L. A., 'Positivism and the Separation of Law and Morals' in H. L. A. Hart, *Essays in Jurisprudence and Philosophy* (Oxford: Clarendon Press, 1983), 49–87

Hayek, F. A., *The Road to Serfdom* (Chicago: University of Chicago Press, 1994)

Hazell, Robert, 'Who is the Guardian of Legal Values in the Legislative Process: Parliament or the Executive?' [2004] *Public Law* 495–500

Hewart, Lord, *The New Despotism* (London: Ernest Benn Ltd, 1929)

Hickman, Tom R., 'Between Human Rights and the Rule of Law: Indefinite Detention and the Derogation Model of Constitutionalism' (2005) 68 *Modern Law Review* 655–68

Hobbes, Thomas, *Leviathan*; edited by Richard Tuck (Cambridge: Cambridge University Press, 1991)

Hobbes, Thomas, *Leviathan*; edited by Richard Tuck (Cambridge: Cambridge University Press, 1996)

Hogg, Peter W., *Constitutional Law of Canada* (3rd edn, Toronto: Carswell, 1992)

Hunt, Murray, 'Sovereignty's Blight: Why Contemporary Public Law Needs the Concept of "Due Deference"' in Nicholas Bamforth and Peter Leyland (eds.), *Public Law in a Multi-Layered Constitution* (Oxford: Hart Publishing, 2003), 337–70

Hunt, Murray, *Using Human Rights Law in English Courts* (Oxford: Hart Publishing, 1997)

Issacharoff, Samuel and Richard H. Pildes, 'Emergency Contexts Without Emergency Powers: The United States' Constitutional Approach During Wartime' (2004) 2 *International Journal of Constitutional Law* 296–333

Kaplan, William, *State and Salvation: The Jehovah's Witnesses and Their Fight for Civil Rights* (Toronto: University of Toronto Press, 1989)

Kelsen, Hans, *Introduction to the Problems of Legal Theory. A Translation of the First Edition of the Reine Rechtslehre or Pure Theory of Law*; translated by Stanley L. Paulson and Bonnie Litschewski-Paulson (Oxford: Oxford University Press, 1992)

Kilroy, Charlotte, '*R. (on the application of Abbasi) v. Secretary of State for Foreign and Commonwealth Affairs*: Reviewing the Prerogative' (2003) 2 *European Human Rights Law Review* 222–9

Lajoie, Andrée, 'The Implied Bill of Rights, the Charter and the Role of the Judiciary' (1995) 44 *University of New Brunswick Law Journal* 337–54

Laskin, B., 'An Inquiry into the Diefenbaker Bill of Rights' (1959) 37 *Canadian Bar Review* 77–134

Lauterpacht, Hersch, *The Function of Law in the International Community* (Oxford: Clarendon Press, 1933)

Lauterpacht, Hersch, 'Is International Law a Part of the Law of England?' (1939) 25 *Transactions of the Grotius Society* 51–88

Locke, John, *Two Treatises on Government*; edited by P. Laslett (Cambridge: Cambridge University Press, 1988)

Loughlin, Martin, *Public Law and Political Theory* (Oxford: Oxford University Press, 1992)

Macklin, Audrey, 'Borderline Security' in Ronald J. Daniels, Patrick Macklem and Kent Roach (eds.), *The Security of Freedom: Essays on Canada's Anti-Terrorism Bill* (Toronto: University of Toronto Press, 2001), 383–404

Maitland, F. W., *The Constitutional History of England* (Cambridge: Cambridge University Press, 1950)

Maravall, José María and Adam Przeworski (eds.), *Democracy and the Rule of Law* (Cambridge: Cambridge University Press, 2003)

Mason, Anthony, 'The Foundations and Limitations of Judicial Review' (2002) 31 *Australian Institute of Administrative Law Quarterly Forum* 1

Mason, Anthony, 'Judicial Review: A View From Constitutional and Other Perspectives' (2000) 28 *Federal Law Review* 331–43

Masur, Jonathan, 'A Hard Look or a Blind Eye: Administrative Law or Military Deference' (2005) 56 *Hastings Law Journal* 441–521

Mathews, A. S. and R. C. Albino, 'The Permanence of the Temporary: An Examination of the 90- and 180-Day Detention Laws' (1966) 83 *South African Law Journal* 16–43

Moncrieff, Scott-Lucy, 'Detention Without Trial' (2004) 26 *London Review of Books* 22

Mullan, David, 'Mr Justice Rand: Defining the Limits of Court Control of the Administrative and Executive Process' (1979–80) 18 *University of Western Ontario Law Review* 65–114

Mullan, David, 'The Role for Underlying Constitutional Principles in a Bill of Rights World' (2004) *New Zealand Law Review* 9–38

'Notes and Comments, The Bounds of Legislative Specification: A Suggested Approach to the Bill of Attainder Clause' (1962) 72 *Yale Law Journal* 330–67

Postema, Gerald, *Bentham and the Common Law Tradition* (Oxford: Clarendon Press, 1986)

Pritt, D. N., *The Autobiography of D. N. Pritt: Part One; From Right to Left* (London: Lawrence & Wishart, 1965)

Rawlings, Richard, 'Review, Revenge and Retreat' (2005) 68 *Modern Law Review* 378–410

Rawls, John, *Political Liberalism* (New York: Columbia University Press, 1993)

Rawls, John, *A Theory of Justice* (Oxford: Oxford University Press, 1980)

Raz, Joseph, 'Authority, Law, and Morality' in Joseph Raz, *Ethics in the Public Domain: Essays in the Morality of Law and Politics* (Oxford: Oxford University Press, 1994), 194–221

Raz, Joseph, 'The Inner Logic of the Law' in Joseph Raz, *Ethics in the Public Domain: Essays in the Morality of Law and Politics* (Oxford: Oxford University Press, 1994), 222–37

Raz, Joseph, 'The Obligation to Obey: Revision and Tradition' in Joseph Raz, *Ethics in the Public Domain: Essays in the Morality of Law and Politics* (Oxford: Oxford University Press, 1994), 325–38

Raz, Joseph, 'The Politics of the Rule of Law' in Joseph Raz, *Ethics in the Public Domain: Essays in the Morality of Law and Politics* (Oxford: Oxford University Press, 1994), 354–62

Raz, Joseph, 'The Rule of Law and Its Virtue' in Joseph Raz, *The Authority of Law: Essays on Law and Morality* (Oxford: Oxford University Press, 1979), 210–29

Roach, Kent, 'The Administrative Law Scholarship of D. M. Gordon' (1989) 34 *McGill Law Journal* 1–38

Roach, Kent and Gary Trotter, 'Miscarriages of Justice in the War Against Terror' (2005) 109 *Penn State Law Review* 967–1041

Rossiter, Clinton L., *Constitutional Dictatorship* (Princeton: Princeton University Press, 1948)

Scalia, Antonin, 'Judicial Deference to Administrative Intepretations of Law' (1989) *Duke Law Journal* 511–21

Scalia, Antonin, *A Matter of Interpretation: Federal Courts and the Law* (Princeton: Princeton University Press, 1997)

Scalia, Antonin, 'The Rule of Law as a Rule of Rules' (1989) 56 *University of Chicago Law Review* 1175–88

Schmitt, Carl, *The Concept of the Political*, translated by George Schwab (New Jersey: Rutgers University Press, 1976)

Schmitt, Carl, *Die Diktatur: Von den Anfängen des modernen Souveränitätsgedankens bis zum proletarischen Klassenkampf* (Berlin: Duncker & Humblot, 1989)

Schmitt, Carl, *Gesetz und Urteil: Eine Untersuchung zum Problem der Rechtspraxis* (Munich: CH Beck, 1969)

Schmitt, Carl, *Der Hüter der Verfassung* (Berlin: Duncker & Humblot, 1985)

Schmitt, Carl, *The Leviathan in the State Theory of Thomas Hobbes: Meaning and Failure of a Political Symbol*; translated by George Schwab and Erna Hilfstein (Westport, Conn.: Greenwood Press, 1996)

Schmitt, Carl, *Political Theology: Four Chapters on the Theory of Sovereignty*; translated by George Schwab (Cambridge, Mass.: MIT Press, 1988)

Sedley, Stephen, 'Everything and Nothing: The Changing UK Constitution' (2004) 26 *London Review of Books* 10

Simpson, Brian A. W., *In the Highest Degree Odious: Detention Without Trial in Wartime Britain* (Oxford: Oxford University Press, 1992)

Stephen, Leslie, *Science of Ethics* (London: Smith, Elder, 1882)

Steyn, Johan, 'Deference: A Tangled Story' [2005] *Public Law* 346–59

Steyn, Johan, 'Guantanamo Bay: The Legal Black Hole' (2004) 53 *International and Comparative Law Quarterly* 1–15

Sueur, Le Andrew, 'Three Strikes and It's Out? The UK Government's Strategy to Oust Judicial Review from Immigration and Asylum Decision-making' [2004] *Public Law* 225–33

Sunstein, Cass R., 'Minimalism at War' (2004) *The Supreme Court Review* 47–109

Sunstein, Cass R., *One Case at a Time: Judicial Minimalism on the Supreme Court* (Cambridge, Mass.: Harvard University Press, 1999)

Tomkins, Adam, *Our Republican Constitution* (Oxford: Hart Publishing, 2005)

Tribe, G. and Gudridge, Patrick O., 'The Anti-Emergency Constitution' (2004) 113 *Yale Law Journal* 1801–70

Tushnet, Mark V., 'Defending *Korematsu?* Reflections on Civil Liberties in Wartime' (2003) *Wisconsin Law Review* 273–307

Vinx, Lars, 'Legality and Legitimacy in Hans Kelsen's Pure Theory of Law', PhD thesis, University of Toronto (2005)

Wade, William, *Constitutional Fundamentals* (The Hamlyn Lectures) (London: Stevens & Sons, 1989)

Wade, H. W. R. and C. F. Forsyth, *Administrative Law* (7th edn, Oxford: Clarendon Press, 1994)

Williams, George, 'Reading the Judicial Mind: Appellate Argument in the Communist Party Case' (1993) 15 *Sydney Law Review* 3–29

Willis, John, 'Administrative Law and the British North America Act' (1939–40) *Harvard Law Review* 251–81

Willis, John, 'Three Approaches to Administrative Law: The Judicial, the Conceptual, and the Functional' (1935–6) 1 *University of Toronto Law Journal* 53–81

Winterton, George, 'The Communist Party Case' in H. P. Lee and George Winterton (eds.), *Australian Constitutional Landmarks* (Cambridge University Press, 2003), 108–44

Winterton, George, 'The Significance of the Communist Party Case' (1992) 18 *Melbourne Law Review* 630–58

Woolf, H. 'Droit Public – English Style' [1995] *Public Law* 57–71

Woolf, H. 'The Rule of Law and a Change in the Constitution' (2004) 63 *Cambridge Law Journal* 317–30

Zarka, Yves Charles, 'The Political Subject' in Tom Sorell and Luc Foisneau (eds.), *Leviathan After 350 Years* (Oxford: Oxford University Press, 2004), 167–82

Zines, Leslie, 'Constitutional Aspects of Judicial Review of Administrative Action' (1998) 1 *Constitutional Law and Policy Review* 50–4

INDEX